The American Bomber Plane

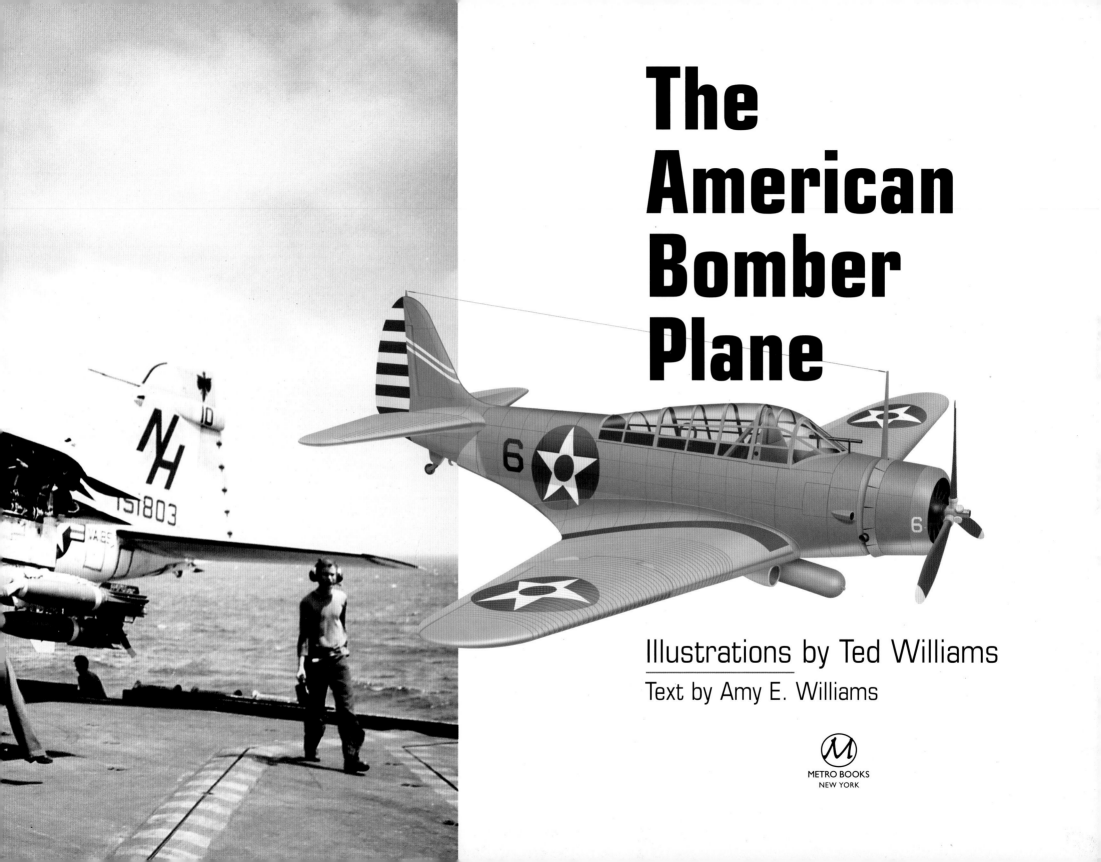

The American Bomber Plane

Illustrations by Ted Williams

Text by Amy E. Williams

METRO BOOKS
NEW YORK

Designed by Kevin Ullrich.
Photo credits appear on page 173.

Metro Books
122 Fifth Avenue
New York, NY 10011

ISBN: 978-1-4351-1008-3

Printed and bound in China

10 9 8 7 6 5 4 3 2 1

Dedication

As always, for Gail

In memory of Gene DeCook, a good friend, quality craftsman,
and an inspiration

Acknowledgments

With gratitude to Dave Ostrowski, a man of great knowledge and integrity;
we have deep appreciation for his friendship and continuing support. Also,
we are indebted to the fine people at Barnes & Noble Publishing, particularly
Kevin Ullrich and Andrea Rotondo—thanks for taking such good care of us.
And, without a doubt, David Malpass requires an extra-special recognition:
without his encouragement, this book would not exist.

Contents

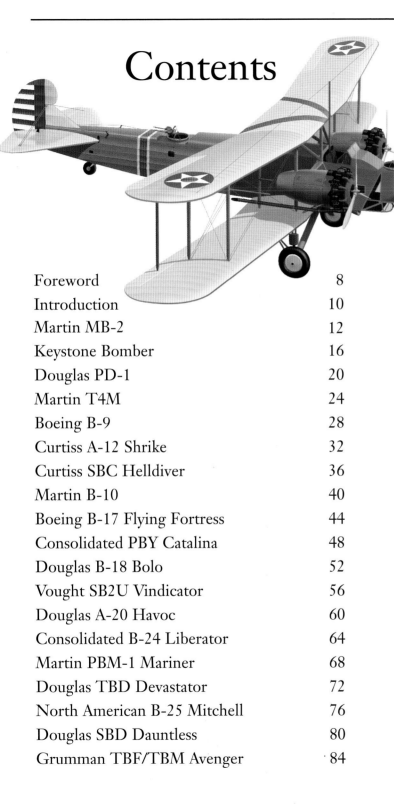

Foreword

Bomber plane! Mention of these words elicits images of very powerful, swift, and dangerous aircraft capable of bringing terrific destructive power to far-away enemies in time of war. Bombers can also serve as a deterrent to war, and they have fulfilled both of these roles in our history. Many Americans today are not aware of how significant an impact the American bomber has had on our nation and the freedom and liberty

we enjoy. Now, in *The American Bomber Plane*, Ted Williams and Amy E. Williams have brought us the fascinating story of the American bomber and its significance in our lives.

Born of necessity in a world that sometimes erupts in conflict, the bomber combines the best technology talented designers and engineers can incorporate in an airplane with the skills of highly trained and motivated airmen to bring war to an enemy. Even the names of these planes—Helldiver, Devastator, Flying Fortress, Liberator, Stratofortress, Intruder, Thunderbolt II—speak to their power and dangerous capabilities.

American bomber planes are the product of a blending of private enterprise with government assistance and oversight. In 1915, the U.S. government established the National Advisory

Committee for Aeronautics (NACA, now NASA) to conduct research and advance the science of aeronautics. Information obtained from this extensive research effort coupled with the results from military tests and development projects are freely provided to aircraft designers and manufacturers. This system has allowed for continuous improvement in bomber plane technology. Bomber development has always attracted people who want to push the envelope, who thrive on challenges, who won't take "no" for an answer, who will always achieve the impossible.

Competition has also played a major role in the American system of bomber plane development. Once our military services establish a requirement and a design specification for an

BELOW: An A-10 pilot assigned to the 354th Expeditionary Fighter Squadron signals that he is "good to go" prior to a flight at Bagram Airfield, Afghanistan. The 354th EFS is deployed from Davis-Monthan Air Force Base, Arizona.

advanced bomber plane, manufacturers are invited to compete for the contract. A "paper competition" in the form of proposals usually comes first, followed by the flight-testing and evaluation of prototype bombers. Finally, the much-sought-after production contract is awarded to the winner.

In austere times, such as the period between the world wars, in particular during the Great Depression, bomber plane production runs have been small. During World War II, however, many manufacturers turned out large quantities of bombers, a feat that is unlikely to be repeated with today's modern, highly complex, and extremely expensive jet aircraft. But each production run furthered the advancement of bomber plane technology and each new design or refinement of an existing model improved upon its predecessor. This approach has resulted in some truly great bombers, and the story of their development and evolution is a fascinating one.

That saga is told with great style in *The American Bomber Plane* by Ted and Amy Williams, perhaps the only father/daughter team of aviation authors anywhere. Ted and Amy have combined their individual talents to create a unique perspective on American bomber planes and the great people associated with them.

Amy is the writer and researcher on the team and, having earned a master's degree in Scientific and Technical Communication from Bowling Green State University in Bowling Green, Ohio, is well qualified for the task. Ted is the artist on the team, and I have had the distinct and very rewarding experience of working with both Amy and Ted on earlier projects including their highly successful book, *The American Fighter Plane*. As editor of *Skyways*, I have worked closely with Ted for over thirteen years as he created many fine aircraft illustrations for our articles, including 3-view drawings, centerfold portraits, and spectacular, full-color, wrap-around covers featuring aircraft of aviation's Golden Era, the 1920s and '30s.

Ted brings to his portraits a rare combination—the soul of an artist and a love of aviation. An artist will capture the grace, the beauty, the smooth or perhaps purely functional lines of an airplane; Ted does this as well, but he adds a close-up dimension, rich in detail. In *The American Bomber Plane* we see the airplane not at a distance as we would see it in flight, but close up, as if we had walked up to it on an airfield flight ramp or perhaps in the hangar undergoing maintenance. Ted's 3-view drawings give us an excellent idea of what the bomber looks like from not just one, but many perspectives. Each color portrait depicts an airplane as it appeared in service, complete with authentic service markings, insignia, and camouflage. Some readers might be surprised to see single-engine airplanes such as the Curtiss SBC Helldiver included in a book of bombers that are often considered to be large twin or four-engine machines. The authors' thoroughness would not permit single-engine dive-bombers, torpedo bombers, or attack airplanes to be left out, as they are aircraft designed and used for bombing, and they have played an important role in the history of American bombers.

Ted's color portraits of 1920s and '30s bombers have a special appeal and give us a new perspective on early American bombers, which, dating from an era before color photography became commonplace, are usually depicted only in black-and-white photographs. Ted brings these classic aircraft to life in full color. And what a colorful lot of planes they were! We had gotten through the "war to end all wars" and another war was not yet on the horizon. There was no pressing need for military planes to be camouflaged to blend in with their surroundings, so many of them sported wonderful color markings—yellow wings and tails; blue fuselages; bands, stripes, and chevrons of all colors. The advantage of camouflage later became apparent and today's bombers are mostly painted in shades of gray—what a contrast with the colorful biplanes and early monoplane bombers of the '20s and '30s. *The American Bomber Plane* allows us to turn back the hands of time and see the many-hued biplane bombers of yesteryear: the U. S. Army Keystone B-6A bomber with its huge yellow upper wing; and the navy Martin T4M with yellow wing and red tail were typical of early biplane bombers.

The early monoplane bombers of the late 1930s were as colorful as their biplane predecessors, and Ted has captured this era with his portraits of the army yellow-and-blue Martin B-10 and Curtiss A-12 Shrike; and the navy silver-and-yellow PBY Catalina and Vought SB2U Vindicator. In the early 1940s, as the reality of war loomed, we began to see the reemergence of camouflage on bomber planes. This is also accurately portrayed by Ted in his illustrations of the Douglas A-20 and Douglas TBD Devastator.

Interestingly, toward the end of World War II, as the Allies achieved air superiority, camouflage became unnecessary again, and warplanes began to exhibit a wide variety of colorful markings as shown in Ted's rendering of the famous Boeing B-17 Flying Fortress. The jets, too, had their own distinctive markings and are well represented in this book. One can see in this single volume, the evolution of American bomber planes in all their colorful glory, from the earliest wood-and-fabric biplanes to the latest stealth jet bomber, the Northrop B-2.

The medium in which Ted works to create the wonderful images in *The American Bomber Plane* is quite remarkable. A talented artist, Ted has executed many airplane portraits in such traditional mediums as pencil, ink, airbrush, watercolors, and oils. In more recent years, applying his skills as an artist, Ted has perfected the digital techniques necessary to create works of art using a computer. What Ted does is not just reworking or colorizing some existing image of an airplane with the computer. All of Ted's color portraits and 3-view drawings in this book were done from scratch by painting with what I would describe as an electronic paintbrush on a computer screen.

This book also shows the aviation historian side of Ted. With a lifelong interest in aviation, Ted has read everything he can get his hands on about airplanes and the people associated with them. He thoroughly researches each of his aircraft portraits, so we see not only an accurate rendering of lines and shapes, but also the correct colors, unit markings, and squadron insignias. Amy's attention to research and detail keeps the subject matter focused and fresh, and, combined with Ted's illustrations, her illuminating text leads the readers through the rich history of the American bomber plane. In addition, the book is filled with archival photographs that further illustrate the story of these aircraft and the people who designed, flew, and maintained them.

With this volume, Ted and Amy Williams have given us a rich, colorful, and accurate portrait of the fascinating world of the American bomber plane. I hope we will see more from this talented team.

—Dave Ostrowski
Editor Emeritus, *Skyways, The Journal of the Airplane, 1920–1940*

Introduction

Nearly every American is aware of the B-17, the big four-engine bomber with brazen nose art that is almost as famous today as the aircraft itself. A hero of World War II, the image of hundreds of B-17s darkening the sky, as flak and the explosions of felled bombers fill the frame, is preserved in our American memory—an enduring symbol of American tenacity.

Today, when we have slick bombers with advanced computer systems and stealth technology, it is amazing to think back to the crews of ten impossibly brave, and unbelievably young, American men who flew in hordes of heavy bombers over Germany, armed only with incendiary bombs and ideology. However, even before the B-17, the United States and other militarized nations had begun to investigate the idea of dropping explosives from aircraft during World War I.

From the start of military aviation, the American government struggled with the role of the bomber. It questioned whether a civilized nation could consider itself civilized if it dropped fire from the sky. Yet, as our enemies developed the competency, and another world war mounted, the United States was forced to take the argument out of the think tank and into the factory.

One of the earliest documented proponents for strategic bombing was Giulio Douhet (1869–1930), an Italian general who paved the way for strategic bombing supporters around the world. Douhet's career included a post with Italy's Aeronautical Battalion, the Italian army's first air service. World War I and his military experiences quickly shaped Douhet's revolutionary ideas about war and the value of ending conflict quickly. He firmly believed strategic bombing was an efficient way to ensure a speedy victory, thereby saving thousands of lives, even if in the process it was necessary to strike populated areas.

His masterwork, *Il dominio dell'aria* or "The Command of the Air," was first available in the 1920s. It is the culmination of his ideas on strategic bombing, air superiority, and the introduction of a distinct air force assembled from a lifetime studying the subject. The main ideas within his treatise are still called upon today, as Douhet continues to be revered as a leading theorist on the philosophy of strategic bombing.

The first historically important American advocate for air superiority was General William "Billy" Mitchell (1879–1936). Mitchell's early career was distinguished by his service in World War I as an aviator with the United States Army Air Service, where he experienced firsthand the aircraft's invaluable contribution to ground activities. After his service in Europe, he brought back with him the firm conviction that the United States needed to create a separate, autonomous air force—an idea that the United States Navy strongly opposed. When Mitchell asserted that the airplane was better at delivering ordnance than a battleship, he set into motion a series of events that would indeed validate his claim, but also ruin his career.

In July 1921 an elaborate strategic bombing test was staged off the coast of Virginia. Mitchell led a specially modified force of Martin MB-2s in a demonstration that proved aircraft were capable of sinking a ship. The *Ostfriesland*, a prized German battleship that was in the United States's possession after the Armistice, along with five other obsolete vessels, were sunk by Mitchell's bombing aircraft—absolute evidence that Mitchell was correct. (Mitchell also accurately predicted how the Japanese would raid Hawaii, well in advance of the 1941 events at Pearl Harbor.)

Through it all, Mitchell's undoing was his staunch, unwavering nature. He was court-martialed and cashiered out of the army in 1925. It was not until years later that his ideas were revived and he was posthumously awarded a Congressional Medal of Honor in 1946, ten years after his death. Today he is credited as the "father" of the United States Air Force.

BELOW: One of eleven YB-58As is being readied for a test flight. The Hustler was the U.S. Air Forces's first Mach 2 bomber.

this book traces the development of the American bomber aircraft through to the $1 billion Northrop B-2—the most advanced and expensive aircraft of all time.

It's the story of how the Boeing, Curtiss, Douglas, Grumman, Martin, and Northrop companies—and the famous men behind the nameplates: William Boeing, Glenn Curtiss, Donald Wills Douglas, Leroy Grumman, and Jack Northrop—surmounted engineering challenges to build aircraft that met army and navy specifications, fostered the survivability of the crew, and pushed the envelope to make bigger, faster, more lethal aircraft.

The American Bomber also touches upon the development of the United States's air arm and the creation of a wholly independent air force—changing bomb and weapons technology, including the nuclear threat—and the evolving political tensions that shape our world. Unlike a fighter aircraft with its one pilot and one mission, a bomber typically has many jobs to do, a crew that can be in the double digits, and it must always carry a heavy load—all engineering obstacles that require thoughtful consideration.

Consolidated, General Dynamics, Lockheed, and Republic are just a few more examples of American companies that dedicated engineers and considerable man-hours in the quest to develop premier bombing aircraft for the United States. It's an ever-evolving story that plays out in the air, but starts on the drawing board.

The bombers and attack aircraft in this volume were selected and depicted in detail by aviation artist Ted Williams. Each aircraft represents an undeniably historically significant, inventive solution for its day and situation, and is a benchmark in the evolution of the American bomber, boasting advancements in aerodynamics, propulsion, construction, avionics, and weapons systems.

As a final note, the data listed in each specification section only details the variant illustrated. A brief overview for each design program appears in the text. Although every aircraft in this book has numerous prototype, evaluation, and production models, the entire variant history is not included with the specifications.

Giulio Douhet and Billy Mitchell are two of the most recognizable catalysts in the development of strategic bombing doctrine. Once established, however, it became the domain of the manufacturers to develop aircraft that could deliver on their promise.

In 1941 an advertisement for Ryan, builder of Charles Lindbergh's "Spirit of St. Louis" and today a part of Northrop Grumman, placed an ad for its School of Aeronautics in the magazine *Flying and Popular Aviation*. It proclaimed: "In no other industry does the engineer play so important a role as in aviation." *The American Bomber* attempts to tell that story. From the World War I–era Martin MB-2 of Billy Mitchell lore, through the growing pains of the 1930s with its numerous Curtiss, Douglas, and Martin designs, into the prolific World War II–era when iconic aircraft of all sorts were produced at a rate unlike anything before or since,

TOP: B-1Bs under construction at Air Force Plant 42 in Palmdale, California.

BOTTOM: An MB-2 has dropped a white phosphorus incendiary bomb on the decommissioned battleship USS *Alabama* during the 1921 bombing test off the coast of Virginia.

Martin MB-2

It was originally believed that the airplane would never be suitable for bombing. At the start of World War I, the few airplanes that saw combat were used primarily for scouting or ground support. These early aircraft were simply not strong enough to reliably deliver a heavy load of bombs to a target, or fast enough to return safely after provoking an enemy.

However, over the course of World War I, European aircraft designers did indeed develop airplanes that could carry bombs. Russian designer Igor Sikorsky engineered a very large airplane, the first with four engines that could transport bombs and protect itself with mounted machine guns; similarly, the Germans built a devastatingly successful line of heavy bombers called the Gotha G series.

Meanwhile, a continent away, the United States had formed its own military air service, the Aeronautical Section of the United States Army Signal Corps, in as early as 1907; although pre–World War I American military doctrine did not condone strategic bombing, especially over cities or populated areas. By 1914 a more advanced Aviation Section grew out of the Aeronautical Section, but the future of American bombing tactics was still unclear. Undeniably, though, the events of the First World War had proved the viability of bombing aircraft, and the United States needed to keep up with its European counterparts.

In 1918 the Glenn L. Martin Aircraft Company was contracted to build an American-designed bomber for the United States government—one that could outperform the British Handley Page and Italian Caproni models. What developed was the Martin MB-1 (Martin Bomber 1), the progenitor of the American bomber. Like most early bombers, the MB-1 was chiefly designed to perform reconnaissance and ground support with bombing considered a secondary mission.

Glenn Luther Martin began his career selling automobiles. He learned to fly in 1909 and soon started building aircraft with auto mechanics from his dealerships. Not technical himself, he relied on talented and hardworking individuals to execute his ideas. The ability to find and retain qualified engineers helped him grow an aircraft company that produced many landmark designs under the Martin name.

Lured to Cleveland by city financiers, Martin convinced several of his key employees, including Donald Wills Douglas and Lawrence Bell, to move with him from California to the Midwest. In time, both Douglas and Bell would go on to start their own successful firms, the Douglas Aircraft Company and Bell Aircraft Corporation, respectively.

96th Bomb Squadron

OPPOSITE: This aircraft, AS64195, is the first of twenty MB-2s built by Martin. Later designated NBS-1, these bombers are best remembered today as being the aircraft that participated in the famous Billy Mitchell demonstration of 1921 when the ex-German battle cruiser *Ostfreisland* and other ships were sunk by aerial bombardment using special 2,000-pound bombs.

The Cleveland factory, a brand-new building with an adjoining airstrip, was constructed and fully operational in only six weeks. Getting an American-designed bomber assembled and to the front was paramount. The world conflict—the War to End All Wars—would continue to rage until November 11, 1918, but, despite the Martin company's heroic efforts, the MB-1 was not ready in time. The army continued with its order for the bomber from Martin, though in greatly reduced quantities.

The MB-1 was a wooden biplane covered in fabric and designed to carry a crew of four. The airframe was designed by Donald Douglas to use two American-made Liberty engines. The Liberty engine was a marvel in its time. The 400 horsepower V-12 air-cooled in-line power plant was robust and easily accessible. It was mass-produced by most major American automotive manufacturers, and it was used extensively throughout the First World War, with more than 20,000 built by 1919. Even after the war, the Liberty engine was used in everything from airplanes to high-speed boats.

Initially, four versions of the MB-1 were planned: a day and night bomber, an offensive gun ship version, and an observation variant with cameras and guns for defense. The MB-1 was equipped with flexible-mounted Lewis machine guns; an early lightweight air-cooled machine gun named after United States Army colonel Isaac Newton Lewis, who perfected Samuel McClean's design for the weapon.

The first Martin bomber to fly on September 1918 at McCook Field in Dayton, Ohio, impressed the army with its speed. Fifty were ordered, but only ten were delivered, most after the Armistice. Three of these MB-1s, often called GMBs—Glenn Martin Bombers—went to the Smithsonian, while the remaining military variants were outfitted for record-breaking stunt attempts or for other nonmilitary or experimental service. Some were refitted to carry mail and passengers, but, overall, the aircraft's military career was less than stellar, until Brigadier General William "Billy" Mitchell brought his design ideas to the development of the MB-2 bomber.

Billy Mitchell, the "father" of the United States Air Force, was a powerful, yet derisive voice in early airpower. During World War I, Mitchell served in the U.S. Army Air Corps. He was a tireless advocate for airpower, particularly strategic bombing and a move away from battleship warfare—ideas the U.S. Army and U.S. Navy were unwilling to support. Later, in 1925, Mitchell wrote a missive that accurately predicted the Japanese attack on Pearl Harbor. Mitchell's

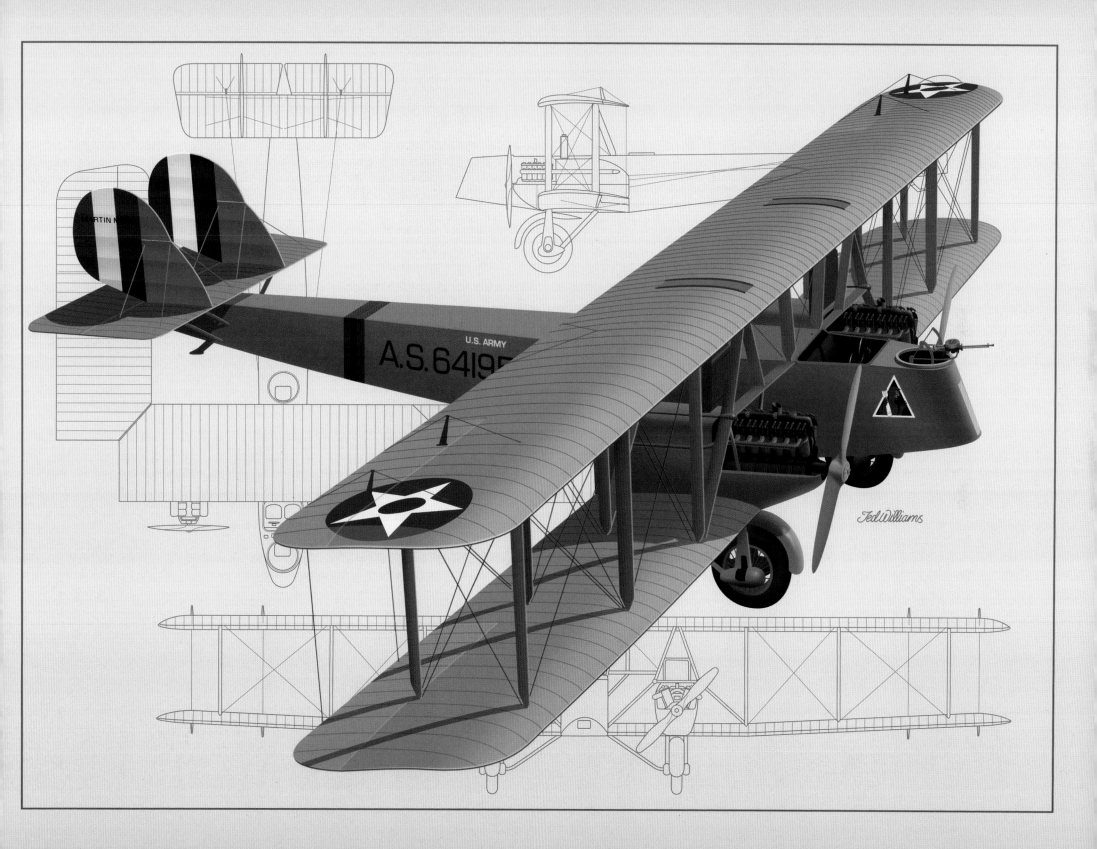

U.S. ARMY
A.S. 6419

Ted Williams

Martin MB-2 Specifications

Type: Land-based bomber
Crew: Four
Power plant: Two 420-horsepower Packard Liberty 12-cylinder liquid-cooled engines
Performance: Maximum speed, 99 miles per hour at sea level; service ceiling, 8,500 feet; maximum range, 560 miles
Weight: Empty, 7,864 pounds; maximum takeoff weight, 13,695 pounds
Dimensions: Span, 74 feet, 2 inches; length, 43 feet, 7 inches; height, 15 feet, 7 inches; wing area, 1,121 square feet
Armament: Five .30-cal Lewis machine guns, up to 2,000 pounds of bombs or one 1,650-pound torpedo

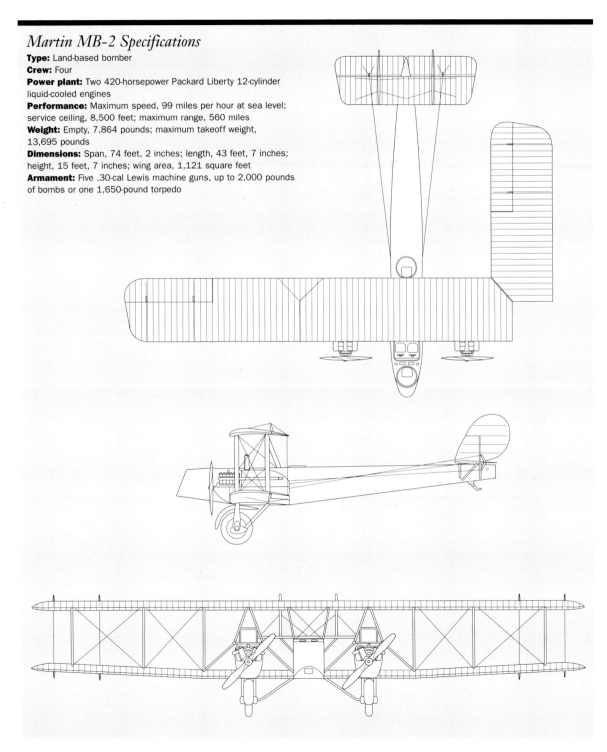

outspoken beliefs led to a court-martial and his subsequent resignation from the army. It was not until years later that his ideas were praised.

The Mitchell-influenced MB-2 had larger wings, but it was slower than the MB-1 because it could carry a larger payload, improving its military function as a strategic bomber. The two Liberty engines, which had been suspended between the wings, were moved into two newly created nacelles mounted on the lower wing. This engineering change eliminated the need for the struts that had previously suspended the engines in place between the wings.

The MB-1's original four-wheel landing gear was replaced by a more efficient two-wheel system with bigger wheels and pneumatic shock absorbers. Now, since there was more distance between the two wheels, the MB-2 had room for internal bomb stowage. Also, new hinges behind the nacelles permitted the wings to fold for easier storage. Based on these improvements, the United

States Army Air Service (the USAAS, as the Aviation Section of the Signal Corps was renamed in 1918) ordered twenty in 1920.

In 1921 Mitchell proved his theory that strategic bombing was indisputably a feasible military technique, and the air tactic of the future. In front of an audience made up of prominent army and navy officials and the press, Mitchell's collection of specially outfitted MB-2s sank ex-German and other war surplus ships, including the famous German battleship, *Ostfriesland*, which the Treaty of Versailles had turned over to the United States as war reparations.

On the cusp of Mitchell's dynamic bombing experiment, the army ordered another 110 Martin bombers. These were designated as NBS-1s, Night Bombers for Short distances, but these planes were not built by the Glenn L. Martin Aircraft Company. Government procurement practices of the time stipulated that any request for any aircraft could be bid on by any

BELOW: A Curtiss-built MB-2 bomber awaits delivery to the U.S. Army. The MB-2 was discernable from the MB-1 by its wing-mounted engines and two-wheel landing gear.

OPPOSITE: Larry Bell, Eric Springer, Glenn Martin, and Donald Douglas (l-r), the design team for the first American bomber, pose for the camera in front an early MB-1.

firm, no matter who originated the design. As such, Aeromarine built twenty-five, Curtiss built fifty, and L.W.F. Engineering built thirty-five, all undercutting Martin's $23,485 per plane price. This was not unusual for the day. Often the company that spent money to innovate something new, and took the time to convince the government that it needed the something new, did not recoup its initial investment.

The Martin NBS bombers saw military service until 1928; none are in existence today. Unfortunately, the three MB-1s earmarked for the Smithsonian did not survive, nor did the original Cleveland factory. We may only have photos of the MB-1 and MB-2, but its service life spawned the development of American bombers, as well as the careers of several prominent aviation pioneers who, in their own time, would all leave an indelible mark on the time-line of bomber development.

Keystone Bomber

In 1920 Thomas Henri Huff partnered with Elliot Daland to form an aviation company in Ogdensburg, New York. Both men were educated at Massachusetts Institute of Technology and had successful aeronautical careers before starting a joint venture. Known for its sturdy crop-dusting aircraft, their little self-named company was the precursor to Delta Air Lines and the progenitor of the Keystone bomber.

Huff-Daland and Company received an order from the U.S. Army in 1923 to build a light bomber for a crew of three that was to supersede the Martin MB design. Huff-Daland's first attempt was the XLB-1. Already faster than the wooden Martin NBS-1, the Huff-Daland biplane bomber featured a fabric-covered steel tube frame with 66 feet of tapered wings and five .30-caliber machine guns, but only one engine—a large Packard radial with 800 horsepower. Since the immense engine and propeller occupied the nose area, an aiming window on the underside of the aircraft was used to drop the bombs, which were housed internally.

The XLB-1 aircraft led to the development of the LB-1, which had a larger Packard engine, larger bomb load capacity, and a crew of four. However, doubts remained about the endurance and security of a single engine. The XLB-1 and LB-1 would be the last single-engine bombers considered by the U.S. Army Air Service.

Before completely abandoning the single-engine configuration, Huff-Daland produced a heavy bomber version. An even larger variant of the LB-1, the XHB-1 could carry 4,000 pounds of bombs—almost double the weight of the light bombers. Only one was built. Later, Huff-Daland created another heavy bomber design for evaluation, a twin-engine monoplane, but it was also never produced in quantity.

The Huff-Daland XLB-3 assuaged the army's single-engine concerns. It had two inverted Liberty engines with 420 horsepower each, which were mounted to the lower wing; now bombs could be aimed more accurately from the nose. But soon the Liberty engines proved insufficient for this variant and they were replaced by two Pratt & Whitney R-1340-1 Wasp radial engines. Designated XLB-3A, the Pratt & Whitney version carried a crew of five.

When the XLB-3A was introduced in 1927 the Huff-Daland company was undergoing a transformation. Absorbed by the Keystone Aircraft Corporation, the new company continued its dedication to bomber development and the line of Huff-Daland–inspired light bombers.

RIGHT: A Keystone bomber under construction; note how the exhaust collectors are mounted in front of the radial engine, an improvement used on later variants.

OPPOSITE: The Keystone B-6A was the last of America's biplane bombers. A big aircraft by the standards of the day, the B-6A could take off at over 13,000 pounds gross weight. Here it is shown with yellow wings and empennage. As early as 1924 yellow was used on the flying surfaces to increase visibility in the event the aircraft went down in a remote area. In 1927, yellow wings and tail became the standard paint scheme for all U.S. Army aircraft.

The next significant variants were the Liberty-powered XLB-5 with a single tail and the LB-5 with a triple vertical tail, but the bulk promised to the army in 1928 was the Keystone LB-5A bomber, distinguishable by its twin vertical tail. In total, thirty-five aircraft resulted from the LB-5 (ten) and LB-5A (twenty-five), yet the solitary XLB-5 remains notable because of a tragic accident. On May 28, 1927, an XLB-5 crash caused by a propeller malfunction killed one man, Private Daniel Leroy Yeager. The four other crew members jumped from the doomed aircraft. In 1927 these four brave men became the largest group involved in a single aviation disaster to survive by using parachutes.

In 1928 Keystone provided the army with the XLB-6, which would be produced in a quantity of eighteen as the LB-6. It featured straight-chord wings, as opposed to the previous version's tapered wings, and two Wright Cyclone radial engines. The Wright engines were an improvement over the Liberty in-line engines—the Liberty engines on the LB-5A had been acquired as war surplus; they could only operate to World War I specifications. To further enhance the aircraft's structural performance, the Wright Cyclone engines were suspended between the wings.

The Keystone bomber was the U.S. Army's primary bombing aircraft for most of the 1920s and '30s. The design of the LB-5 and -6 remained the basis for all other aircraft in the series. Modifications through to the LB-14 were built on the -5 or -6 platform. The most successful was the Keystone LB-10A with sixty-three ordered in 1930. These planes were designated as B-3A because, in 1930, the U.S. Army Air Corps discontinued the distinctions for light (LB), medium (B), and heavy (HB) bombers. Henceforth all bombers, no matter their size or strategic or tactical purpose, would carry a "B" for bombing.

The 1930s would challenge Keystone's tired engineering principles as newer, more radical all-metal monoplanes came off the drafting tables and into reality. Despite being produced in the greatest quantity of the series, the LB-10A/B-3A was limited by its 1920's technology. It could reach a top speed of only approximately 114 miles per hour, with a typical cruising speed of 98 miles per hour; these speeds were nearly identical to the speed

BELOW: Keystone Bombers of the 91st Bombardment Squadron have assembled in formation over the Hudson River, New York, for a dynamic public relations photo.

OPPOSITE TOP: Early flight crews were exposed to the elements in open cockpits as in this Keystone bomber from the 23rd Bomb Squadron stationed in Hawaii.

OPPOSITE BOTTOM: This photo of the forward fuselage of a Keystone bomber, taken in 1929, clearly shows the aircraft's tubular construction and fabric covering.

specifications for all previous variants. The same was true for its bomb load capacity, service ceiling, and range—they were all about the same for any aircraft in the series, no obvious improvement in nearly a decade.

Keystone bombers flew with several Bomb Groups, including the 2d, 7th, and 19th, headquartered in the United States and overseas. Most Keystone bombers were retired from actual service by 1936, but a few were still being used for reconnaissance duty as late as the 1940s. It has been estimated that some two hundred Keystone bombers were produced overall. Today, none survive. The Keystone bomber was the army's last biplane bomber.

Huff-Daland's influence on early aviation is irrefutable. Although not much better than the Martin bomber it had been designed to replace, the Huff-Daland Keystone bomber became the standard for an entire era. The light bomber series went through many different engine refittings, tail configurations, and variants to produce a very conservative machine. It was the U.S. Army's darling and a very successful product for Keystone.

Keystone Bomber B-6A Specifications

Type: Bomber
Crew: Five
Power plant: Two 575-horsepower R-1820 air-cooled radial engines
Performance: Maximum speed, 121 miles per hour at sea level; service ceiling, 14,100 feet; maximum range, 363 miles
Weight: Empty, 8,037 pounds; maximum takeoff weight, 13,374 pounds (gross)
Dimensions: Span, 74 feet, 9 inches; length, 48 feet, 10 inches; height, 17 feet, 2 inches; wing area, 1,137 square feet
Armament: Three .30-cal Browning machine guns, up to 2,500 pounds of bombs

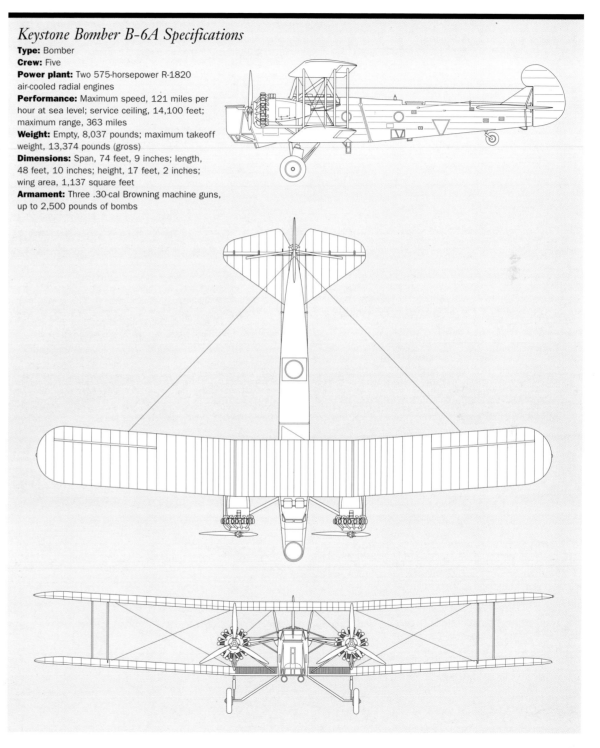

Douglas PD-1

One of the more interesting ideas to emerge during the early days of aviation was the concept of the flying boat. A hybrid of sorts, a flying boat is an airplane with a fuselage akin to the hull of a ship. This distinctive characteristic means a flying boat can function on water. Typically, pontoons on both sides of a flying boat's fuselage support its wings and enable the airplane to float, take off, and land on the water's surface—a unique advantage that eliminates the aircraft's reliance on traditional runways.

Glenn Curtiss was at the forefront of the flying boat. He designed a large biplane flying boat that ultimately found a home with the British Royal Naval Air Service. The basis for the British version was a design Curtiss had intended to be flown from the United States to Europe in what he had hoped would be a celebrated transatlantic crossing. When that stunt flight was cancelled due to the onset of World War I, Curtiss was not deterred. His design still made its way to England.

The British took Curtiss's design, originally called the Curtiss America, and refitted it for military use. Over the course of the First World War, the Curtiss America–styled flying boat continued to be refined and changed to meet the British government's wartime needs. Flying boats were most often used as patrol bombers for antishipping missions. They could easily cover large expanses of ocean, seeking and destroying the enemy's merchant and hostile vessels. Soon the U.S. Navy looked to acquire its own flying boats, ordering its own militarized versions of the Curtiss America, which came to be designated with the identifier PN.

By 1927 the U.S. Navy needed to refresh its supply of PN flying boats, which had been depleted by constant use and war. The Douglas Aircraft Company was one of the American manufacturers selected to build more flying boats for the navy. Contracted to produce twenty-five of the PN-12 variant, the engineers at Douglas altered the 1914 design into a new and improved version.

Like Curtiss, Donald Wills Douglas was one of aviation's most successful pioneers. Douglas's early credits included studying and teaching aeronautics at Massachusetts Institute of Technology, working on the Connecticut Aircraft Company team that crafted the navy's first dirigible, and being the principal design engineer for the Martin MB-1. After leaving the Glenn L. Martin Company, Douglas joined forces with the wealthy sportsman David R. Davis to start an aircraft company. Their enterprise, the Davis-Douglas Company,

RIGHT: Identical to the PD-1, this Martin PM-1 features an enclosed cockpit. The navy used flying boats for long-range reconnaissance and patrol missions over water.

OPPOSITE: The Douglas PD-1 was the last of a core design that dated back to World War I. This successful Douglas version of the Curtiss flying boat was operational from 1930 to 1936. Here it is shown in the markings of VP-6. Large fuselage side identification numbers were used through the mid thirties; however, the use of the red, white, and blue rudder stripes was discontinued on patrol aircraft in 1934.

promptly reorganized into the Douglas Company in July 1921, after Davis lost interest in the aviation industry. Today, the Douglas Aircraft Company is best known for its successful DC series of transport aircraft.

For the PN-12 project, the Douglas Company modified the aircraft's wing-support system. The excess struts and wires were removed; more modern ailerons were used instead. Although still a biplane with fabric-covered wings and a metal-clad hull, the sleek ailerons improved the aircraft's aerodynamics. Other enhancements included tapering and tweaking the shape of major airframe features, such as the engine nacelles, to improve aerodynamics. Douglas engineers also implemented newer technology, such as adjustable-pitch metal propellers, a rudimentary gyroscope-controlled automatic-pilot mechanism, and newer instrumentation, such as modernized radio equipment. For power it used two 525-horsepower nine-cylinder Wright radial engines that were later increased to 575 horsepower.

Now called PD-1 (Patrol Douglas), the aircraft required a crew of five with accommodations for another five men to allow duty rotation during long sorties. It could maintain a top speed that was comparable to the Keystone bomber, while carrying up to 2,000 pounds of torpedoes or bombs on external racks located under the bottom wing. It was armed with two .30-caliber machine guns.

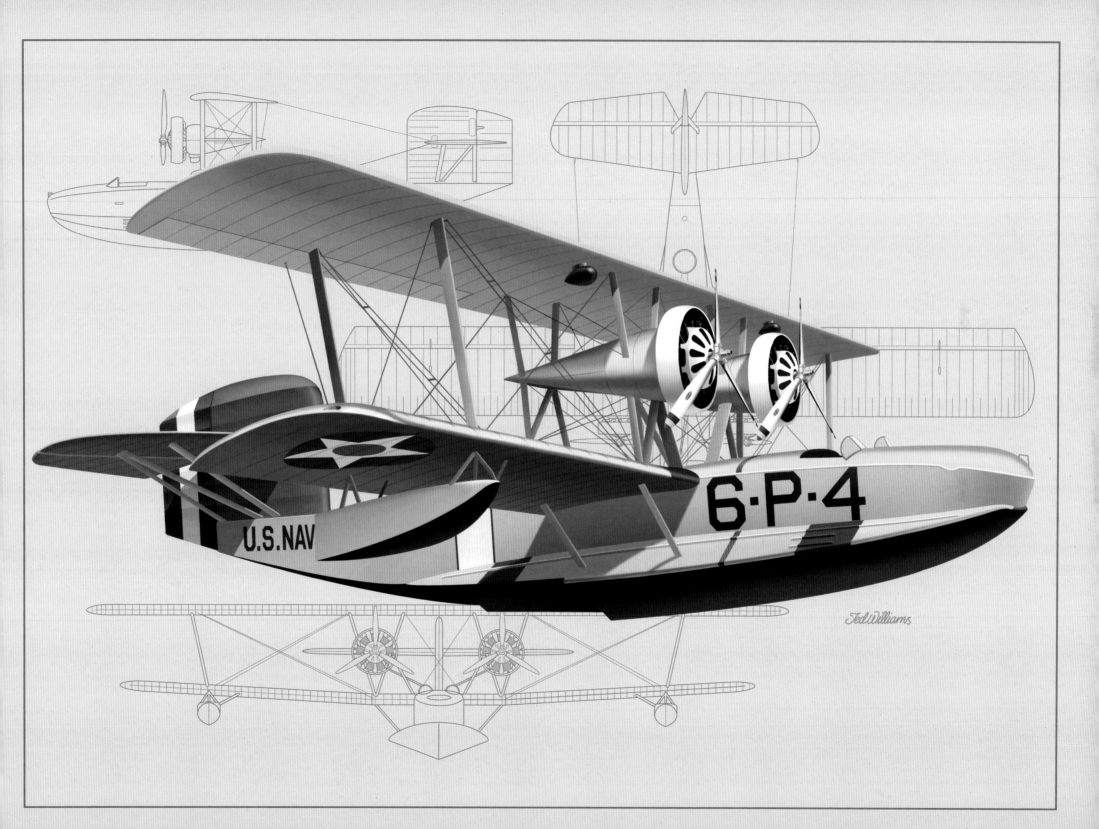

Douglas PD-1 Specifications

Type: Long-range patrol bomber
Crew: Five with five-person relief crew
Power plant: Two 575-horsepower Wright R-1820-64 air-cooled radial engines
Performance: Maximum speed, 114 miles per hour at sea level; service ceiling, 10,900 feet; maximum range, 1,309 miles
Weight: Empty, 7,453 pounds; maximum takeoff weight, 14,122 pounds
Dimensions: Span, 72 feet, 10 inches; length, 49 feet, 2 inches; height, 16 feet, 4 inches; wing area, 1,162 square feet
Armament: Two .30-cal machine guns, 2,000 pounds of bombs, torpedoes, or mines

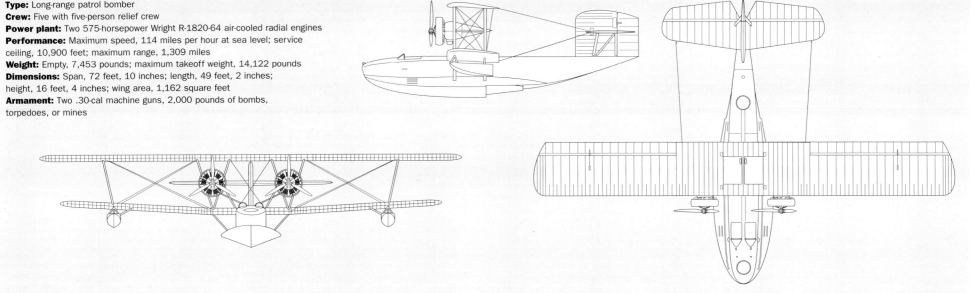

It was a challenging project for Douglas, in part because its facility in California was not located near water. For evaluation, aircraft had to be shipped to San Diego in crates and then reassembled before testing could commence. Later, Douglas would move its factory to Santa Monica.

The Douglas PD-1 saw service with several U.S. Navy patrol squadrons, including the One, Four, Six, and Seven, but it was only operational for six years, from 1930 through 1936; some were used for training exercises through 1938. Just like the U.S. Army's Keystone bomber, the PD-1's core design was defined by its World War I limitations. It quickly became obsolete.

In 1929 the Glenn L. Martin Company was hard at work on its own government-sponsored revision of the PN-12. The Martin version, known as the PM-1, was another twin-engine biplane with fabric-covered wings and metal construction that incorporated "Alclad," an aluminum alloy with corrosion repelling attributes. As with the PD-1, the Martin design debuted many

OPPOSITE BELOW: This overhead view of a Martin PM-1 clearly displays the classic planform of the Curtiss flying boat. The structures above the ailerons were an improvement added to balance the excessive aerodynamic forces experienced by the control surfaces.

BELOW: The last improvement to the PM/PD/PN series of flying boats was the incorporation of twin vertical stabilizers as shown on these Martin PM-2s.

of the same types of changes: adjustments to reduce drag-inducing structures, increased power from nine-cylinder engines, and the implementation of newer materials and technologies. Thirty PM-1s were built and delivered, and an additional twenty-five PM-2s became operational in 1931.

The U.S. Navy would continue to embrace the flying boat long after the demise of the PD-1 and PM-1 programs. Escalating tensions with the island nation of Japan was one motivation for development of versatile waterborne aircraft. That the Douglas and Martin companies, as well as the Keystone Aircraft Corporation with its PK-1, all built and supplied the U.S. Navy with adaptations of Curtiss's flying boat well into the 1930s is a testament to his vision.

Glenn Curtiss may not have won the *Daily Mail*'s prize for crossing the Atlantic with his Curtiss America in 1914, but he certainly earned the U.S. Navy's esteem. In 2007, the Glenn H. Curtiss Museum in Hammondsport, New York, completed a functional reproduction of the 1914 Curtiss America.

Martin T4M

A bomber's purpose is to drop something; it can be anything from propaganda pamphlets to something more lethal and explosive. Why that item gets dropped is either strategic or tactical. Strategic bombing is an attack on an enemy's ability to wage war by destroying infrastructure or manufacturing assets. Tactical bombing supports ground army operations, disrupting enemy lines of supply and communications by attacking enemy assets beyond the reach of artillery.

Naval bombing operations are primarily tactical. A naval bomber's overall task is to extend the fleet's offensive firepower, and to seek out and destroy enemy vessels. In addition, a naval bomber requires a more robust design to withstand the rigors of aircraft carrier operations and long-range missions over broad expanses of ocean.

In 1922 the U.S. Navy Bureau of Aeronautics (BuAer) sent out a request for a biplane that could "scout" and drop bombs or torpedoes. BuAer selected a Curtiss design—designated CS-1 (Curtiss Scout)—and commissioned Curtiss to build six.

The CS-1 had a riveted steel-tube fuselage with room for a crew of three: a pilot, rear gunner, and bomber or torpedoman. The CS-1's bottom wingspan was greater than the top, the wings folded for storage, and the torpedo could be partially stowed in a hollow cavity fashioned into the underside of the fuselage.

In 1923 the Glenn L. Martin Company stepped in with a lower per-unit cost and won the contract to build another thirty-five CS-1s for the U.S. Navy. Turnabout is fair play: Only two years prior, Curtiss had swooped in to build a large order of Martin's night-bombing configuration of the MB-1. The procurement practice that allowed any manufacturing company to bid on any military project would last until World War II when the government would finally acknowledge how the company that engineered an aircraft should keep the rights to build it.

The Martin-built version was designated SC-1. It retained features and construction details from the CS-1, such as the distinctively longer bottom wingspan and single Wright in-line liquid-cooled engine. Like its antecedent, the SC-1 had either wheels for land operation or floats for use on water. In time, an enhanced version of the aircraft was developed by Curtiss: two were built by Curtiss as the CS-2 and forty were built by Martin as the SC-2.

In 1925 Martin received another order from the U.S. Navy to build more scout bombers, but the navy wanted changes to the platform. In 1926 Martin

VT-2B Torpedo Squadron 2

RIGHT: A T4M-1 with extended tail hook prepares to enter the pattern for landing on board the USS *Saratoga* in January 1929. The decks of early aircraft carriers could quickly become over-crowded with parked aircraft, which only left a small area for the pilot to make a safe landing.

OPPOSITE: Although not the only torpedo-delivering aircraft used by the U.S. Navy in the 1920s, the Martin T-4M was arguably the best. It even became a Hollywood celebrity. Here a dashing T4M-1 is shown in the 1932 markings of VT-2B. The bright red tail indicates it is stationed aboard the aircraft carrier, USS *Saratoga*.

U.S. NAVY

2-T-15

Ted Williams

completed twenty-four T3M-1s, the aircraft that evolved from the SC design. This next-generation scout bomber had several considerable improvements over the SC. Now, the steel frame was welded not riveted, the wooden two-bladed propeller was swapped out for a metal three-bladed propeller, and the crew increased to four. A T3M-2 was also developed with a Packard engine.

In total, Martin built 124 T3M-1s and T3M-2s. T3Ms equipped squadrons on the U.S. Navy aircraft carriers the USS *Saratoga* and USS *Lexington*. The -2s were distinguishable from the previous variant by their wings; on the T3M-2, the upper and lower wings were of equal span.

Improvements continued. The navy urged the Martin company to update the T3M's engine for even better carrier performance. The nine-cylinder 525-horsepower Pratt & Whitney R-1690 Hornet engine was tested and accepted into service in the T4M. The Pratt & Whitney radial engine was lighter and easier to maintain than the twelve-cylinder liquid-cooled Packard engine. In addition, the T4M incorporated newer lightweight metals and materials and the wings were shorter with rounded tips. All of these changes helped to improve the aircraft's speed and performance. Martin built 102 T4M-1s.

The T4M-1 was used in the U.S. Navy's annual grand-scale training exercises. In 1929 a simulation presupposed the Panama Canal was being attacked. The T4M-1 was an important player in this mock scenario devised to measure the airplane's effectiveness during an actual hostile encounter. The T4M, along with other fleet aircraft used for the elaborate exercise, helped reinforce the concept that bombing aircraft could extend the fleet's striking power.

The T4M also became a celebrity on the silver screen when it was featured in the 1931 MGM film *Hell Divers*. The movie starred Clark Gable as a dashing naval officer.

While the T4M was out serving its country, changes were happening back at the factory. In 1929 Glenn Martin sold his entire Cleveland operation and the rights to the Cleveland-developed designs to a company called Detroit Aircraft, which operated the factory under its Great Lakes Aircraft Company subsidiary. Great Lakes would continue to build the T4M for the navy, but now designated as the TG-1 and TG-2. In all, eighteen TG-1 and thirty-two TG-2 aircraft were built. Glenn Martin relocated his enterprise to Baltimore, Maryland, where he built a new facility that was the first aircraft factory completely dedicated to manufacturing all-metal aircraft. Martin also tried unsuccessfully to sell the T4M outside of the United States.

The T4M saw service with the U.S. Navy until 1937. Overall, it was a successful design and it was one of the most widely used naval bombers of the interwar period. Like the Douglas PD-1 and Martin PM-1, which flew to success on a Glenn Curtiss design, the Martin T4M's ancestry was Curtiss, but Martin made the design its own. An impressive pedigree and a Hollywood leading role make for one interesting story indeed.

Martin T4M-1 Specifications

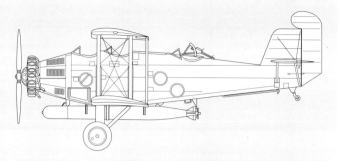

Type: Torpedo bomber
Crew: Three or four
Power plant: One 525-horsepower Pratt & Whitney Hornet R-1690-24 air-cooled radial engine
Performance: Maximum speed, 114 miles per hour; service ceiling 10,150 feet; maximum range, 656 miles
Weight: Empty, 3,890 pounds; maximum takeoff weight, 7,387 pounds
Dimensions: Span 53 feet; length, 35 feet, 7 inches; height, 14 feet, 9 inches; wing area, 656 square feet
Armament: Three .30-cal machine guns and one 1,600-pound torpedo

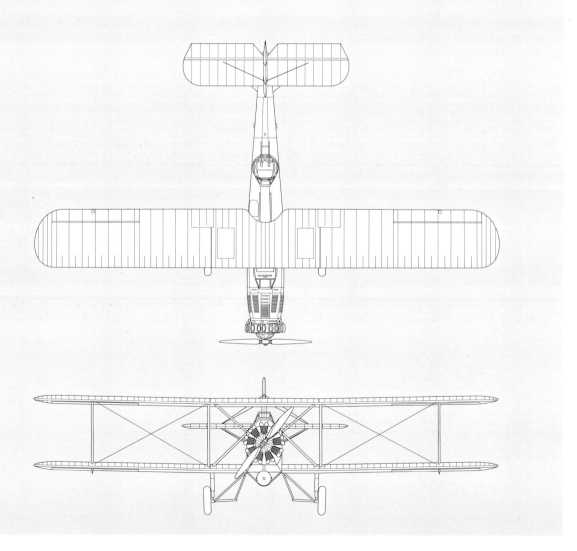

LEFT: This T4M-1, mounted on floats, is one of two assigned to the USS *Heron* on station with the Asiatic Fleet in 1932.

BELOW: The T4M-1 was later built as the TG-1 by Great Lakes Aircraft. This T4M-1 has been assigned to the Naval Reserve Air Base in Seattle, Washington.

Boeing B-9

Although quickly outclassed by the Martin B-10, the Boeing B-9 is still regarded as an evolutionary milestone on the timeline of American bomber aircraft development. The B-9 was an internally-braced cantilevered (no struts needed) low-wing all-metal monoplane bomber made for the U.S. Army, and it caused quite a sensation despite its limited production run.

At only twenty-two years of age, William E. Boeing was drawn to flight during the exciting pioneering days of aviation. Bolstered by money from his family's Minnesota lumber and mining operations, and with an engineering education from Yale, Boeing headed west to Seattle, Washington.

In the Pacific Northwest, Boeing started his own company. The fledgling manufacturing firm managed to stay alive during the World War I production boom and postwar bust by manufacturing everything from boats to wooden furniture. Ultimately, Boeing's unwavering determination and aptitude for recruiting skilled talent put the Boeing Airplane Company back on the path to becoming a premier aircraft supplier to the U.S. Army and Navy.

Military contracts were the bread and butter of every airplane business during the 1920s and '30s. Like everyone else in the industry, Boeing's firm built several approved designs at the request of the military; but Boeing was not satisfied. He wanted his company to originate its own designs.

The B-9 was unlike anything attempted in the bombing category. It was a Boeing original and it did not stem from a military request, although it was based on the need for a better bomber. Amazingly, after the end of World War I and before World War II there had been very few advances in bomber development; the entire category was held to the standards set by the Keystone bomber and early Martin designs.

Boeing introduced two prototypes in 1930, Models 214 and 215—one with two liquid-cooled Curtiss Conqueror engines and the other with Pratt & Whitney Hornet radial engines and anti-drag NACA cowlings. The National Advisory Committee for Aeronautics (NACA), precursor to NASA, tested and developed flight engineering concepts.

Closely based on the silhouette of the Boeing Model 221 Monomail six-passenger transport aircraft, the prototypes were capable of carrying a maximum 2,400-pound payload or six 400-pound bombs, which were carried on external mounts under the wings. The design also featured novel retractable landing gear—the wheels could be situated partially inside the engine nacelles during flight for improved aerodynamics.

OPPOSITE: There are two features of the B-9 that immediately impress the viewer: the first is its aerodynamic cleanliness—a sensation in 1930; second is its single cantilevered wing that could lift a great load like a biplane, yet give the bomber unprecedented speed. It is obvious why this aircraft is considered the grandsire of the modern bomber.

The U.S. Army evaluated the Pratt & Whitney–powered Model 215, designated XB-901, in 1931 and praised it highly. It was faster than the pursuit aircraft of the day and it exceeded the army's expectations for handling, speed, and armament capabilities. One flaw was a wrinkling characteristic that plagued the thin metal covering. The semi-monocoque fuselage's external metal skin absorbed motion stress, creating a furrowed appearance. Pilots also complained about poor visibility.

These objections aside, the army bought the two prototypes based on the XB-901's initial favorable flight tests and designated them YB-9 and Y1B-9 (formerly Models 215 and 214). In 1932 the army ordered five additional service test aircraft with superchargers and other modifications. This lot was labeled Y1B-9A.

YB-9 and Y1B-9 continued to undergo examinations by the engineers at Wright Field in Dayton, Ohio. Through exhaustive testing and comparisons, the YB-9 was determined to have better overall performance than its sister ship, mostly attributed to its Pratt & Whitney Hornet radial engines that could move larger propellers than the ones on the Y1B-9. As a result, the Y1B-9's Curtiss Conquerors were exchanged for Pratt & Whitney Hornets.

All aircraft from the initial order were delivered to the army by March 1933. Over the course of manufacturing, subtle improvements were initiated. These included a redesign of the vertical fin, rudder, and wheel coverings; updates to the nacelles; and the addition of powered landing gear. Prior to the electrical assist, it would take the muscle of two men to raise and lower the gear.

The aircraft was originally designed to accommodate four men positioned in a line and widely separated from each other, but the army insisted on a five-person crew made up of a gunner/bombardier located in the nose, and a pilot, copilot, radio operator, and rear gunner with a flexible .30-caliber machine gun, who each sat in individual open-air cockpits. An enlargement to the wing allowed for the added radio operator's weight. The crew had to use a ladder to board the plane, and once in, communication was challenging because of the seating arrangement in exposed cockpits along the slender fuselage. The gunner in the nose had an aiming sight for dropping bombs and a .30-caliber machine gun.

Both the YB-9 and Y1B-9 flew their entire careers at Wright Field. The five Y1B-9As spent the majority of their time continuing to perform testing. Only one succumbed to tragedy. The last aircraft from the batch of five crashed during a night training mission, killing its entire crew.

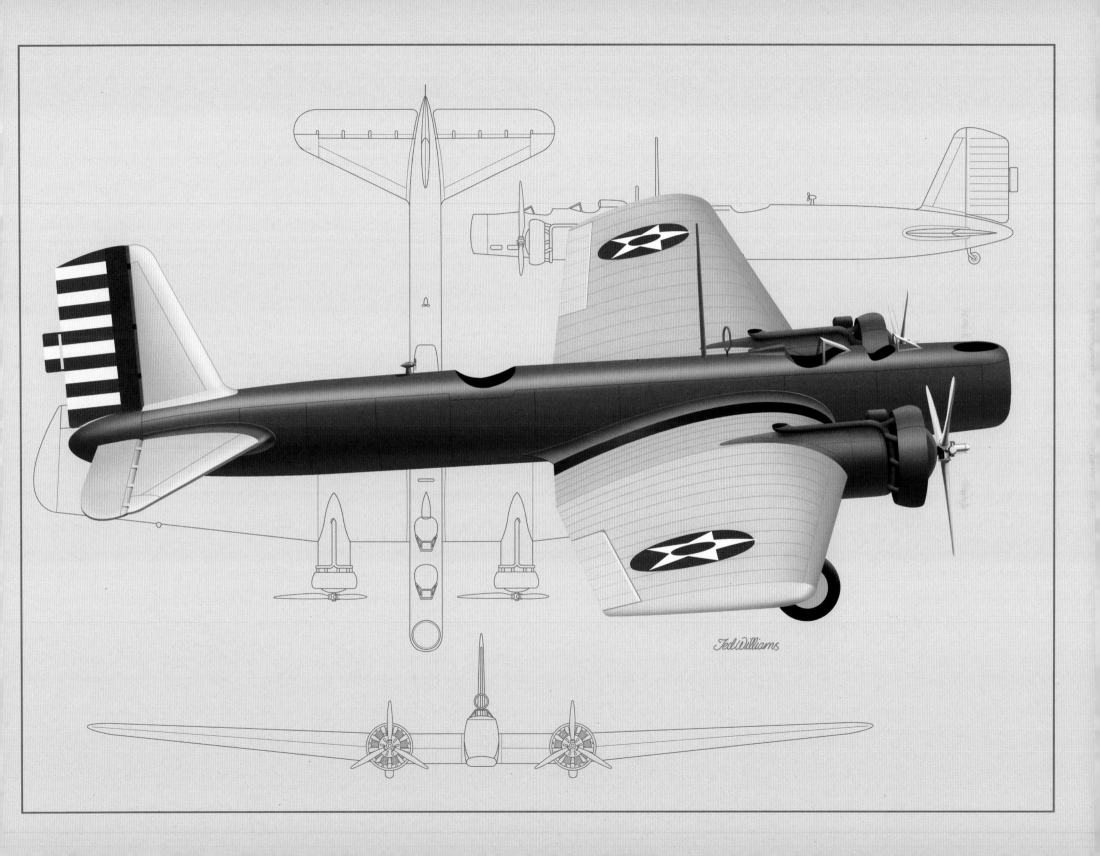

Ted Williams

LEFT: The rear gunners open position in a Boeing B-9 had a flexible .30-cal gun mount. It was located in the slender fuselage aft of the wing.

OPPOSITE: The all-metal monocoque construction, pioneered in the Boeing Monomail, gave the Boeing B-9 its unprecedented strength and performance.

BELOW: The temporary War Games camouflage applied to this Boeing B-9 could be easily removed with soap and water.

On the whole, the B-9 acquitted itself well. It performed admirably at a military competition in 1933 and it far exceeded the army's active bombers' performance specifications, despite a few flight characteristics that were criticized by pilots. Furthermore, design improvements, such as sliding greenhouse-style canopies to protect the crew from wind and weather and a B-9B model were being discussed. Boeing fully expected the army would make a large bulk purchase, but the B-9 missed its moment. The Martin B-10 had already been brought to the U.S. Army Air Corps's attention and Martin's aircraft was faster, bigger, and, maybe most important to the government, more economical to produce.

All seven B-9s were out of service by 1935. None are in existence today. An ignoble end to such a promising design, yet its forward-thinking innovations led to newer, faster bombers, and helped to push the U.S. Army toward considering monoplane bomber designs. Popularly known as the "Death Angel," it never had the chance to earn the moniker.

Boeing B-9 Specifications

Type: Bomber
Crew: Five
Power plant: Two 600-horsepower Pratt & Whitney Hornet R-1860-11 air-cooled radial engines
Performance: Maximum speed, 188 miles per hour at 6,000 feet; service ceiling, 20,750 feet; maximum range, 540 miles
Weight: Empty, 8,941 pounds; maximum takeoff weight, 13,932 pounds
Dimensions: Span, 76 feet, 10 inches; length, 52 feet; height, 12 feet; wing area, 954 square feet
Armament: Two .30-cal machine guns and 2,260 pounds of bombs

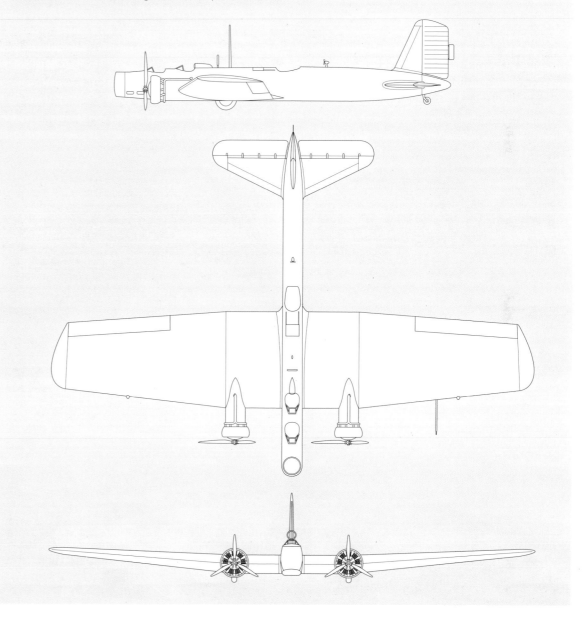

Curtiss A-12 Shrike

Glenn H. Curtiss had been busy during World War I supplying the U.S. Army and Navy with aircraft. Already known for his flying boats, his innovative concepts, and for convincing the navy to accept aircraft into fleet operations, Curtiss was one of early aviation's most celebrated figures.

Curtiss started his aviation career designing engines and building motorcycles in his hometown of Hammondsport, New York. In 1907 Curtiss claimed a land speed record on a motorcycle of his own creation, and nearly all lighter-than-air ships at the time used a Curtiss engine. Curtiss took this notoriety, and everything he knew about engines and powered flight, and joined Alexander Graham Bell's famous Aerial Experiment Association (AEA).

His success with the AEA and, later, with his own designs, put Curtiss at odds with the Wright brothers who claimed patent infringement. Curtiss spent much of his professional life battling the Wrights in court, but the litigious distraction did not keep him from producing several notable aircraft designs, growing his little manufacturing enterprise into an esteemed aviation empire.

Glenn Curtiss died at age fifty-two in 1930 of an embolism shortly after an appendectomy; nonetheless his name lives on. Successful corporate arrangements organized after his death—including a seemingly unlikely alliance with the Wright Aeronautical Corporation—have kept the acclaimed, pioneering Curtiss and Wright legacies in the public eye.

In 1930 the Curtiss company broke new ground. Using specifications from the U.S. Army, it developed an all-new, all-metal low-wing monoplane to succeed the Curtiss Falcon. The Curtiss Falcon biplane had been a very popular observation and attack aircraft. Both the army and the navy flew numerous Falcon variants from 1923 through 1934.

Much like a bomber, an attack aircraft's role is to destroy a target or hinder an enemy's ability to wage war. Mostly tactical, attack aircraft are used to support a ground army's activities. However, unlike a high-altitude bomber, an attack aircraft must get in close to the conflict. For that reason, it must have speed and protection for the crew. Because of this, most attack aircraft take on the look and characteristics of fighters and are sometimes referred to as fighter bombers or attack bombers.

The designers at Curtiss christened the new airplane "Shrike" after a particularly vicious predatory bird that has the appearance of an enchanting songster, but is actually a deadly aggressor; the army called it X8-A.

RIGHT: A look at the left side of an A-12's cockpit. The A-12 Shrike was the first successful aircraft designed for attack missions. Bigger than a fighter, but just as nimble, it could deliver heavy ordnance and withstand the g-forces encountered during steep angles of attack.

OPPOSITE: The Shrike was the U.S. Army's first monoplane attack aircraft. The A-12 was a refinement of the earlier Shrike designs with a radial engine instead of a liquid-cooled inline engine. In January 1934, the army adopted the blue fuselage scheme for all types of aircraft. The yellow cowl shown here identifies this A-12 as being from the 20th Attack Squadron, Hawaii, 1939.

The X8-A was the first monoplane Curtiss supplied to the army. In addition to the metal construction, it featured covered cockpits. The pilot, in the completely enclosed front cockpit, had access to four forward-firing .30-caliber machine guns located outside of the swing of the propeller, while the other crewman (an observer gunner) in the semi-enclosed rear cockpit had a single, flexible machine gun. External racks underneath the wings were capable of supporting more than 450 pounds of bombs.

A Curtiss Conqueror liquid-cooled engine and three-bladed propeller powered the X8-A. Curtiss also gave the X8-A trailing-edge and full-span leading-edge flaps, modern features that were in direct contrast with the antiquated drag-inducing wire bracing used to support the wings. By 1930, wire bracing was already an outmoded concept; however, it was required to meet military strength regulations.

Based on the winning assessment of the X8-A evaluation model, five YA-8s and eight Y1A-8s (designated differently to denote they were purchased through

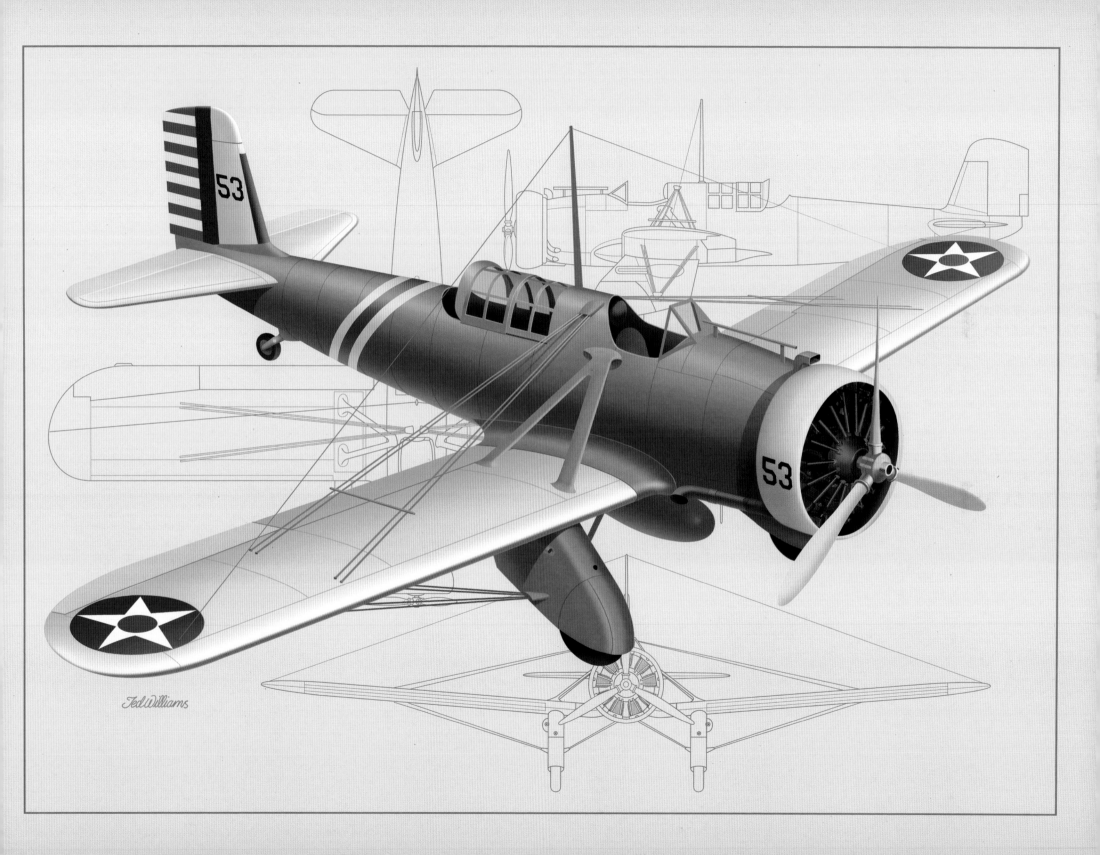

Curtiss A-12 Shrike Specifications

Type: Attack bomber
Crew: Two
Power plant: One 690-horsepower Wright Cyclone R-1820-21 air-cooled radial engine
Performance: Maximum speed, 175 miles per hour; service ceiling, 15,150 feet; maximum range, 521 miles
Weight: Empty, 3,898 pounds; maximum takeoff weight, 5,736 pounds
Dimensions: Span, 44 feet; length, 32 feet, 3 inches; height, 9 feet, 4 inches; wing area, 285 square feet
Armament: Five .30-cal machine guns and over 400 pounds of bombs

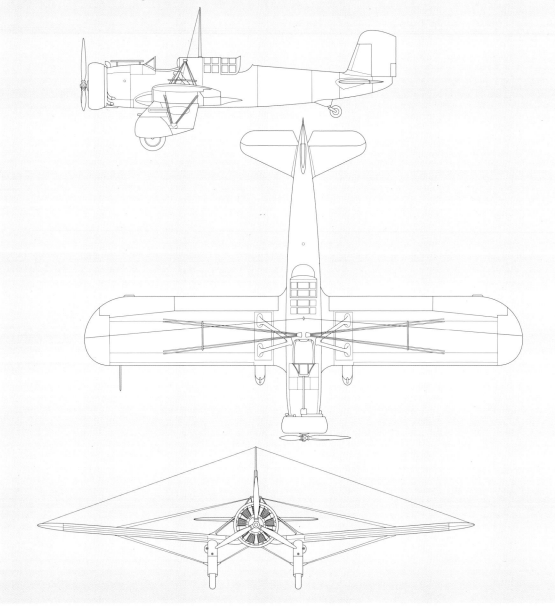

separate funds) were built and accepted into service as A-8s. Otherwise similar to the evaluation model, the A-8s were produced with a newer Curtiss engine. The new engine used the miracle product "Prestone." This was an improvement. Engines with Prestone antifreeze, an ethylene glycol mixture, as the liquid coolant could operate more efficiently with smaller radiators thus reducing drag.

The army continued to work with the Curtiss company to improve the A-8. One of the Y1A-8s was held back from service to test it as an updated Y1A-8A. The Y1A-8A swapped its 600-horsepower engine for a larger 675-horsepower engine that was a geared version of the Curtiss Conqueror, but the monster power plant did little to offset the airplane's increased weight, nor did it noticeably improve performance. The Y1A-8A did, however, pass the evaluation to become the A-8A; forty-six were commissioned but never came to fruition. Instead a new variant was unveiled: the A-12.

The most noticeable difference was the A-12's radial engine. First tested on what was called the YA-10 (a YA-8 modified with a Pratt & Whitney Hornet engine), the radial engine proved a suitable replacement for the liquid-cooled engine previously used for the series. Liquid-cooled engines, no matter the size and placement of the radiator, are always more susceptible to ground fire; and an air-cooled engine is easier to repair and maintain. Other changes to the A-12 included a redesigned fuselage. Plus now, the front and rear cockpits were nearer to each other so crew members could communicate more easily.

Produced in the greatest quantity, forty-six A-12s served the U.S. Army Air Corps until the Second World War. In 1934 they cost the army $19,483 per unit, after the government-furnished equipment was supplied. Curtiss also exported another twenty A-12s to China in 1936. When the Japanese attacked Pearl Harbor on December 7, 1941, nine A-12s were still operational at Hickam Field in Hawaii, but they were not used to engage the enemy. Interestingly, Hickam Field was named for Lieutenant Colonel Horace Hickam, a longtime advocate of military aviation, who died while performing a night landing exercise in an A-12.

RIGHT: An attack aircraft has to be versatile. Its mission may deploy it anywhere from the tropics to the Arctic. Here an A-12 has been fitted with skis allowing it to operate from cold weather bases.

BELOW: Despite external bracing and fixed landing gear, the Curtiss A-12 was a remarkably streamlined design. The large wheel pants contributed to the aircraft's overall aerodynamic efficiency while providing a location for the forward-firing machine guns.

Curtiss SBC Helldiver

The last biplane to serve the U.S. Navy did not start out with two wings. Originally built in response to a specification put out in 1932 by the Bureau of Aeronautics (BuAer) for a two-place naval fighter, the Curtiss-Wright Corporation's Curtiss Aeroplane Division supplied the navy with a design designated XF12C-1. Ready to fly in 1933, the XF12C-1 was a parasol-wing monoplane suitable for carrier operations. (A parasol wing is a single wing positioned above an aircraft's fuselage that is held in place by a series of struts; it affords the pilot good visibility, but it is actually quite similar to biplane construction with its high wing and sturdy braces.)

The Vought and Douglas companies were also invited to supply designs for the navy's consideration. Their submissions were both biplanes. It was apparent that the navy had reservations about a monoplane's suitability for carrier service. A monoplane's flight characteristics were still not understood, whereas the tried-and-true biplane design was well-established. In the lull of peacetime procurement, all three manufacturers were walking a tightrope between encouraging innovation and pleasing a lucrative reactionary client during the height of the Great Depression.

The Curtiss design for the XF12C-1 featured retractable landing gear that was similar to the Grumman F3F fighter. In flight, the wheels would nestle into tire-shaped recesses on each side of the fuselage. A study in contrasts, the XF12C-1was a metal aircraft with fabric-covered control surfaces; it was fitted for carrier duty with an arresting hook and wings that folded rearward for easier storage on and below deck. The XF12C-1's engine was a twin-row air-cooled Wright radial.

Before any of the test aircraft could go into deep evaluation, the navy changed its mind, and the mission request. It decided it wanted the Curtiss fighter to perform as a scout for observation and surveillance, not as a pursuit aircraft. The XF12C-1's identifier was changed to XS4C-1 to reflect its new scouting function. During the transformation from fighter to scout, the aircraft was modified to carry a 500-pound bomb load or an auxiliary, external forty-five-gallon fuel tank, and it received an entirely different Wright engine.

Soon after these improvements were in the works, the navy changed the designation again, from XS4C-1 to XSBC-1. Now the two-place scout was to be a "scout bomber," capable of dive-bombing. These many changes reflected the navy's overall indecision with regards to the airplane's role, not its impression of any individual aircraft. In the 1930s, an American aircraft carrier could transport approximately eighty to one hundred airplanes. It was not unusual for a carrier to

VS-2 Scouting 2

RIGHT: It takes a lot of muscle to crank-up the inertia starter on a big radial engine. Here a pair of aviation machinist mates use the crank to rotate the starter, which will engage the engine.

OPPOSITE: The SBC Helldiver played an invaluable role in the development of dive-bombing tactics and it was the last combat biplane flown by the U.S. Navy. This SBC-4 was flown by VS-2 serving aboard the USS *Lexington* in 1939.

have six different types of aircraft on board (fighters, scouts, and bombers), all exhibiting varying degrees of performance and obsolescence. The navy was still deliberating how to incorporate aircraft into its fleet.

In 1934 the only XSBC-1 crashed outside of Buffalo, New York, just a few miles from the Curtiss facility, during a test flight to study its ability to dive. Later, the cause of the accident was cited as a propeller malfunction. The aircraft was a total loss, but the pilot survived.

Unwilling to have the program end on such a low note, the Curtiss company built a revised XSBC-2 at its own expense. Naval testing had suggested a biplane design would endure the rigors of dive-bombing more successfully. Curtiss responded with a staggered-wing biplane with reinforced "I" struts and a monocoque construction. The top wing was metal, the bottom covered in fabric; they no longer folded.

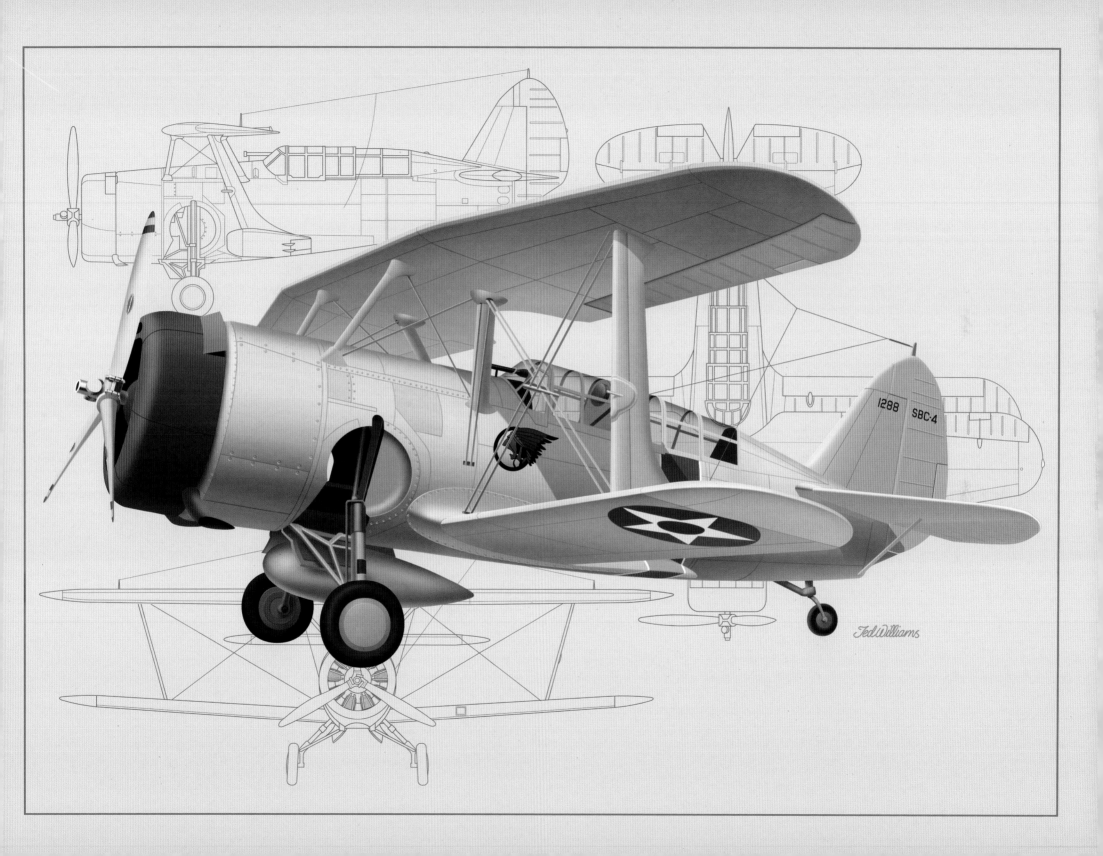

Curtiss SBC-4 Helldiver Specifications

Type: Scout bomber
Crew: Two
Power plant: One 950-horsepower Wright Cyclone R-1820-34 air-cooled radial engine
Performance: Maximum speed, 273 miles per hour at 15,200 feet; service ceiling, 27,300 feet; maximum range, 590 miles
Weight: Empty, 4,841 pounds; maximum takeoff weight, 7,632 pounds
Dimensions: Span, 34 feet; length, 28 feet, 4 inches; height, 12 feet, 7 inches; wing area, 317 square feet
Armament: Two .30-cal machine guns and 1,000 pounds of bombs

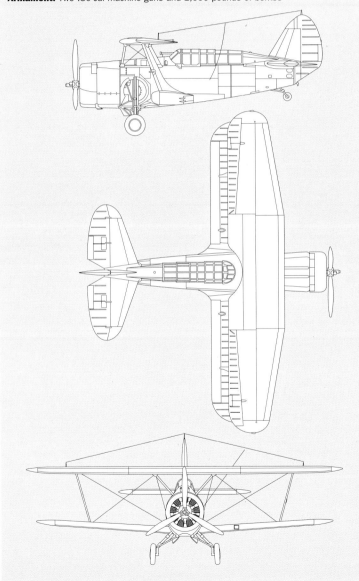

At the behest of the navy, the XSBC-2's undependable Wright radial engine was switched to a Pratt & Whitney R-1535-82 Twin Wasp Junior. The model with the Pratt & Whitney engine was designated XSBC-3. The navy was finally ready to buy from Curtiss. It ordered eighty-three, designated SBC-3. Beginning in 1937, squadrons on the USS *Yorktown*, *Saratoga*, *Enterprise*, and *Ranger* all flew SBC-3s through to the early-1940s. However, by 1941, most surviving SBC-3s were being used for training.

The last upgrade to the line was the SBC-4 in 1938 when the airframe was reunited with a Wright engine. This time it was a large diameter Wright R-1820-22 Cyclone with a staggering 950 horsepower. The large engine necessitated another cowl design, but the increased power allowed the bomb load to increase to 1,000 pounds. Examining drawings, it is easy to discern the most obvious changes between the variants. From the XSBC-2 on, the canopy was modified to incorporate a folding turtledeck. This greatly streamlined the airplane's profile to the look most associated with the SBC-4.

BELOW: Scouting Squadron Two (VS-2) stands inspection at Naval Air Station (NAS) North Island, Coronado, California, prior to being assigned to the USS *Lexington* (CV-2), August 1939.

BELOW: This is an SBC-4 Helldiver of the U.S Fleet Tactical Aircraft Unit that was assigned to the flag unit for Commander Carrier Division Two in 1940. In addition to its tactical duties, the navy used the Helldiver for personnel transport.

The SBC was exported to France, although not put to use. The British also considered its merits, renaming it the Cleveland Mk I, but decided against buying it in quantity.

The SBC-4 found fame at the New York World's Fair, where one was exhibited in 1939, yet its heyday was nearly over. The SBC-4 was the last first-line biplane to serve the U.S. Navy and Marine Corps. The aircraft was dubbed "Helldiver" by the people who built it, and more than 250 were delivered during its production period, but the SBC did not directly contribute to any aerial missions in World War II. Instead, it was used extensively as a trainer to prepare many World War II naval aviators for the conflict, and the equipment, that was to come. In fact, many fresh-from-the-factory SBC-4s were shipped directly to reserve units to meet the needs of the burgeoning Naval Air Reserve programs.

Martin B-10

The Martin B-10 grew out of a 1929 request from the U.S. Army Air Corps; however, like the Boeing B-9 project, the Glenn L. Martin Company produced the B-10 on its own initiative. Still, interplay between the developers at Martin and army engineers drove the B-10 to greatness.

The first attempt at what was to become the legendary B-10 was met with initial displeasure. Martin originally proposed a biplane. The army quickly dismissed Martin's original proposal because it wanted an all-metal monoplane modeled after the Boeing B-9. What was to come out of the Martin factory next turned out to be one of the last, and most revered, bombers of the interwar years.

Martin's Model 123 was a modern all-metal twin-engine mid-wing monoplane with corrugated metal panels on the top and underside of the fuselage. It had an obvious rounded underbelly that could conceal 2,200 pounds of bombs in an internal bomb bay with mechanical hand-crank doors. A pair of Wright R-1820 Cyclone air-cooled radial engines provided power.

The Model 123 was designed to be armed with a .30-caliber Browning machine gun in a nose turret, floor, and rear canopy location. An ingenious system of bungee cords in the turret kept the gun properly oriented. The aircraft was originally designed to be operated by a crew of three, but the crew was expanded to include a pilot, a copilot who would operate the radio, a bombardier/gunner, and a rear gunner.

In 1932 the Model 123 was delivered to the army's Wright Field for testing. Designated XB-907, it impressed the army with its speed—an unprecedented 197 miles per hour, which was faster than the B-9. And soon the B-10 would be able to best 210 miles per hour, climb to an altitude of 22,000 feet, and demonstrate a range of 1,360 miles.

Nevertheless, despite its many attributes, the prototype had some serious problems. Its handling instability, undue vibration characteristics, and treacherously high landing speed, were all decreed by test pilots as unacceptable. Not surprisingly, these early difficulties, complicated by numerous change requests from the army, nearly ended the B-10 program prematurely.

But the engineers at Martin persevered. They continued to adapt and change, if grudgingly at times, their design to meet the army's expectations, while the army did its part testing emerging aeronautical concepts. This collaborative spirit helped the B-10 develop into a better bomber than originally conceived. The redesigned XB-907A had longer wings, NACA-designed short-chord cowlings that covered the engines and reengineered landing gear. In addition, its most

RIGHT: The Martin B-10's NACA cowlings could be removed to fully expose the aircraft's Wright Cyclone engines for maintenance.

OPPOSITE: The Martin B-10 was a leap forward in bomber design. It was not only revolutionary in its design as an all-metal monoplane, but it out-performed the pursuit aircraft of the time. The B-10 pioneered many modern design features found standard on later bombers, such as a rotating nose turret, retractable landing gear, and internal bomb bay and NACA engine cowlings.

distinctive feature, the nose gunner's turret, was redefined. In 1933 the army ordered forty-eight. After years of struggling through the Great Depression to build its state-of-the-art bombing masterpiece, the multimillion-dollar military contract helped pull the Martin company away from the financial doom that was threatening the entire country.

However, conflict ensued. Glenn Martin won the 1932 Collier Trophy for the B-10, an award established in 1911 to honor milestones in aviation, but he neglected to give the government engineers their due. This enraged the army and nearly jeopardized Martin's contract. In the face of this unpleasantness, the Martin bomber went on to additional feats of notoriety.

The original order for forty-eight aircraft produced a selection of variants and the base design continued to undergo developmental improvements throughout its entire career. The first order was made up of thirteen YB-10s for testing, a YB-10A with supercharged Wright engines, seven YB-12s with Pratt & Whitney R-1690 Hornet engines, twenty-five B-12As outfitted with floatation devices and extended fuel capacity for flying over long stretches of water, and an XB-14.

The most-produced U.S. military variant was the B-10B; introduced in 1935, it could climb to 10,000 feet in only seven minutes. In 1935 a B-10 was the first army aircraft to test the famous Norden precision bombsight for high-altitude daylight bombing, which was already in use by the navy. This testing revealed that the B-10's accuracy and speed could extend beyond the range of its escort fighters, securing the Martin B-10's reputation as one of the best purpose-built bombers ever developed.

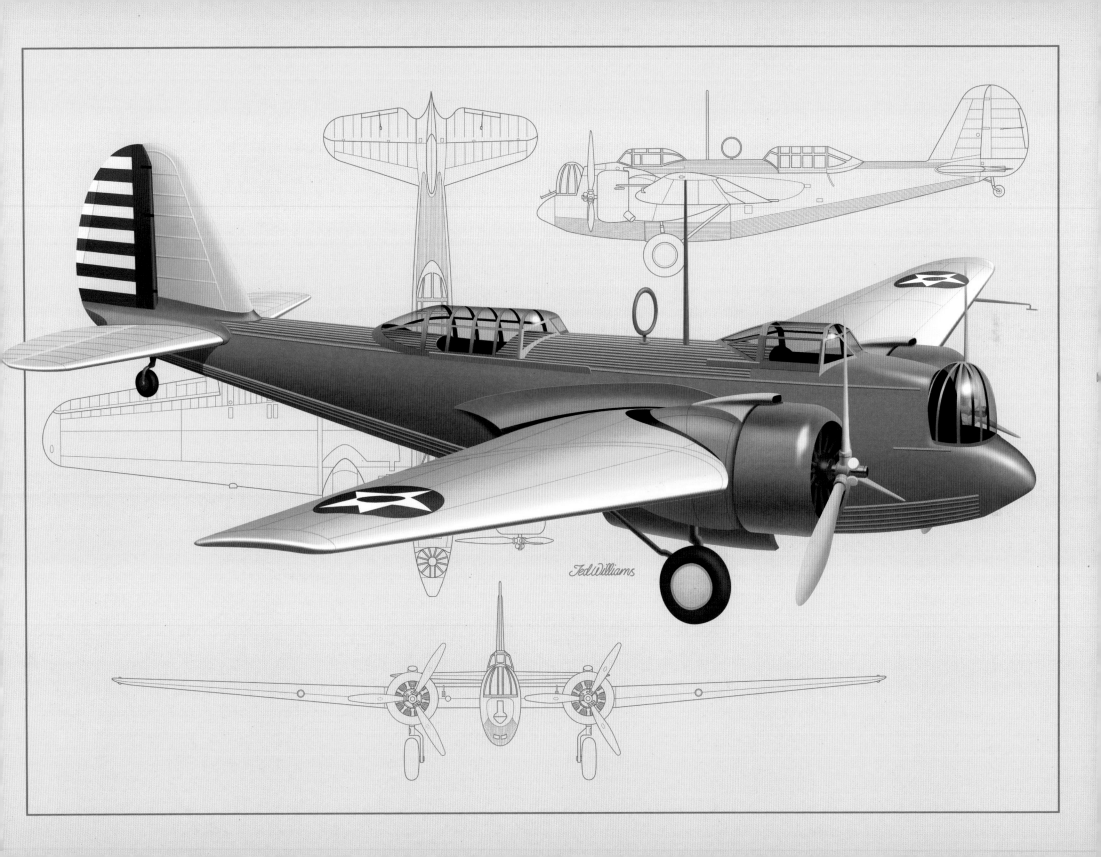

Ted Williams

Ultimately the army would order 155 in a variety of configurations for use in twenty-eight of its bombardment squadrons; 119 of these would still be in use in 1940. After 1936, 192 export versions were sold to seven countries around the world, including Russia, China, and Turkey.

The aircraft truly distinguished itself when, future general of the Air Force, Henry "Hap" Arnold led ten brand-new B-10s on a historic flight from Washington, D.C., to Alaska and back. The capable bombers were used to photograph and survey the uncharted wilds. As flights like the Alaskan journey succeeded, and as pilots familiarized themselves with the B-10, advancements continued. In time, its ability to fly at high altitudes necessitated the inclusion of oxygen equipment, and radios and other newer technology were tested.

ABOVE: A ground crew refuels a Martin B-10. In the early 1930s, the B-10's modern silhouette was a standout at any airport.

RIGHT: B-10s from the 9th Bomb Group gather in an echelon formation for a run on the target.

OPPOSITE: The B-10 had an organized cockpit. The throttle quadrant for the two engines is clearly visible mounted to the left bulkhead. The large diameter of the control yoke wheel indicates how it took strength to move the aircraft's control surfaces.

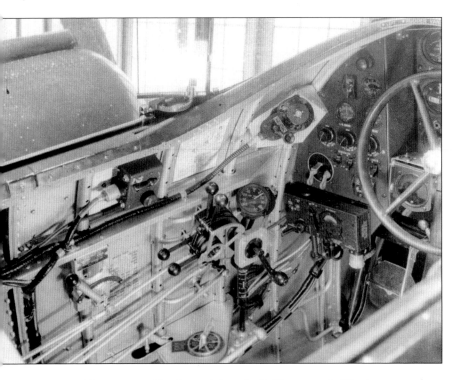

Martin B-10B Specifications

Type: Medium bomber
Crew: Four
Power plant: Two 775-horsepower Wright Cyclone R-1820-33 air-cooled radial engines
Performance: Maximum speed, 213 miles per hour at 10,000 feet; service ceiling, 24,600 feet; maximum range, 1,240 miles
Weight: Empty, 9,681 pounds; maximum takeoff weight, 14,700 pounds
Dimensions: Span, 70 feet, 6 inches; length, 44 feet, 9 inches; height, 15 feet, 5 inches; wing span, 678 square feet
Armament: Three .30-cal machine guns and 2,200 pounds of bombs

But not everything learned from the B-10 was good. After heavy use, common maintenance concerns developed. The landing gear was found to be troublesome, and stress caused wing-spar cracking that was more apparent near the end of its active service life.

During the B-10's lifespan the U.S. Army Air Corps used it for everything from carrying mail (during a brief period in 1934) to developing military bombing procedures. At the start of the United States's involvement in World War II, the B-10 was still being used for nonessential duties. It was obsolete by 1943.

Despite its progressive design and commendable list of achievements for the army, the B-10's career was really quite short. Newer bombers like the Douglas B-18 and the seminal B-17, developed by Boeing, quickly ousted the B-10 from its position as the army's leading frontline bomber. Considering how the Martin B-10 so swiftly overtook the Boeing B-9's career, perhaps it is fitting that a Boeing design eventually won out.

Today, the only B-10 in existence is on display at the National Museum of the USAF near Dayton, Ohio. Argentina gifted the aircraft to the United States in 1970 after friendly negotiations between the two countries. Originally exported to Argentina in 1938, this solitary B-10 is the lone example of an era. It underwent a three-year renovation conducted in the mid-1970s by volunteers from the 96th Mobile Maintenance Squadron, Air Force Reserve, Kelly Air Force Base, in San Antonio, Texas.

Boeing B-17 Flying Fortress

What is a bomber? Despite the examples in this book, and the scores more from around the world, without a doubt, the quintessential American bomber is, and may always be, the B-17 Flying Fortress.

The Boeing B-17 is the epitome of the entire bomber category. Inextricably linked to World War II, the B-17 actually started its career much earlier in 1934 when the U.S. Army Air Corps put out a specification for a large, multi-engine bomber.

At the time of the request, Boeing was already engaged in an experimental project with the army to develop a long-range bomber design known as Model 294. Designated XB-15, it was one of the largest bombers ever evaluated by the army. Only one would be produced; the project was plagued with engine woes, disappointingly low top speeds, and poor fuel economy.

Boeing's next attempt, and its proposal for the 1934 bid, was the Model 299. It drew inspiration from the best aspects of the XB-15, as well as from the Boeing Model 247 transport and airliner. Ready to fly in July 1935, Model 299 faced off against the Martin 146 and Douglas DB-1 (Douglas Bomber) for the opportunity to build the army the multiengine bomber it desired.

The Martin and Douglas models were both designed around two engines, a typical, if tired, solution. The Boeing Model 299 with its four 750-horsepower Pratt &Whitney R-1690 Hornet engines, each paired with a huge 11-foot three-bladed propeller, blew away the competition with its awesome speed, climb, and strength. The Model 299 also featured autopilot, five gun stations, and a larger-than-life stature—its wingspan was over 100 feet. The Model 299 was all but assured the contract, until tragedy struck.

In October 1935 the only Model 299 crashed during a test flight at Wright Field. Because the Model 299's control surfaces were so large, they were locked when the plane was parked. It was determined after the crash that these locks were not disengaged by the crew. While the demolished airplane itself was cleared of any blame, the death of its two test pilots cast a pall over the entire program. In a conservative moment, the army awarded Douglas the production order for 133 of its proposed design, the B-18 Bolo.

However, the army did not forsake Boeing. It contracted for thirteen service test aircraft so further flight testing could be conducted. First designated Y1B-17, then YB-17 ("Y1" indicates an aircraft expenditure outside of that year's operational budget), it was classified as a heavy bomber and christened "Flying Fortress" by Dick Williams, a reporter for the *Seattle Times*. In 1937, most of

RIGHT: The size and power of the B-17 called for a more complex flight deck, which in turn gave rise to the need for a written pre-flight check list. No longer could it be left up to the pilot or co-pilot to remember which functions needed to be performed before the aircraft left the ramp.

OPPOSITE: The Boeing B-17 has become legend in the history of aerial bombardment. It created much excitement when first introduced to the public in 1935 and immediately acquired the name "Flying Fortress." This B-17F is shown in the markings of the 94th Bomb Group, 331st Bomb Squadron. Captain Jack Sprentall stationed at Bury St. Edmunds Airfield, Suffolk, England in 1944, commanded the aircraft.

these evaluation models were delivered as B-17s to the 2d Bomb Group stationed at Langley Field in Virginia for continued testing.

One of the original Y1B-17s went to Wright Field in Ohio for even more testing. Several engines later, it flew as the B-17A, which, in turn, led to the YB-17B and B-17B. In 1939 the army ordered thirty-nine B-17Bs. Updates to the B included: an enlarged rudder, a redesigned Plexiglas nose turret, and supercharged Wright radial engines capable of 1,000 horsepower. Armament was increased from five machine guns to six .50-caliber machine guns with one additional .30-caliber, and the payload could weigh up to 4,400 pounds. The B-17B was the first variant to be supplied to active units.

In 1940 a B-17C was introduced. The army ordered thirty-eight from Boeing. The C was modified to eliminate the bulbous side "blisters" in exchange for flat, streamlined side windows, and a "bathtub" turret was added. This variant was the first Flying Fortress to taste World War II. Twenty were sent to the Royal Air Force (RAF); however the aircraft were delivered without the Norden bombsight. This American top secret precision bomb-aiming technology was an integral part of the B-17 performance as a daylight bomber.

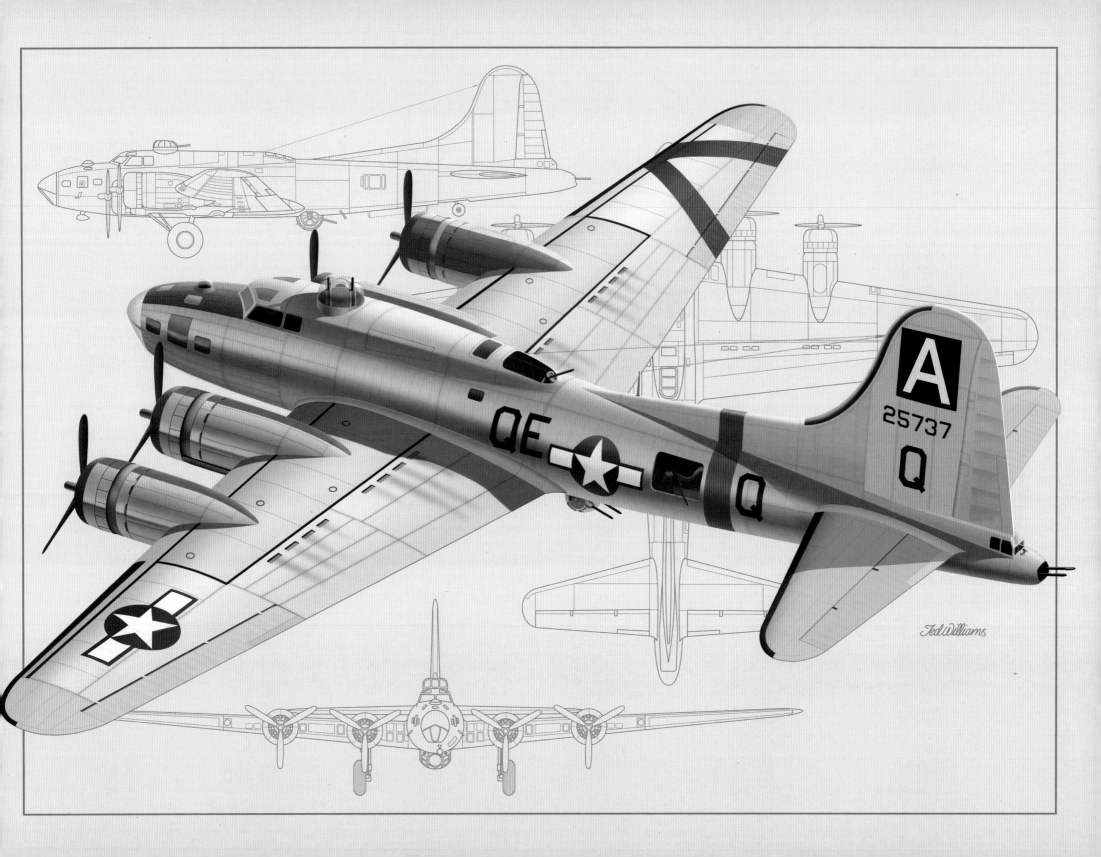

The B-17D received self-sealing fuel tanks and an augmented armor plate in preparation for combat. International tensions were escalating; the likelihood of the United States entering the war was imminent. In all, forty-two B-17Ds were built or converted from Cs.

The next version, the B-17E, was updated to receive the tail design most associated with the Flying Fortress. Additional alterations were made to the orientation of the waist gunner positions, also the bathtub turret under the fuselage was replaced by a ball turret, a powered upper turret was placed behind the flight deck, and a tail gunner position was added. Power was provided by four Wright R-1820-65 turbo-supercharged radial engines, each with 1,200 horsepower. As the B-17Es entered combat operations, other changes were initiated. After years of wistful peacetime deliberations about what a bomber should and could not be, real-life conflict necessitated speedy corrections. The need to ensure the crew's survival, and that of the aircraft, became paramount. Five hundred twelve B-17Es were built.

The B-17F and G were the most heavily armed, and were built in the greatest numbers. Before the war's end, a Flying Fortress could carry twelve .50-caliber machine guns and 8,000 pounds of bombs. Demand was so great, other manufacturers had to assist Boeing to meet the army's production requests. In all, between 1934 and 1945, nearly thirteen thousand were built—6,981 by Boeing, 2,750 by Lockheed-Vega, and 2,995 by Douglas.

Perhaps most remarkable are the stories of the crews who flew them. The Flying Fortress was conceived to perform daylight bombing missions. In 1942 B-17s started to fulfill that destiny by targeting German sites of military importance. At first, without escort fighters, hundreds of B-17s were downed and thousands of men perished. Later, P-51 Mustangs would accompany the Flying Fortresses on long bomb runs and bomber losses were reduced.

There are countless stories of the "Forts" and the American heroes who never made it back to base, but there are also numerous stories about the B-17s that limped home in spite of catastrophic battle wounds. Ten men would serve on a B-17, front to back: a bombardier and navigator in the nose, a pilot and copilot on the flight deck, a flight engineer who manned the top turret, a radio operator stationed amidships, a ball turret gunner, two waist gunners, and a lone tail gunner. It was not easy duty. The high-altitude conditions were extremely cold and uncomfortable for these men. Ice would form on weapons and equipment, and oxygen was required. Plus, it was the bombardier's avowed responsibility to destroy the Norden bombsight should the airplane be in peril, to ensure the enemy did not obtain the technology.

One of the more enduring memories of the B-17 is not a feature from the factory. Rather it is the nose art that was applied in the field. Many crews painted outrageous glamour girls and patriotic images on their B-17s. Partly for morale, partly for menace, the art that accompanied B-17s on their sorties over Europe and Japan is almost as legendary as the aircraft itself.

Boeing B-17F Specifications

Type: Heavy bomber

Crew: Ten

Power plant: Four 1,200-horsepower Wright R-1820-97 air-cooled radial engines

Performance: Maximum speed, 325 miles per hour at 25,000 feet; service ceiling, 37,500 feet; maximum range, 2,800 miles

Weight: Empty, 35,728 pounds; maximum takeoff weight, 56,500 pounds

Dimensions: Span, 103 feet, 9 inches; length, 74 feet, 9 inches; height 19 feet, 1 inch; wing area 1,420 square feet

Armament: Eleven .50-cal machine guns and 8,000 pounds of bombs

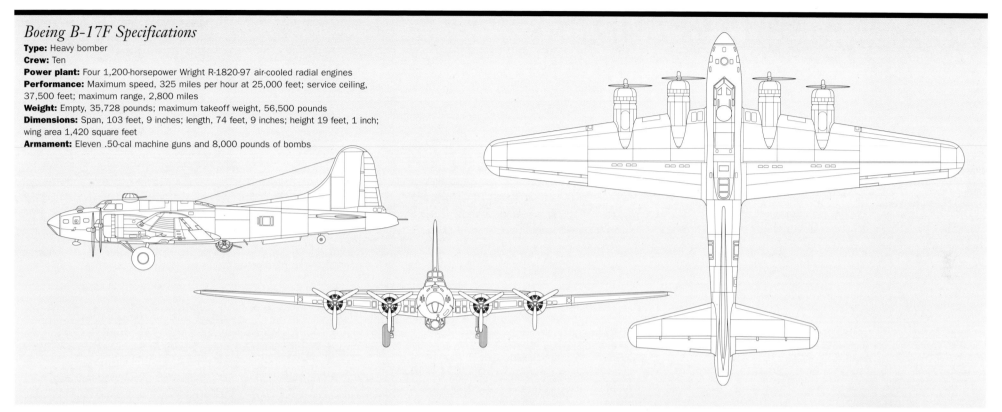

OPPOSITE TOP: These early B-17s do not have the same silhouette as later World War II-era Flying Fortresses. Advances in armament, powerplants and aerodynamics considerably changed the look of this legendary aircraft.

OPPOSITE BOTTOM: B-17 fuselage assembly area at a Boeing facility in Seattle, Washington.

LEFT: Waist gunners were likely to get into each other's way, as shown in this photo of waist gunners in action in a B-17F. In the later B-17G, the windows were staggered, fore and aft, to give the gunners more room.

RIGHT: This B-17 received a direct hit by flak. Remarkably, the bomber made it back to base with its entire crew unharmed.

Consolidated PBY Catalina

In 1933 the U.S. Navy entered into a contract with Consolidated Aircraft Corporation to build a next-generation flying boat. The navy was looking for a patrol bomber with a range of 3,000 miles at a cruising speed of 100 miles per hour, and Consolidated delivered. Douglas was also approached, but its submission was not accepted into service. The flying boat was not new to the navy. It had flown several designs, mainly Curtiss models, since the advent of heavier-than-air powered flight. Most recently, Douglas, Martin, and Keystone had already supplied patrol bomber flying boats to the navy.

Consolidated was founded in 1923 by Reuben H. Fleet. It was a merger of Gallaudet Aircraft Corporation, a manufacturer of early Curtiss floatplanes, and Dayton-Wright Aircraft. Later, Consolidated would earn its reputation engineering its own large flying boats, including the PBY Catalina.

In 1929, Thomas-Morse, designers of the first American pursuit airplane, the MB-3, merged with Consolidated. Other mergers and acquisitions followed. Consolidated joined with Hall Aluminum Aircraft in 1940, and Vultee in 1943, to form Consolidated Vultee Aircraft Corporation.

Model 28, designated XP3Y-1, was designed by Isaac "Mac" Laddon, the engineer who is also credited with bringing to life many other influential aircraft for Consolidated, including the B-24 Liberator, the most-produced heavy bomber of World War II. At its core, the Model 28 was based on a previous biplane flying boat, the BuAer-designed and Consolidated-built P2Y, but the similarities ended quickly. For the new version, Laddon engineered an all-metal monoplane with a semi-cantilevered parasol wing that did not require extensive external bracing. Another unique design feature was the dual-purpose wing tips. In flight they appeared innocuous enough, but for sea operation they could be deployed downward for use as stabilizing floats. Laddon's design was so inventive he sought and received a United States patent.

The fuselage, true to its nautical origins, was hull-shaped with provisions for a crew of seven: a pilot, copilot, bombardier/navigator, radio operator, flight engineer, and two waist gunners. As on a boat, bulkheads divided the aluminum alloy hull into five separate sections. The ship was powered by two 825-horsepower center wing-mounted Pratt & Whitney R-1830-58 Twin Wasp engines with NACA cowlings. They turned three-bladed Hamilton Standard propellers featuring a new constant-speed mechanism that hydraulically controlled the pitch of the blades.

Initial armament included one .30-caliber gun in the nose and two additional machine guns, either .30- or .50-caliber, at waist position. Bombs were attached

RIGHT: A PBY-5A Catalina overflys a United States Navy K Class blimp on submarine patrol in the South Atlantic. The Catalina's best attribute was its range and duration. In the Pacific Theater, Catalinas were known to have flown reconnaissance missions lasting up to twenty-four hours.

OPPOSITE: The PBY Catalina became the U.S. Navy's most indispensable patrol bomber of World War II. It had the capability of flying very long missions over large expanses of ocean. It also gained a reputation as an effective search-and-rescue aircraft, earning the affectionate nickname "Dumbo." Introduced in 1939, the PBY-5 was the first Catalina to have the distinctive rear fuselage gun turret blisters

to racks on the underside of the wings. Depth chargers could also be carried. (A depth charge is a type of explosive weapon that is released into the water to destroy enemy submarines; not by a direct hit, but from the concussion of the blast.)

Successful flight evaluation of prototype models led to a 1935 production order for sixty, which were designated as a bomber, PBY-1. Soon, in 1936, Consolidated received another production order for fifty of the improved PBY-2. Later, in 1936, 1937, and 1939, an enhanced -3 (in a quantity of sixty-six), -4 with its distinctive "blisters" at the waist gun locations (in a quantity of thirty-three), and -5 (in a quantity of two hundred), were produced and delivered to the navy. Each variant received updated Pratt & Whitney engines that could offer greater horsepower.

In 1939 the -5A variant launched the "amphibian" version. Retractable landing gear in a tricycle configuration complemented its boat characteristics. Now a PBY could take off and land on the ground or water for greater operational flexibility. Plus, it was easier to get the aircraft on to shore for maintenance and for cargo and ordnance loading. In 1940 the navy ordered 134 new PBY-5As and converted several additional -5s. This is also about the time that the U.S. Navy officially recognized the "Catalina" moniker, which was already used by the factory and the RAF.

Ultimately, the -5 variant was the most modified and the most successful. The navy ordered 979 PBY-5s and 782 PBY-5As from Consolidated in 1941.

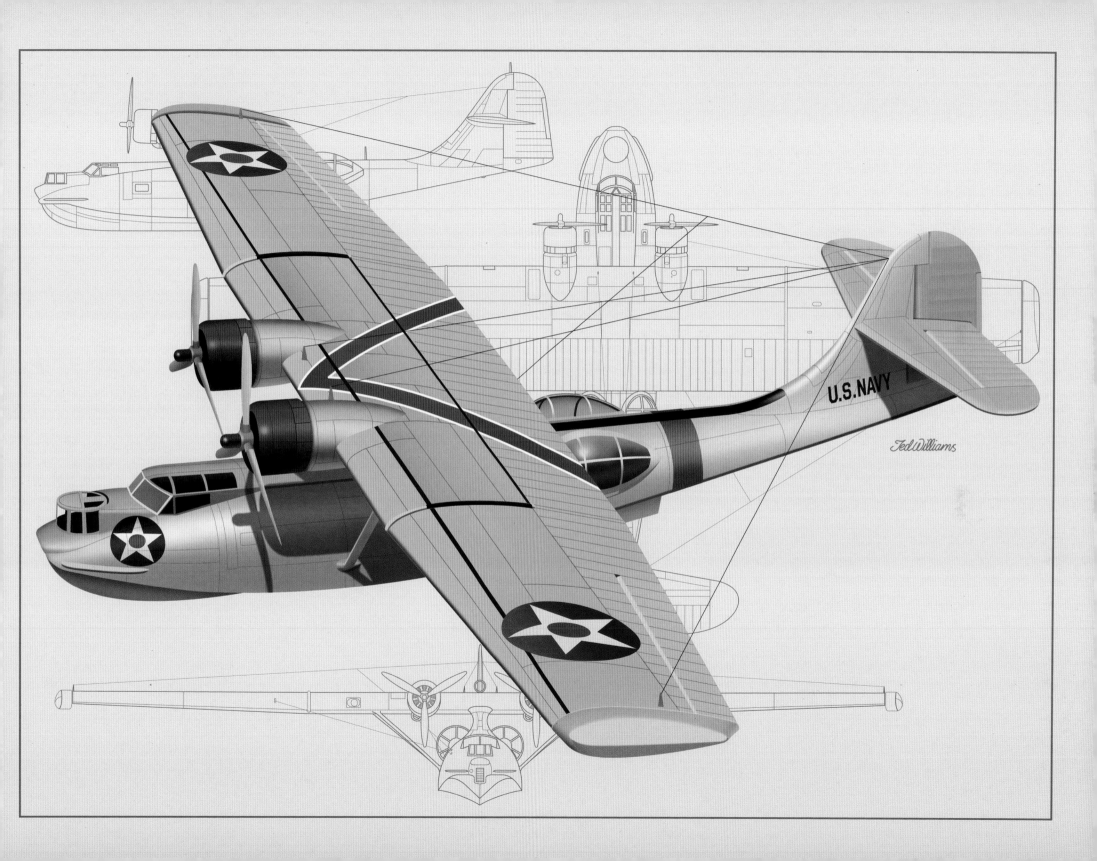

A Boeing manufacturing facility in Canada and Canadian Vickers Ltd. also built several variants for the American, Canadian, and British militaries, totaling nearly 750 more aircraft. Furthermore, a PBN-1 Nomad version with several enhancements and changes was built by the Naval Aircraft Factory in 1941.

The Catalina was used extensively throughout the Second World War; twenty-nine naval patrol squadrons would eventually be equipped with the Catalina. It was used in both the European and Pacific theaters. Later variants could carry up to nine men, deliver 4,000 pounds of bombs or torpedoes, and mount five machine guns.

The Catalina was the first U.S. military aircraft to have onboard radar. In 1942 some navy PBYs were coated in a dull, non-reflective black paint for nighttime operations in the Pacific. These PBY-5s were known as "Black Cats." Used extensively throughout the Pacific Theater, these cloaked cats used radar to seek out Japanese ships and mines. The radar was also valuable to search out and rescue survivors from downed ships and aircraft.

By 1948 most PBY Catalinas were no longer in active service roles; although the navy used some for secondary training and transport activities until 1957. The majority of World War II military aircraft were scrapped after the war; luckily many PBY Catalinas were spared this indignity. Because of its size and range, plus its versatile amphibious nature, the PBY was sold as surplus for civilian transport and cargo purposes. The Smithsonian and National Museum of the United States Air Force both have one for display, and there are others around the world that have been preserved to this day.

BELOW: With the wing tip floats extended, this Catalina begins its high speed take-off run.

OPPOSITE TOP: PBY Catalinas were indispensable during World War II. Because the PBY was required to log long missions, facilities were set up to refit and refurbish these aircraft. This aviation mechanic works on a war weary PBY at a Naval Air Station in Seattle, Washington.

ABOVE: A PBY crewman is about to install a .30-cal machine gun into the port-side blister turret of this aircraft. The PBY's blisters were a great vantage point for observers during reconnaissance and air-sea rescue missions.

Consolidated PBY Catalina Specifications

Type: Patrol bomber
Crew: Seven to nine
Power plant: Two 1,200-horsepower Pratt & Whitney R-1830-82 air-cooled radial engines
Performance: Maximum speed, 189 miles per hour; service ceiling, 21,500 feet; maximum range, 2,990 miles
Weight: Empty, 17,526 pounds; maximum takeoff weight, 34,000 pounds
Dimensions: Span, 104 feet; length, 63 feet, 10 inches; height, 18 feet, 6 inches; wing area, 1,400 square feet
Armament: Two .30-cal machine gun, two .50-cal machine guns, and 4,000 pounds of bombs or torpedoes

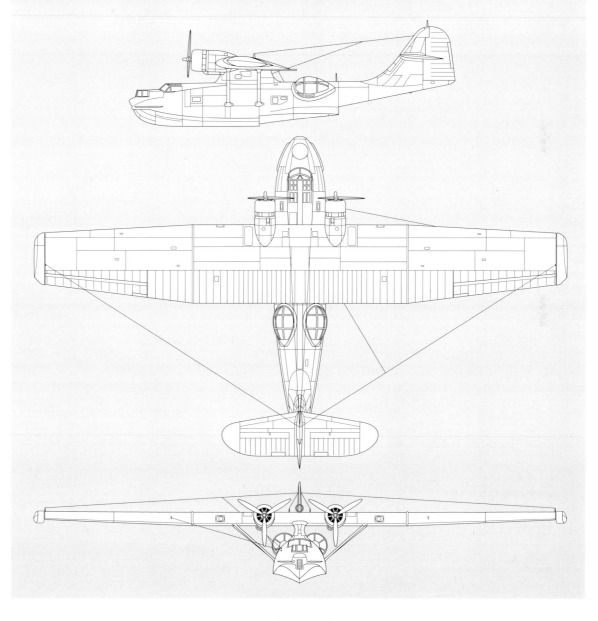

Douglas B-18 Bolo

In 1934 Douglas went head to head against Boeing and Martin in an attempt to provide the U.S. Army Air Corps with a multiengine bomber to replace the Martin B-10. The Douglas entrant had two advantages over the clear favorite, the Boeing B-17: The Douglas two-engine design was cheaper to produce than the Boeing, and it survived the competition. Had the Boeing Model 299 (precursor to the Flying Fortress) not crashed on a test flight, the outcome may have been different for Douglas.

Douglas's premise was a bomber based on its popular DC transport. The DC-2 was a twin-engine civil airliner with seats for fourteen passengers in its elongated cabin. Commercial variants of the DC-2 were exported around the world and it was also modified for use as a military transport. Douglas's latest incarnation, the DB-1, was true to its DC heritage, but it had an even larger fuselage fortified to carry 2,000 pounds of bombs, as well as rounded wing tips and larger tail control surfaces. Hinged bunks, a feature from its origin as an airliner, were supplied so the crew could rotate during long missions.

The B-18 was powered by two 930-horsepower Wright R-1820-45 Cyclone engines that rotated large, broad-bladed propellers. Each engine had its exhaust vented above the nacelles. This made the aircraft more difficult to observe in dark skies.

It took six men to crew the B-18: a pilot, copilot, bombardier/navigator, and three gunners who each operated one of the three .30-caliber machine guns, located in the nose, in a retractable dorsal turret behind the wing, and aft in a specialized hatch. At the time, the army's backing of the B-18 was questioned in light of the superiority of Boeing's prototype. While not as leading-edge as Boeing's, the Douglas design did meet the 1934 specifications set by the army; and perhaps the army's most compelling reason for buying the Bolo in bulk: It could buy two B-18s for only a little more than the price of one Boeing.

The B-18A also had larger engines, two 1,000-horsepower Wright R-1820-53 Cyclones, and the propellers were more advanced and fully feathering. (If one engine was lost in flight, the fully feathering propeller could be adjusted to reduce drag and gain maximum thrust and efficiency from the remaining engine.) Beginning in 1938, 217 B-18As were ordered with a redesigned nose that improved the position of the bombardier/navigator and nose gunner; now the two men had more room to do their jobs simultaneously.

VB-4 Bombing Four

RIGHT: Factory workmen put finishing touches on B-18 wing panels before assembly to the fuselage. The national insignia shown here was used by the U.S. Army from August 1919 to May 1942, when, after twenty-three years, the red center in the roundel was removed.

OPPOSITE: The B-18 Bolo was basically a military adaptation of the Douglas DC-2 commercial airliner. Although it was quickly made obsolete by other bomber designs such as the Boeing B-17, it performed an important role in the defense of the Continental United States in the months after the attack on Pearl Harbor. This B-18 carries the marking of the 88th Observation Squadron, 1940.

Today the Bolo is merely a footnote in history; however, when the United States was drawn into the Second World War it was the most available American bomber. B-18s and B-18As saw service with several units including the 38th and 21st Reconnaissance Squadrons and the 19th, 7th, and 5th Bombardment Groups, the latter at Luke Field, Hawaii.

At the time of the Japanese attack on Pearl Harbor there were thirty-three B-18s at Hickam Field in Hawaii, and another twelve were stationed at Clark Field in the Philippines. Nearly all of these B-18s in the Pacific region were destroyed where they sat on the ground during the surprise raid.

Many B-18As were modified; 122 B-18As went back to Douglas to be refitted with radar and Magnetic Anomaly Detection equipment for use during night operations to search for German U-boats in Caribbean, Gulf, and American waters. This variant was called the B-18B; its mission was anti-submarine warfare. These B-18Bs helped to develop and perfect airborne radar techniques. Earlier, in 1939, another B-18 had been refitted to test an onboard cannon, and yet another was used to judge different aerial cameras. These types of evaluations helped to engender systems and equipment that would help the United States win the war.

In 1939 a contingent of twenty Bolos, called the Digby Mk I, were purchased by the Royal Canadian Air Force for reconnaissance and bombing. The RAF considered the Digby, but declined.

Another thirty-eight B-18As were delivered as B-23s. The B-23 Dragon was an updated version of the Bolo but with different wings and a tail modeled after the DC-3, Douglas's most successful aircraft. One of the primary complaints about the B-18 was its inability to surpass 200 miles per hour. To remedy this, the B-23 had two 1,600-horsepower Wright R-2600 Cyclone engines to help it achieve a top speed of 280 miles per hour. It also incorporated a machine gun position in a tail turret to better protect it from rear attacks.

The B-23 began serving reconnaissance squadrons in 1940, but it was quickly outmoded. Instead, most B-23s were refitted for the transport role, where they served admirably. After the war, many surviving aircraft found work as civil transports; some were even updated with luxurious cabins for corporate executives. Many B-18s were also sold as surplus and used for civilian transport or by foreign militaries.

By 1943 the B-18 and B-23 were made obsolete by the Consolidated B-24 Liberator, and by medium bombers like the North American B-25 and Martin B-26. Today, the National Museum of the United States Air Force has a restored B-18 from 1939 and a B-23 in its collection.

The Douglas B-18 Bolo is not a standout in history, but at the start of World War II it was the U.S. Army's primary bomber. Too soon it proved to be underpowered and, when compared against the best of the Axis, it was outgunned and inadequately armored. It was quickly eclipsed by the Boeing B-17. In hindsight, the Bolo's greatest achievement may have been its readiness. It was available in great numbers to prepare legions of future B-17 pilots when Flying Fortresses were just leaving the factory. The B-18's only failing was that it was exactly what the army wanted at a time when funds and peace were in a precarious position.

OPPOSITE TOP: Final production of a Douglas B-18A Bolo. The airframe in the foreground has had its wing panels delivered from the wing shop to the factory floor in preparation for assembly in the relaxed atmosphere of a prewar aircraft manufacturing plant.

OPPOSITE BOTTOM: For the 1938 General Headquarters of the Air Force (GHQAF) Maneuvers, ground crewman of the 7th Bomb Group apply water-soluble camouflage paint directly over the natural aluminum finish of this B-18.

BELOW: Formation of B-18s from the 7th Bomb Group, December 1939. The aircraft's DC-2 lineage is apparent. Because the Bolo was based on the successful DC-2 commercial airliner, Douglas could consolidate the bomber's production, drastically reducing its per unit price.

Douglas B-18 Bolo Specifications

Type: Bomber

Crew: Six

Power plant: Two 930-horsepower Wright R-1820-45 air-cooled radial engines

Performance: Maximum speed, 217 miles per hour at 10,000 feet; service ceiling, 24,200 feet; maximum range, 1,200 miles

Weight: Empty, 15,719 pounds; maximum takeoff weight, 27,087 pounds

Dimensions: Span, 89 feet, 6 inches; length, 56 feet, 8 inches; height, 15 feet, 2 inches; wing area, 959 square feet

Armament: Three .30-cal machine guns and a maximum 4,400 pounds of bombs

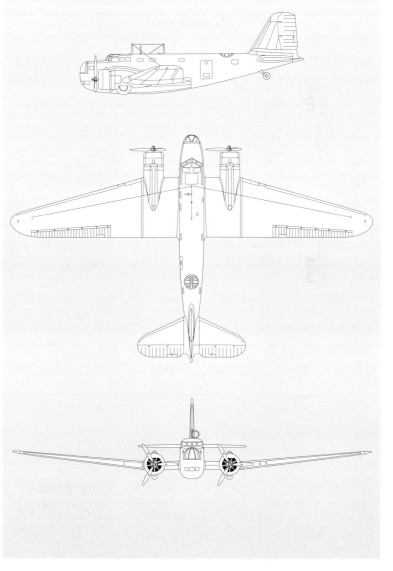

Vought SB2U Vindicator

The Vought name has been a part of aviation history almost as long as Boeing and Curtiss. Dynamic aviation pioneer Chauncey "Chance" Vought and the company he founded in 1917 were involved in several fruitful aviation partnerships until his sudden death in 1930. Yet, the Vought name lives on, most famously tied to important World War II aircraft such as the inverted gull-winged Corsair and the venerable F8U Crusader, a favorite fighter among Vietnam-era pilots.

In 1922 a Vought VE-7 biplane took off from the American aircraft carrier the USS *Langley* heralding the start of aviation's impending contribution to the fleet. So it's no surprise that Vought was called upon to produce the first naval monoplane scout bomber, the XSB2U-1; however, in 1934 the monoplane concept was not completely uncontested by the U.S. Navy. Just four months into the monoplane project, the navy put in another order. The XSB3U-1 was a scout bomber just like the XSB2U-1, but with one crucial difference—it was a biplane.

The XSB2U-1 and XSB3U-1 were evaluated against each other in April 1936. As a result, fifty-four of the monoplane design were ordered from the Vought-Sikorsky Division of the United Aircraft Corporation, while all continuing efforts with the biplane model were discontinued. The monoplane acquitted itself well during testing, proving its dominance over the older and inferior biplane technology.

The XSB2U-1, named the Vindicator, was an all-metal low-wing monoplane with parts of the aircraft, such as the control surfaces and areas of the wings and fuselage, covered in fabric. On the two-place aircraft, the crew, made up of a pilot and gunner-observer, was enclosed under a sliding-glass canopy. The production model, the SB2U-1, was powered by a single twin-row fourteen-cylinder Pratt & Whitney R-1535-96 Twin Wasp Junior engine with 825 horsepower that could generate a top speed approaching 250 miles per hour. It also featured folding wings for carrier storage and retractable landing gear. Bombing Squadron VB-3 was the first navy squadron to take delivery of the SB2U-1.

In 1938 the navy ordered more Vindicators, but with equipment changes that raised the aircraft's gross weight. Externally, the SB2U-2 was identical to the -1. In total, fifty-eight -2s were built.

In 1941 the navy made its last order. Designated SB2U-3, fifty-seven were built, primarily for the Marine Corps. It was the variant that truly earned

VB-4 Bombing Four

OPPOSITE: The Vought SB2U Vindicator was the U.S. Navy's first monoplane dive-bomber. The Vindicators of both the U.S. Navy and Marine Corps bombing units saw extensive action in the beginning months of the War in the Pacific, including the historic naval engagement at Midway. After the Battle of Midway, all SB2Us were relegated to rear echelon duties. This SB2U-2 flew with VB-4 assigned to the USS *Ranger*, 1939.

the Vindicator moniker because of its increased firepower from both forward-firing and rear-mounted .50-caliber machine guns, and its ability to carry up to 1,000 pounds of bombs and increased armor. This final SB2U variant was redesigned to be suitable for long-range operational flights. The -3 had larger fuel stores and could carry optional external auxiliary tanks.

A scout-bomber is a dive-bomber. Dive-bombing is a risky proposition for a pilot and his aircraft. Not only must the aircraft withstand nearly unbearable stress loads, but the pilot's mettle is tested as his aircraft bears down on a target like a hawk zeroing in on its prey. To complicate matters, the bomb must be released at an altitude that allows the pilot enough time to escape the blast's effect; if it is let go too closely to the target, the pilot is in jeopardy of perishing in his own destruction.

At the same time, a dive-bomber must be fast to enhance maximum survivability. While the aircraft needs the structural integrity to handle the extreme forces of a near vertical dive, it must also withstand the g-forces sustained during pullout. To add to the list of requirements, armor plating is essential since a dive-bomber gets within close range of antiaircraft fire.

Despite being built for the purpose of dive-bombing, the SB2U was already considered outdated by World War II. It was slower than other aircraft being built in preparation for the war. The reality of World War II put pressure on aircraft manufacturers to build more innovative aircraft, not just designs that placated the army and navy's reactionary thinking and outdated requirements of the 1930s.

Nor did the SB2U come equipped with self-sealing fuel tanks or dive brakes. (Dive brakes would become a standard innovation on later dive-bombers such as the Douglas TBD Devastator and SBD Dauntless.) These drag-inducing flaps helped control dive speed as the aircraft descended on its target. The story is some Vindicator pilots would lower the landing gear to control dive speeds, simulating the action of dive brakes.

Despite its shortcomings, the SB2U did see combat during the Battle of Midway, but its performance was not stellar. The Vindicator was simply not up to the task of challenging superior fighter aircraft like the Japanese Zero. Meanwhile, a few SB2Us were used in service, but without success, by the RAF. These were known as the "Chesapeake." Another export version was used by France. However, by 1943 the SB2U was relegated to a secondary training role or scrapped.

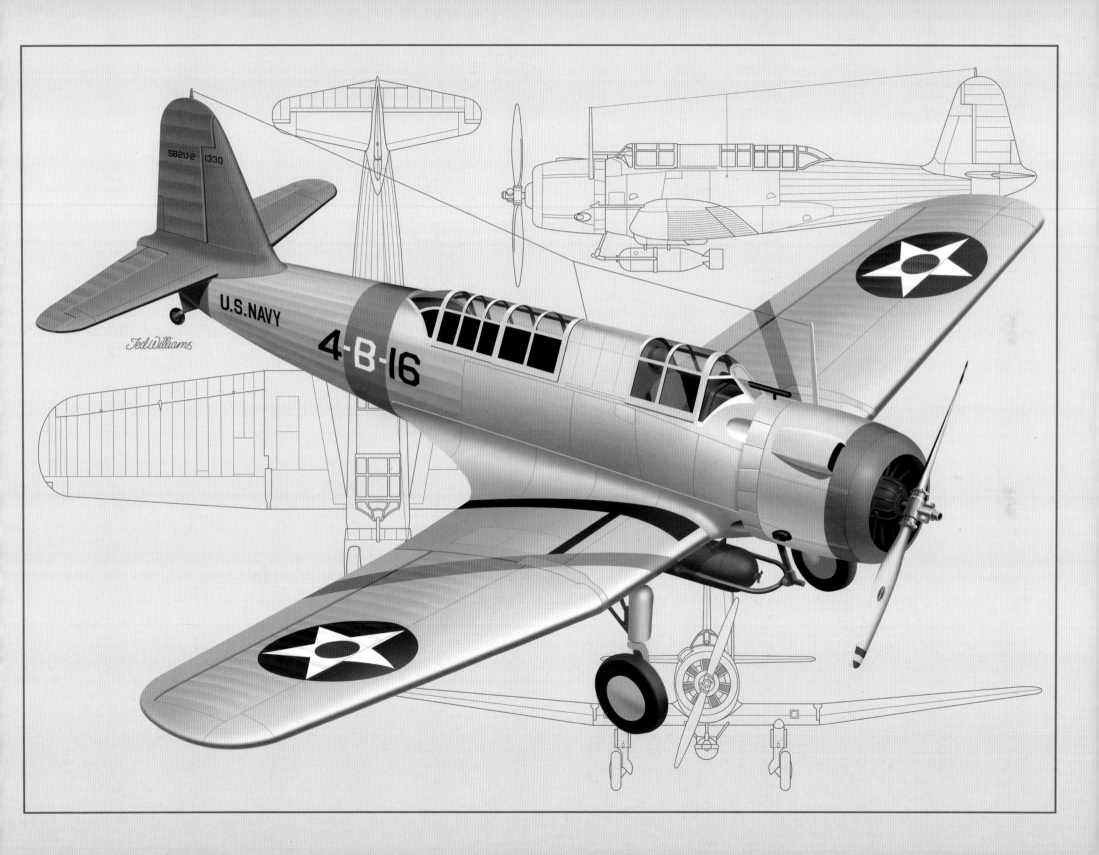

Vought SB2U-2 Specifications

Type: Scout bomber
Crew: Two
Power plant: One 825-horsepower Pratt & Whitney R-1535-96 air-cooled radial engine
Performance: Maximum speed, 251 miles per hour at 9,500 feet; service ceiling, 27,500 feet; maximum range, 1,002 miles
Weight: Empty, 4,713 pounds; maximum takeoff weight, 6,379 pounds
Dimensions: Span, 42 feet; length, 34 feet; height, 10 feet, 3 inches; wing area, 305 square feet
Armament: Two .50-cal machine guns and up to 1,000 pounds of bombs

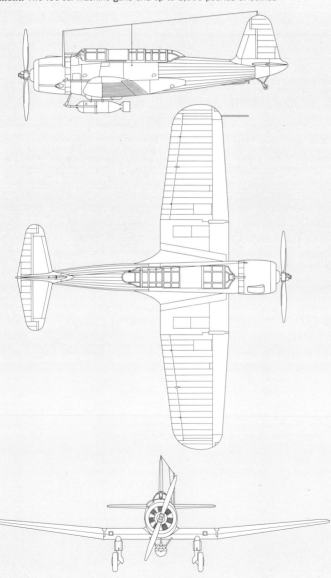

OPPOSITE: It's March 1941 and already the Vought factory is overcrowded. By the end of the year, many aircraft manufacturers would outgrow their manufacturing facilities.

BELOW: With World War II on the horizon, the U.S. Navy needed a long-range scout reconnaissance aircraft to serve with the fleet. A few combat designs were fitted and tested with floats, like this SB2U Vindicator photographed in 1939.

Today, the National Naval Aviation Museum in Pensacola, Florida, has the last SB2U of its kind. It was reclaimed from the depths of Lake Michigan in 1990, where it had been submerged for almost fifty years after a carrier crash landing during a training exercise. The solitary existing scout-bomber has been painstakingly restored—the last example of 1930's navy dive-bombing technology. A story of important engineering milestones, the SB2U was the first monoplane to serve the navy, while its previous shipmate, the SBU, was the navy's last biplane.

Douglas A-20 Havoc

The Douglas Aircraft Company, already a quality player in the aviation industry, came into its own during World War II. On the wings of its enormously successful DC series of transport planes, Douglas was one of the most prolific war-era suppliers for the United States. Many aircraft bearing the Douglas name came into being during the 1940s.

After years of developing serviceable but mediocre peacetime aircraft for a military with its head in the sand, another world war had erupted and manufacturing had to step up—and quickly. The army was forcibly shaken out of its complacency toward aircraft innovation. Obsolete airplanes built to antiquated performance standards were suddenly unacceptable; American lives were at stake. The United States needed to measure its meager air arm against the best of Germany and Japan.

Now the army was looking for record-breaking performance: faster speeds, extensive armament, offensive punch, heavier ordnance—all aviation achievements it had intentionally shied away from throughout most of the decade preceding World War II.

The Douglas A-20 Havoc started out as yet another unremarkable design of 1936, but it evolved into one of the most successful American attack aircraft of the early years of the war. Designed by Jack Northrop and Ed Heinemann, a noted engineer who was also the genius behind Douglas's SBD Dauntless and A-26 Invader, the Havoc began its career as the Northrop 7A.

The 7A attack/observation aircraft was designed to attain 250 miles per hour from two 425-horsepower Pratt & Whitney R-985 Wasp Junior radial engines, but the aircraft proved to be an under-performer. A 7B attack bomber version was developed in 1937; it was larger and faster, and it caught the eye of the French Armée de l'Air. Designated DB-7, the French versions, the DB-7A and DB-7B, incorporated many changes that improved flight characteristics and performance. However, two hundred of the 270 aircraft ordered by France were routed to the RAF after the fall of France to Germany. The RAF operated several variants under the names Boston I, II, and III and as the Havoc I, II, and III for night operations. The United States called them A-20, later adopting "Havoc" for all variants.

In 1939 the U.S. Army Air Corps ordered sixty-three A-20s and 123 A-20As based on improvements Douglas had implemented from the USAAC evaluations and from European DB-7 models. The A-20 was equipped for high-altitude bombing, while the A-20A was designed for low-altitude activities. The American

VB-4 Bombing Four

RIGHT: A "Rosie the Riveter" works inside the wing of an A-20 at the Douglas Aircraft Company plant in Long Beach, California.

OPPOSITE: United States Army Air Force crews carried out the first American bombing mission over Europe in August 1942, flying the British version of the Douglas A-20 named "Boston" by the RAF. All major Allied Air Forces, with the Soviet Union having the most, flew the Douglas A-20. This A-20G— "Little Joe" of the 5th Air Force, 312th Bomb Group, 389th Bomb Squadron— has completed 150 missions.

A-20 fuselage was still narrow as the original design stipulated, but it was deeper to allow for a larger bomb or fuel load.

The A-20 was originally intended to have superchargers, but they did not work well and were deemed unnecessary as the U.S. Army Air Corps decided to use the aircraft at lower altitudes, where the turbo burst was unnecessary. Only one of the A-20s received the superchargers. Instead the majority of the aircraft from this order were delivered as A-20As powered by Wright R-2600-11 Cyclone engines with 1,600 horsepower. Some A-20s were refitted as P-70s, a specialized night-fighting version with radar. The RAF had already used the aircraft for night operations. Now the United States would do the same. Although the P-70's career was brief, soon the superior purpose-built Northrop P-61 Black Widow took over nighttime operations.

Finished A-20As began shipping in 1941. The 3d Bombardment Group, in Savannah, Georgia, was the first to receive them. This year saw other important changes. Namely, the U.S. Army Air Corps reorganized into the U.S. Army Air Forces on June 20, 1941. General "Hap" Arnold was appointed as commander of the newly established organization. The Army Air Forces' charter was to tame air operations by consolidating all aircraft combat, procurement, and training activities into one body.

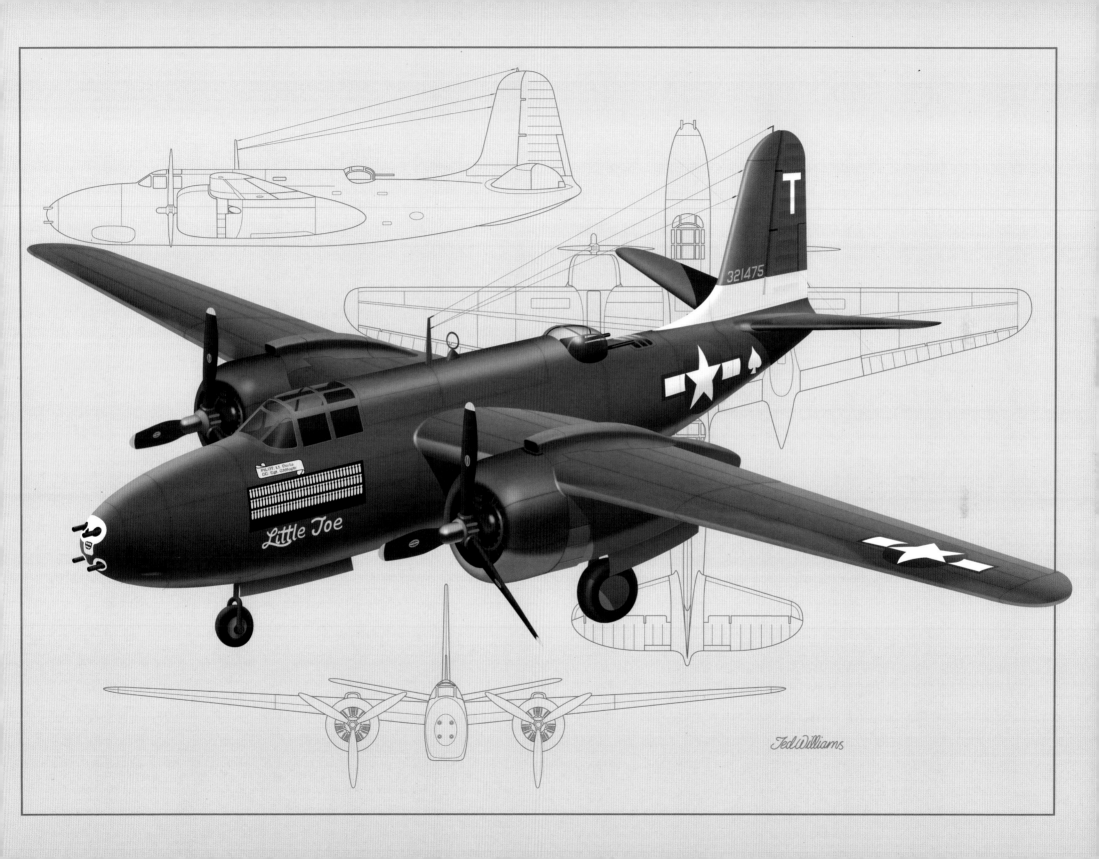

Little Joe

321475

T

Ted Williams

The A-20's armament consisted of four forward-firing .30-caliber machine guns, two dorsally located guns, and one rearward firing machine gun in the belly of the aircraft. Additional guns could be mounted in the nacelles. Although seldom installed, they would be activated by foot pedals in the rear gunner's area. The aircraft was operated by a three-man crew: a bombardier/navigator, pilot, and rear gunner. The men were situated in separate compartments, widely spaced from each other. This was the only practical solution in the slender fuselage. The bombardier's position was the most insecure. In the event of a crash, there was little protection for the man in the Plexiglas nose.

By 1942 all A-20As were removed from combat. Other variants took their place. Almost one thousand each of the A-20B and A-20C were built. The -B would introduce .50-caliber machine guns, and the A-20C variant initiated the use of self-sealing tanks and external auxiliary drop fuel tanks. Orders from the United States continued through to a -K variant, the -G version being the one produced in the greatest quantity—nearly three thousand (2,850) were built. The A-20G featured four 20-mm cannons that were mounted in the nose; these were later switched to the more reliable .50-caliber machine guns. The -G variant also received more armor and a powered gun turret. The first A-20s could carry 1,600 pounds of bombs; later variants were capable of up to 2,400 pounds and had a larger crew of four.

TOP LEFT: As the need for more aircraft increased, factories operated around the clock, seven days a week. Here, Douglas employees diligently work to complete another A-20 Havoc for the war effort.

TOP RIGHT: "Eloise," an A-20G, has six forward-firing .50-cal machine guns in a solid nose, which replaced the glazed nose bombardier position of previous variants. The G model was the most produced Havoc.

During its service, this aircraft served in every theater of the war, with numerous allied armies, and the platform continued to adapt, creating newer variants and specialized functional capabilities, throughout its tenure. It was a very successful aircraft for Douglas, the U.S. Army Air Forces, and for several other nations, including Great Britain, Australia, and Russia. Through lend-lease arrangements, scores of A-20 Havocs went to Russia to help stop Adolf Hitler and his advancing aggression. Overall, nearly seventy-five hundred were built by Douglas, with 380 contracted under license by Boeing. The last Havocs were built in 1944.

Originally conceived for observation and attack, the A-20 developed into a premier light bomber—it was the American World War II attack bomber produced in the greatest quantity. With the Second World War a reality, bomber aircraft development and production was more rapid and vital than ever. Today an A-20G can be viewed at the National Museum of the U.S. Air Force in Dayton, Ohio.

BELOW: A night-fighting version of the Havoc was designated P-70. Note the radar antenna on both sides of the forward fuselage. The radar was used to search out enemy aircraft in the darkness. Also note the suppressors on the guns used to reduce muzzle flash.

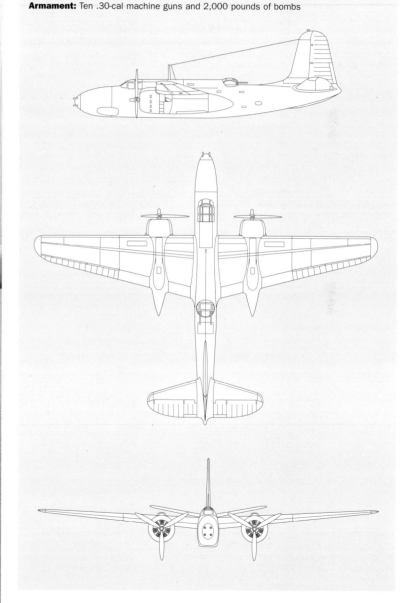

Douglas A-20C Specifications

Type: Attack bomber
Crew: Four
Power plant: Two 1,600-horsepower Wright Cyclone R-2600-23 air-cooled radial engines
Performance: Maximum speed, 342 miles per hour at 13,000 feet; service ceiling, 25,320 feet; maximum range, 2,300 miles
Weight: Empty, 15,090 pounds; maximum takeoff weight, 21,500 pounds
Dimensions: Span, 61 feet, 4 inches; length, 47 feet, 4 inches; height, 17 feet, 7 inches; wing area, 464 square feet
Armament: Ten .30-cal machine guns and 2,000 pounds of bombs

Consolidated B-24 Liberator

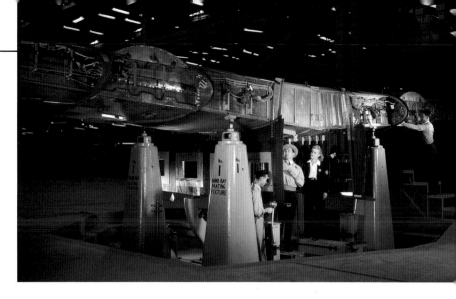

Produced in greater quantity than any other American military aircraft, the Consolidated B-24 Liberator contributed mightily to the United States's victory in World War II. The Liberator was used in every theater over the entire duration of the war for a multitude of roles. Thousands of American airmen flew in them overseas, while even more Americans worked on them in home-front factories, as numerous manufacturers, such as Consolidated, Ford Motor Company, North American, and Douglas, hurried to build or assemble them in time to fulfill the awesome wartime need.

Isaac "Mac" Laddon, Consolidated engineer of the B-24, drew from his experience with the Consolidated PBY Catalina to craft the new design. In 1939 Consolidated provided the U.S. Army with a new long-range heavy bomber that it said would surpass the B-17's abilities. Developed out of a desire to improve the range and payload capabilities of the Flying Fortress, the B-24 was designed around four Pratt & Whitney engines and a wing called a Davis airfoil. The wing was mounted high on the fuselage to enable it to support bomb loads directly, rather than by the fuselage's structure; and the wing's contour and Fowler flaps were engineered to increase lift and reduce or create drag as needed. The Davis wing's teardrop shape could maximize lift in the thin atmosphere at high altitudes. In this "wet wing" design, the fuel was carried in open spaces inside of the wing without additional containment structures. This helped the aircraft hold the quantity of fuel required for long-range missions.

The B-24 prototype featured unique-looking twin vertical stabilizers and retractable tricycle landing gear with a nose wheel of the type also used on the Douglas A-20 Havoc. The all-metal heavy bomber had an extraordinarily deep fuselage that could carry cargo or up to 8,000 pounds of bombs in its two separate compartments. The aircraft's ten crewman could walk between the bomb storage compartments by way of a specially crafted walkway. The bomb bay roll-up doors slid aside, instead of opening outward, to preserve aerodynamics in flight. Most astounding, the B-24 had the unprecedented capacity to lift an enormous weight of crew, cargo, fuel, and bombs, largely made possible by the innovative wing construction and design.

France, Great Britain, and the U.S. Army Air Corps ordered production models based on the XB-24 prototype. The RAF ordered 164 for itself, and took delivery of the remaining French supply after the fall of France in 1940. The British called it the LB-30A Liberator I and II. Later improved Liberators III and IIIAs were employed; these were primarily B-24Ds using British equipment.

RIGHT: A B-24 wing assembly is mounted on a fixture that properly aligns the bomb bay subassembly to the wing. A proper alignment is critical to the flight characteristics of the aircraft.

OPPOSITE: The B-24 Liberator was the most produced American aircraft of World War II. The lumbering Liberator carried out far more bombing missions than the more photogenic B-17. Designated as the PB4Y-1, the U.S. Navy used the Liberator for long-range reconnaissance and bombing patrols in the Pacific Theater. This B-24J, "Fearless Fosdick," was commanded by Lt. Bud Farnsworth of the 8th Air Force, 445th Bomb Group, 702nd Bomb Squadron stationed at Tibenham, England, 1944–45.

The first American B-24s consisted of seven YB-24s and thirty-six B-24As. The majority of these airplanes were not delivered as originally specified. Six of the YB-24s were sent to Great Britain and the majority of the B-24As were produced as B-24Cs or as British Liberators.

Improvements and evaluation variants followed. The B-24D was the first variant to undergo mass production. Starting in 1940, an order for 2,698 of the -D version commenced.

The B-24D initially mounted eight guns, two in the nose, two in the top turret, two waist guns, one in the belly, one in the rear; and it featured updated Pratt & Whitney R-1830-42 Twin Wasp engines. The B-24E followed, it continued to use Pratt & Whitney engines. The bulk of these were built by or from subassemblies from Ford at its Willow Run factory near Detroit, Michigan. A new facility, Willow Run boasted more than 2 million square feet and an assembly line that was as long as a mile. By war's end, the Willow Run plant could cost-effectively produce one bomber every hour.

The next production variant, the B-24G and the B-24G-1, was built by North American in 1942. Later the B-24G-1 was built to the specifications of the B-24H. Another 3,100 B-24Hs were built by Consolidated, Ford, and Douglas. Ultimately, 6,678 of the B-24J, 1,667 of the B-24L, and 2,593 of the B-24M would be produced. In all, more than 18,000 B-24s were built—8,685 at the Ford Willow Run factory alone.

Standard armament for later B-24s included ten .50-caliber machine guns and 12,800 pounds of bombs. The 1942 attack of the Ploesti oil refineries is one of the most-publicized events of the war attributed to B-24s. B-24 Liberators of all variants also provided strategic bombing and offered antisubmarine protection in the Atlantic and Pacific regions, and flew reconnaissance missions.

A naval version of the B-24, called the Consolidated PB4Y Privateer, was developed. It had an enlarged single tail and a longer wing; 740 were built in this configuration for Navy and Marine Corps operations, in particular for antishipping

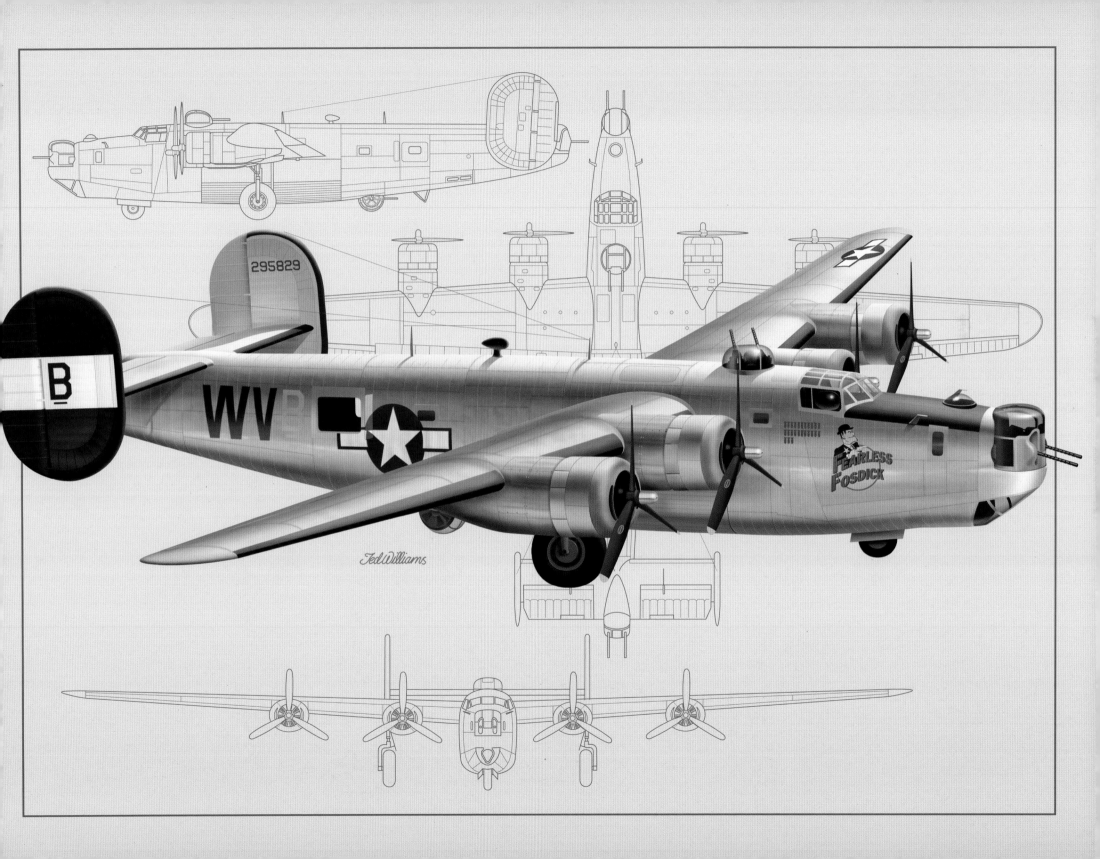

295829

WV

B

FEARLESS FOSDICK

Ted Williams

and antisubmarine low-altitude bombing. The Coast Guard also operated the PB4Y on search-and-rescue missions. Some Privateers were active through to 1954, even serving in the Korean War. Privateers would also be used for transport and refitted to carry various electronic devices.

The B-24 Liberator had several advantages over the B-17 Flying Fortress. It was faster and it could cross the Atlantic Ocean in one hop. Lumbering B-17s would have to take off hours earlier than the B-24 to reach the same target destination at the same time. Also, a man could stand upright in the B-24's deep, wide fuselage.

The B-24's Davis wing was a blessing and a curse. It allowed B-24s to lift huge payloads, but the high wing was not well-suited to withstand extreme g-force, and wheels-up landings could be catastrophic. Not always easy to fly, it is true that a B-24 could not take as much punishment as the B-17; however, an American in a B-24 had the same, if not a slightly better chance at surviving his mission in a B-24 than in a Flying Fortress.

Looking back at the World War II experience, the Consolidated B-24 Liberator does not have the same mystique, nor has it received the same high regard as the Boeing B-17 Flying Fortress, but the numbers don't lie. From 1939 to 1945, more than 18,000 B-24s were built. The B-24's contribution is immense. No other aircraft, before or since, has been produced in such a large quantity.

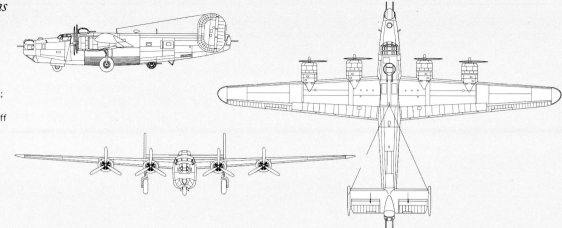

Consolidated B-24J Specifications

Type: Heavy Bomber
Crew: 10
Power plant: Four 1,200-horsepower Pratt & Whitney Twin Wasp R-1830-65 air-cooled radial engines
Performance: Maximum speed, 300 miles per hour at 30,000 feet; service ceiling, 28,000 feet; maximum range, 2,100 miles
Weight: Empty, 36,500 pounds; maximum takeoff weight, 65,000 pounds
Dimensions: Span, 110 feet; length, 67 feet, 8 inches; height, 18 feet; wing area, 1,048 square feet
Armament: Ten .50-cal Browning machine guns and 12,800 pounds of bombs

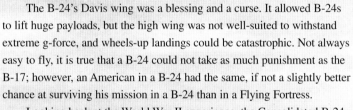

OPPOSITE: A B-24J at a Pacific island base is about to take on a full load of fuel as ground crews button up and prepare the aircraft for its next mission. A total of ten bombardment groups from the 5th, 7th, and 13th Air Forces participated in the island campaigns in the Pacific Theater during the Second World War.

LEFT: A bird's-eye view of B-24s nearing completion. The Liberator was the most produced United States aircraft of World War II. The B-24 was also used as a passenger transport (C-87) and fuel tanker (C-109). The navy also pressed the Liberator into service as the PB4Y Privateer.

Martin PBM-1 Mariner

The Martin PBM-1 Mariner was not anything like Athena—the Greek goddess of wisdom and war who, legend tells it, sprang fully grown from her father Zeus's head. No, the Mariner started its life in quarter-scale miniature.

The Martin Model 162A flew in 1937. It was Martin's response to the navy's request for a new twin-engine patrol bomber. Martin envisioned a mammoth all-metal gull-winged flying boat that was even bigger than the Consolidated PBY Catalina. To prove its concept, Martin took a different tack. Martin built a prototype that was only one-quarter the size of the actual aircraft. Its wingspan was just 43 feet and it could scarcely seat one pilot.

The quarter-sized prototype was fully functional, and a cost-effective way for Martin to build and test its proposed design, but it was not without its engineering challenges. The fabricators at Martin had to devise a way to place one smaller-scale engine inside the hull-like fuselage because petite, quarter-sized radials simply did not exist. The gamble worked. The Navy ordered twenty-one full-size production aircraft based on the evaluation of the diminutive test model.

A full-scale prototype called XPBM-1 was reviewed in 1939 to authenticate the mini-version. This time the wingspan was 118 feet. It had two Wright R-2600-6 Cyclone engines with 1,600 horsepower. The XPBM-1 prototype had machine guns at the waist, in the tail, and in nose and dorsal gun turrets. To perform the duties of a patrol bomber it could carry 2,000 pounds of depth charges or bombs. It was manned by a crew of seven. Like the PBY Catalina, the first XPBM-1's floats were retractable. On later variants they would become fixed structures.

The most unique feature on the XPBM-1 was its gull wing. The high gull wing kept the wing-mounted engines sufficiently above the water line, and it easily attached to the top of the fuselage without any additional drag-inducing parasol construction. A parasol wing was the inferior solution seen on the Catalina and other flying boats of the time. The gull wing was also cantilevered; it did not need any external bracing, further reducing drag. The Vought F4U Corsair is another well-known World War II–era gull-wing aircraft.

The production-run version was similar to the XPBM-1, which had introduced improvements to the design of the original smaller scale model. In 1941 the first production PBM-1s were delivered to Navy Patrol Squadron VP-74 for use on antisubmarine patrols. The PBM-1 was built with the improved dihedral tail of the XPBM-1. Now the tail's horizontal surfaces had a visible upward

angle that helped increase flight stability. One of the original twenty-one was converted to be an XPBM-2. It was used to test a larger fuel capacity for extreme-range maneuvers and for compatibility with a catapult-launching system the Naval Aircraft Factory was erecting; however, production PBMs never used catapult launching in the field.

The PBM-1 became known as the Mariner. In 1941 the government officially recognized the use of popular names for its military aircraft. While most aircraft already had names, they were usually a suggestion from the manufacturer, since the military had a standardized system for identifying designation numbers. Using a generic name allowed the government to provide news about its deployments and aircraft without publicizing specifics, such as variant or type.

The next sizable production run was the PBM-3. It was ordered in the quantity of 379. These were the first models to premier the fixed floats, larger Wright R-2600-12 Cyclone engines, four-bladed Hamilton Standard propellers, and larger, elongated nacelles that had space for internal bomb storage—a vast improvement over the external racks. A fraction of this order (274 units, the PBM-3C) was considered for export to the RAF; while another 201 units were built as the PBM-3D. This variant had more armor plate, increased armament, self-sealing fuel tanks, and Wright R-2600-22 Cyclone engines. As a consequence, the -3D was heavier and slower. Some of these PBM-3Cs and -3Ds carried radar aboard in a radome, the bulge above the cockpit where electronics and antennae were housed. This structure protected the sensitive instrumentation from environmental conditions. Another variant, the PBM-3R, was a transport with a reinforced deck to support cargo or seats for twenty people. It was not armed.

The next variant built in quantity was the PBM-5. It was the last major revision and the one built in the largest numbers. It featured eight .50-caliber machine guns and could haul 4,000 pounds of bombs, torpedoes, or depth charges. The crew could consist of as many as thirteen men depending on the type and duration of the mission. The -5 used Pratt & Whitney Double Wasp engines, the eighteen-cylinder R-2800-22 with 2,100 horsepower.

The -5 variant was active from 1944 to the war's end. Thirty-six amphibious PBM-5As were built, as were several other incrementally improved versions of the -5 platform. The majority of PBM-5s served over the Pacific Ocean where they were well-suited; however, they also saw action over the

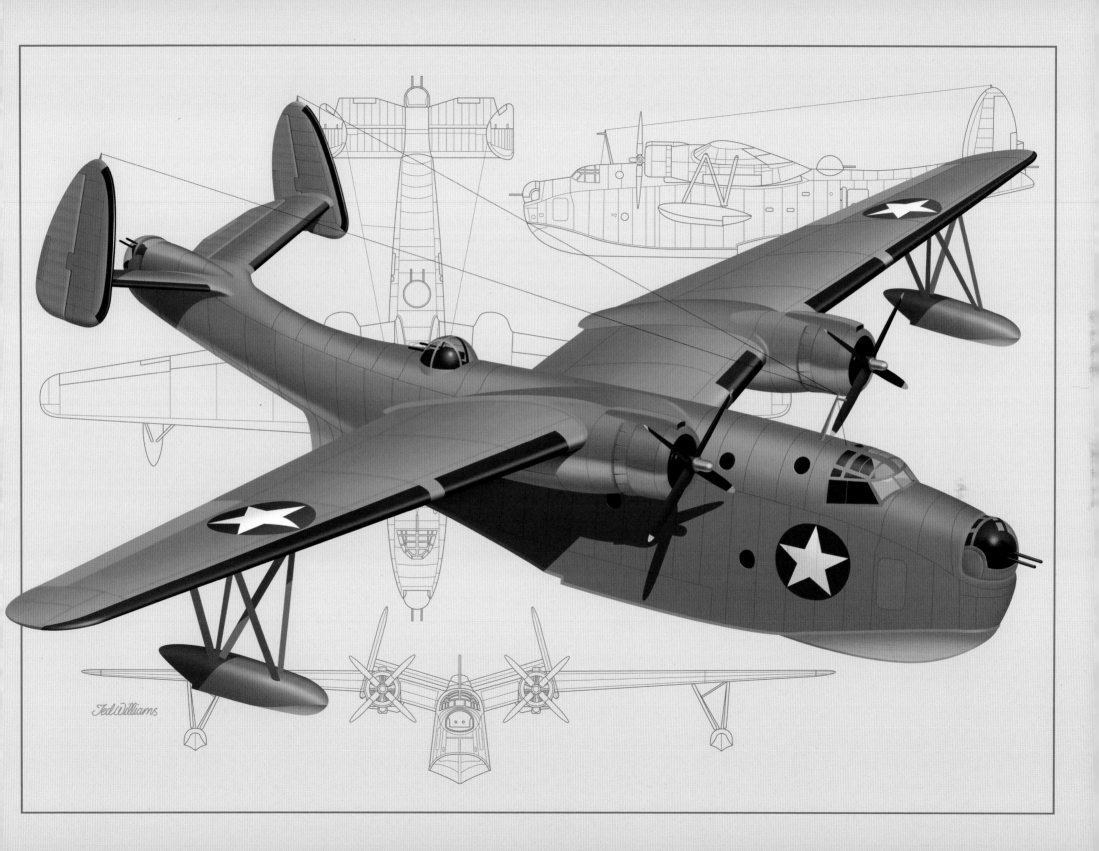

Ted Williams

Martin PBM-3 Mariner Specifications

Type: Patrol bomber
Crew: Seven to ten
Power plant: Two 1,700-horsepower Wright Cyclone R-2600-12 14-cylinder air-cooled radial engines
Performance: Maximum speed, 211 miles per hour; service ceiling, 19,800 feet; maximum range, 2,240 miles
Weight: Empty, 33,175 pounds; maximum takeoff weight, 58,000 pounds
Dimensions: Span, 118 feet; length, 79 feet, 10 inches; height, 28 feet, 10 inches; wing area, 1,400 square feet
Armament: Eight .50-cal machine guns and 8,000 pounds of bombs

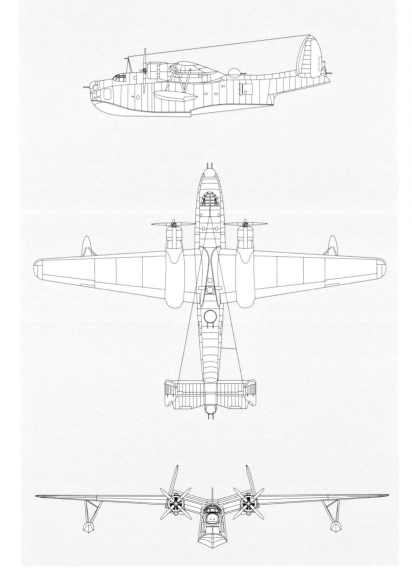

Atlantic where they were used to deter German U-boats and for antishipping. In all, 628 of various -5 models were built. In grand total, 1,366 PBM Mariners were produced over the course of the entire program, the last one leaving the Martin Middle River, Maryland, factory on March 9, 1949. A World War II aircraft, the Mariner was equipped with Norden bombsights.

Some later Mariners received a boost from equipment for jet-assisted takeoff (JATO). The Mariner was used to evaluate whether JATO could speed

OPPOSITE TOP: A PBM-5 Mariner is lowered over the side of its seaplane tender after having been re-armed and repaired for its next patrol mission.

OPPOSITE BOTTOM: PBM hull assemblies await the next step of production. The quality craftsmanship is evident in the sheet metal work. The Mariner was the successor to the Catalina; although not as well known, its versatility kept it in production for several years after the Second World War.

BELOW: This PBM-5 has been winched down the seaplane ramp into the water. Naval Air Station personnel work to remove the lines and beaching gear.

takeoff in rough seas. Others observed missile testing, previewed advanced electronics, or tested technological advancements.

In the 1950s the PBM Mariner served in Korea, when many were pressed back into active duty from reserve units. The Coast Guard also employed the Mariner for search-and-rescue. By 1958 all Mariners were retired from military service. The Martin PBM Mariner was never as lauded as the Consolidated PBY Catalina, but its contributions were just as noteworthy.

Douglas TBD Devastator

The first monoplane to be used for naval carrier-based operations was the Douglas TBD Devastator.

In 1934 the U.S. Navy was looking for a torpedo bomber that operated almost exclusively from an aircraft carrier. The navy's fleet of carriers was evolving and improving; now it needed more modern planes for its decks. The navy sought new ideas from Douglas and the Great Lakes Aircraft Company. When Douglas presented its idea for the all-metal Devastator, Great Lakes offered a biplane design which was handily rejected. The U.S. Navy was finally ready to acknowledge the monoplane's superiority.

The Douglas prototype, the XTBD-1, was a cantilevered low-wing monoplane powered by a single 800-horsepower Pratt & Whitney engine with a three-bladed propeller. The aircraft's crew of three—a pilot, bombardier/navigator, and gunner/radio operator—sat underneath a long, continuously enclosed greenhouse-style glass canopy. Armament was made up of a fixed forward-firing machine gun (either a .30- or .50-caliber) and a flexible rear-firing .30-caliber gun. More than 1,000 pounds of bombs or a Mark XIII aerial torpedo could be carried underneath the fuselage. During missions, the bombardier would move from his seat to lie underneath the cockpit to have access to the Norden bombsight aiming window.

Other features included a rearward retractable undercarriage and wings that used hydraulic power to fold for easier storage on the aircraft carriers. Once folded, the 50-foot wingspan was shortened to 26 feet; and the wings folded upward toward each other, not rearward as was more typical for folding wings of the time.

In 1935 the prototype underwent flight testing and participated in carrier trials on the USS *Lexington*. This trial period was crucial because a carrier-based aircraft must be more rugged than a land-based model. Airframe structures need to withstand the rigors of carrier takeoffs and landings. Space and supplies are also at a premium onboard a ship; maintenance must be easy and self-contained. Case in point, the navy preferred air-cooled radial engines to anything liquid-cooled because radials did not require a supply of coolant and they typically needed to have fewer parts replaced.

The navy ordered 114 TBD-1s in 1936. The production version had a revised rounded canopy that was recommended after preliminary evaluations determined the first design was restricting the pilot's view, especially at landing. The TBD, christened Devastator, had a slightly larger Pratt & Whitney

VT-8 Torpedo Eight

RIGHT: This factory photograph of a Douglas TBD Devastator shows the graceful curve of the wing fillet as it creates a smooth transition between the fuselage and the wing. All three crew members would have good visibility through the large Plexiglas green house canopy. The crew entered and exited the cockpit through the canopy's sliding panels.

OPPOSITE: The Douglas Devastator was the U.S. Navy's first all-metal monoplane torpedo-bomber. Although obsolete by 1941, it saw extensive action immediately after Pearl Harbor at the Battle of the Coral Sea and at Midway. At Midway, thirty-five Devastators were lost, including all of the aircraft and crews of Torpedo Squadron 8 commanded by Lt. Cmdr. John C. Waldron. This TBD-1 is shown in the paint scheme of VT-6 serving aboard the USS *Enterprise* in February 1942.

R-1830-64 Twin Wasp radial engine and improvement to the tail. Production aircraft started arriving onboard U.S. carriers in 1937. The USS *Saratoga* was the first to receive the new torpedo bomber.

In 1938 Douglas received the order to build another fifteen TBD-1s. By that year, the USS *Yorktown*, *Enterprise*, and *Lexington* aircraft carriers had already received Devastators. Soon the USS *Ranger*, *Hornet*, and *Wasp* would be similarly equipped.

Devastators participated in the 1938 Fleet Exercise, the Navy's annual fleet-wide training event. That year the scenario included a mock attack on Pearl Harbor. While the United States military did little based on the data from the exercise, the Japanese used this information as it prepared and planned for the 1941 surprise attack on Pearl Harbor.

The Devastator's greatest achievement came during the Battle of the Coral Sea in 1942, the first large-scale World War II air and sea battle between Japan and the United States. The USS *Yorktown* and *Lexington* launched several aircraft, including twenty-two torpedo bombers. American aircraft attacked and sank the Japanese aircraft carrier *Shoho*.

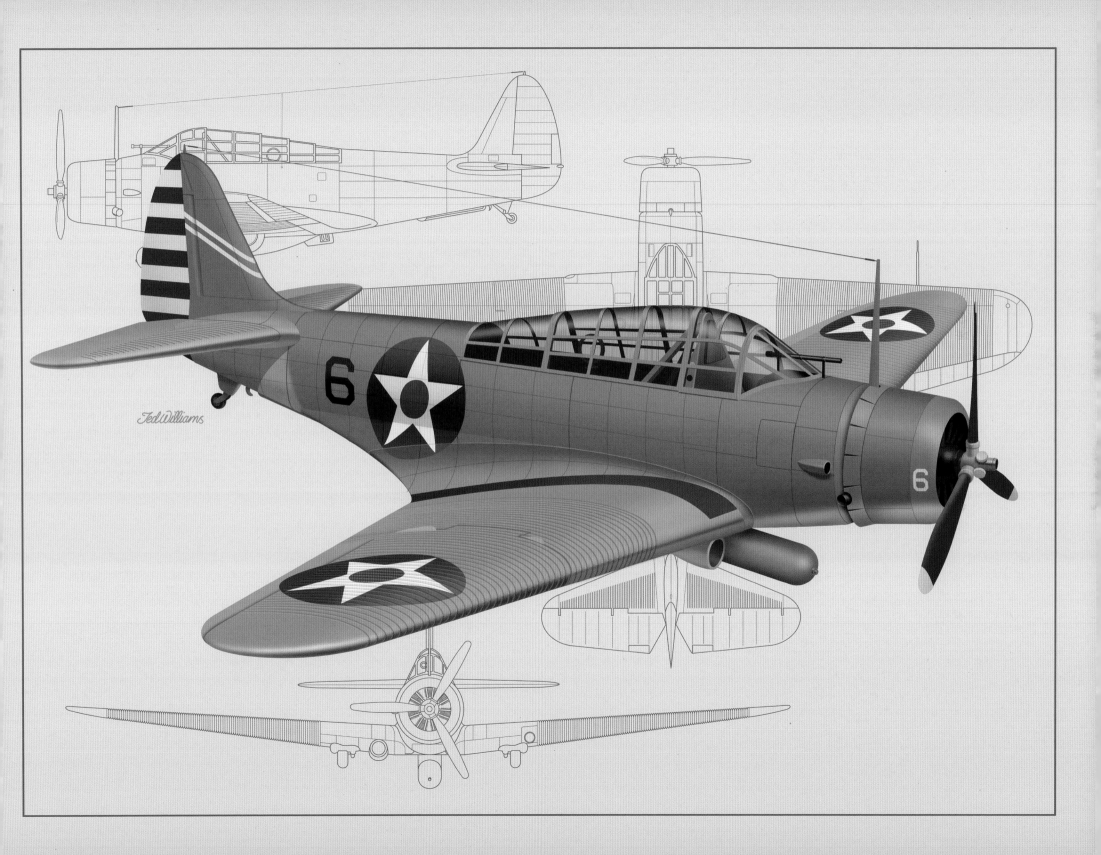

TOP LEFT: With the USS *Yorktown*'s island in the background, deck crews right a TBD Devastator after a landing accident. Assigned to Torpedo Squadron Eight (VT-8), this aircraft was later destroyed in the Battle of Midway.

TOP RIGHT: The Douglas TBD Devastator was the U.S. Navy's first carrier-based monoplane. Because a monoplane's wingspan was greater than the biplanes of the era, the Devastator's wings folded for stowage aboard the aircraft carrier. Hydraulically operated, when folded the span was reduced from 50 to 26 feet.

Douglas TBD-1 Specifications

Type: Torpedo bomber
Crew: Three
Power plant: One 900-horsepower Pratt & Whitney Twin Wasp R-1830-64 air-cooled radial engine
Performance: Maximum speed, 221 miles per hour at 8,000 feet; service ceiling, 19,500 feet ; maximum range, 716 miles
Weight: Empty, 6,183 pounds; maximum takeoff weight, 10,195 pounds
Dimensions: Span, 50 feet; length, 35 feet; height, 15 feet, 1 inch; wing area, 422 square feet
Armament: Two machine guns, either .30- or .50-cal, and 1,500 pounds of bombs or an 1,850-pound torpedo

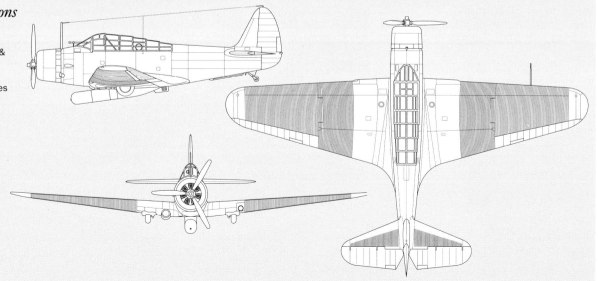

The TBD-1 Devastator was an aircraft of many firsts, but one of its firsts worked to speed its demise. The undercarriage intentionally left the wheels partially exposed in the upward position. It was thought this would aid in the event of a wheels-up landing, when, in reality, the drag-inducing effect mitigated any benefits it could potentially provide during an emergency landing. As a result, the Devastator's top speed was stuck at 206 miles per hour, which was considerably slower than emerging Japanese and German aircraft.

There was another issue with the type of torpedo the Devastator was equipped to carry. While no fault of the aircraft, launching data for the torpedo was incorrect, causing targeting inaccuracies. The torpedo would release as specified, but it would not always detonate upon impact. This put many Devastators in harm's way to no purpose.

But the true test of the Devastator's limitations came in 1942, just one month after its success at the Battle of the Coral Sea. Forty-one Devastators from the USS *Hornet*, *Enterprise*, and *Yorktown* valiantly participated in the Battle of Midway along with many other American carrier-borne aircraft. Only

ABOVE: Gone forever were the bright, highly-visible yellow-and-silver paint schemes that had adorned prewar naval aircraft. This TBD Devastator from Torpedo Squadron Three (VT-3) displays a muted gray-and-blue experimental camouflage design created by artist McClelland Barclay in 1940.

six Devastators survived. The Japanese pursuit plane, the Zero, was faster and more maneuverable and, this time, the Japanese ships were ready with dense antiaircraft fire. The Devastator, with its 1934 origins, was not in a fair fight.

After such heartbreakingly poor performance at Midway, all remaining active service Devastators were taken from the frontline and reassigned to a training role. Other more advanced dive-bombers with faster speeds and more protection for all occupants were rapidly coming to the fore. In 1940 President Franklin Delano Roosevelt had challenged the military and American manufacturers to produce 50,000 aircraft a year. Aircraft updates and design changes were stepping up to meet wartime needs.

The Douglas TBD Devastator came at the time when the U.S. Navy was finally warming to the airplane and its role in the fleet. Produced in limited numbers, the Devastator's most important contribution to aircraft evolution was the fact that it persuaded the navy to consider newer technologies. The Devastator put itself out there in uncertain times, and against the best of its enemies, to ensure the navy would continue to develop newer aircraft.

North American B-25 Mitchell

North American Aviation opened its doors in 1928 as an investment holding company for various aviation interests. Although successful, the Air Mail Act of 1934 dissolved all aviation holding companies. The mega company was forced to spin off its assets. The manufacturing arm retained the name North American. James Howard "Dutch" Kindelberger left his job at Douglas to run the new company.

The B-25 was derived from a design called the NA-40, which, in turn, drew inspiration from another earlier aircraft, the XB-21. In 1937 the XB-21 had competed for a U.S. Army contract and lost to the Douglas B-18A Bolo. Later, a variant of the NA-40, the NA-40B, was evaluated alongside the Douglas A-20 Havoc. Coming up the loser in the attack bomber competition, the NA-40B was revived as a potential candidate for a medium bomber contract.

Now called NA-62 by the factory, the aircraft had a wider fuselage than the attack version. Since the wartime need was so great, the U.S. Army ordered 184, designated B-25, based on previous evaluations. Instead of a lengthy evaluation period, changes occurred while in production. As a result, the first run included twenty-four B-25s, forty B-25As with more armor and self-sealing fuel tanks, and 120 B-25Bs with two turrets.

The first production B-25 flew on August 19, 1940. All of the B-25s had tricycle landing gear, shoulder-mounted wings, two Wright Cyclone engines, and a large, twin tail. The B-25 was named "Mitchell" after General Billy Mitchell, the famously outspoken advocate for military aviation and strategic bombing during the 1920s and 1930s. As early as 1924, Mitchell had suggested the possibility of a Japanese attack on Hawaii. Mitchell was posthumously awarded the Congressional Medal of Honor in 1946 for his contribution to American military aviation, and, to date, the B-25 is the only military aircraft named after a person.

The B-25B is most famous for Lieutenant Colonel James H. "Jimmy" Doolittle's Tokyo Raid on April 18, 1942. On that day, as retribution for the attack on Pearl Harbor, sixteen B-25Bs launched from the USS *Hornet* aircraft carrier on a top secret mission to bomb Japan. Amazingly all sixteen large, land-based army aircraft took to the air from a carrier deck. It was a dangerous maneuver. The bombers were heavy with bombs and fuel, exceeding the maximum takeoff weight of 28,460 pounds, with only 500 feet of deck in front of them. The raid impressed upon the Japanese that the United States was a worthy foe, and led to the Battle of Midway.

RIGHT: An experimental scale model of the B-25 is prepared for wind tunnel tests. The model maker holds an exact miniature of the type of bomb carried by the bomber.

OPPOSITE: The B-25 is best remembered for performing the first bombing raid on Tokyo in 1942, however it was used extensively in all theaters of operation in World War II. The Mitchell was named in honor of Brig. Gen. William "Billy" Mitchell and is the only U.S. aircraft named after a person. This B-25 carries the black-and-white wing and fuselage stripes applied to all Allied aircraft during the Invasion of Normandy on June 6, 1944.

In 1941 and 1942 the B-25C was the first variant to be produced in great quantity. It had two Wright R-2600-13 Cyclone engines and equipment to remove ice from the leading edges. The B-25C could carry more fuel, thereby increasing the aircraft's range. The -C variant also had provisions for external bomb racks in addition to the bomb bay; the B-25C could carry up to 5,200 pounds of bombs. It was armed with six .50-caliber machine guns and carried a crew of five. A total of 1,625 were built in the -C configuration.

Next, 2,290 B-25Ds were built. Identical to the -C variant, all -Ds were built in North American's new facility in Kansas City, Missouri; the B-25C was built in Inglewood, California.

The next production variant was the B-25G, of which four hundred were built. The Plexiglas nose was replaced by a solid redesigned nose that could house two .50-caliber machine guns and a 75-mm M4 cannon. Intended for ground attack and strafing, it had more armor plate on the underside of its fuselage than the previous model. Soon after, another one thousand B-25Hs were built as an improvement to the -G version. The last variant built by North American, the B-25J, had twelve .50-caliber machine guns and a crew of six; 4,318 were built.

Over the course of the program, many B-25s were converted and used for transport or trainers. The Commander of the U.S. Army Air Forces, General "Hap" Arnold, kept a B-25 as his personal staff transport. Allied nations also flew B-25s. Great Britain, the Netherlands, China, Brazil, and the Soviet Union all flew B-25s at some point during the war.

In 1945 a B-25 en route to Newark Airport got lost in a dense fog. The pilot dropped below 1,000 feet trying to regain his visibility, not realizing he was directly over New York City. The army pilot was able to avoid several skyscrapers, except for the Empire State Building. The impact ripped into the seventy-ninth floor, killing eleven people inside the building, as well as the pilot, Lieutenant Colonel William Smith, and his two crewmen.

The B-25 was not as fast, nor could it carry as much weight, as its fellow medium bombers, the Martin B-26 Marauder and the Douglas A-26 Invader. Yet it was a pilot favorite. B-25s saw more activity and covered more ground in World War II than the other two medium bombers. Its two engines were loud; it was tough, and it was battle worthy, able to withstand a lot of damage.

Nearly ten thousand (9,816) were built overall—the largest quantity of all World War II twin-engine military aircraft. Mitchells served with every Allied

North American B-25J Specifications

Type: Medium Bomber

Crew: Six

Power plant: Two 1,700-horsepower Wright Double Cyclone R-2600-29 air-cooled radial engines

Performance: Maximum speed, 272 miles per hour at 13,000 feet; service ceiling, 24,200 feet; maximum range, 1,350 miles

Weight: Empty, 19,480 pounds; maximum takeoff weight, 35,000 pounds

Dimensions: Span, 67 feet, 7 inches; length, 52 feet, 11 inches; height, 16 feet, 4 inches; wing area, 610 square feet

Armament: Twelve .50-cal machine guns and 3,200 pounds of bombs

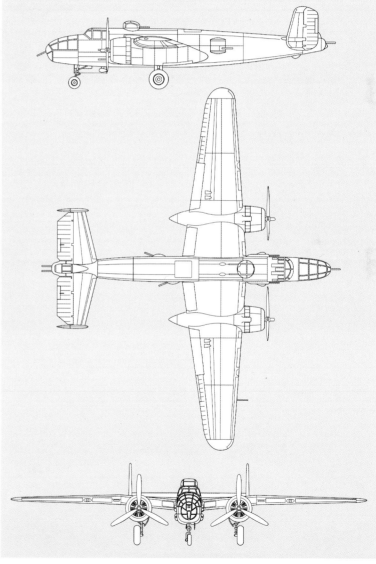

air force and at every theater, doing everything from testing to reconnaissance to bombing and strafing. After the war, some B-25s flew as transports or trainers until as late as the 1970s.

North American provided thousands of aircraft to the war effort, and the North American B-25 Mitchell was the apex of medium bomber development. Dutch Kindelberger and North American would go on to produce the P-51 Mustang, the most-beloved World War II fighter plane. North American airplanes were known for being quality product, born of efficient manufacturing techniques, and easy to maintain in the field; they were adaptable for multiple roles and well liked by the men who used them.

ABOVE: B-25Hs nearing completion at a North American production facility. As the Allies gained air superiority it was no longer necessary to apply camouflage paint. By 1944 aircraft were leaving the factories with a bare aluminum finish.

OPPOSITE: Armors ready a B-25H. This included cleaning and lubricating the 75-mm cannon, laying out the 3-inch ammunition, and loading the .50-cal ammunition belts.

Douglas SBD Dauntless

In 1934 the U.S. Navy evaluated proposals for a new scouting dive-bomber. Vought, Northrop (then a subsidiary of Douglas), Martin, and Brewster complied with designs. Curtiss and Great Lakes also submitted plans; both biplanes, they were rejected early in the selection process.

The navy produced two of the designs from the 1934 competition. The Vought prototype went on to become the SB2U Vindicator. The Ed Heinemann–designed Northrop prototype, the XBT-1, would evolve into the Douglas SBD Dauntless—the most effective dive-bomber of World War II.

In 1936 the navy ordered fifty-four of the Northrop prototype, designated BT-1, but XBT-1 had already started to exhibit weaknesses; in particular, it did not dive well. This is when the aircraft received its most identifiable feature: perforated dive flaps. Jokingly referred to as "Swiss cheese," three rows of three-inch holes were drilled into each flap to prevent the buffeting that was impairing the aircraft's dive performance.

Still not satisfied with the underpowered BT-1, another prototype was developed. The XBT-2 had a larger 1,000-horsepower Wright R-1820 Cyclone engine and a three-bladed propeller. To assess its stability issues, the XBT-2 was sent to the National Advisory Committee for Aeronautics (NACA) laboratory in Langley, Virginia for testing inside the incomparably large—97´ by 222´—wind tunnel. Numerous evaluations led to an improved tail configuration and more predictable control surfaces.

In 1937 Jack Northrop left Douglas to start another independent venture. Douglas resumed control of the XBT-2 project, calling it XSBD-1 to more accurately reflect its scout-/dive-bombing function and its new Douglas parentage. Ed Heinemann elected to stay with Douglas, continuing to lead the engineering team responsible for the dive-bomber.

The navy ordered 144 of the improved design in 1939. By 1940, fifty-seven SBD-1s were delivered to the Marine Corps for land-based use, while another eighty-seven SBD-2s went to the navy for use on aircraft carriers. Named the SBD "Dauntless," it was a two-place, all-metal low-wing monoplane. The pilot and the radio operator/gunner sat under an enclosed greenhouse canopy. The -2 was identical to the -1 except for its larger self-sealing fuel tanks. The -2 also had two forward-firing .50-caliber guns, one more than the -1. Both the SBD-1 and -2 had a flexible .30-caliber machine gun in the rear.

VB-6 Bombing Six

OPPOSITE: Originating from a Jack Northrop design, Douglas Aircraft developed the Dauntless into one of World War II's most important aircraft. The sturdy, easy to fly dive-bomber was instrumental in the American victories over the Japanese Fleet, and it continued to serve through the end of the war long after its replacement, the SB2C Helldiver, had been delivered. This SBD-3 was flown at the Battle of Midway on June 4, 1942 by Ensign Lew Hopkins of VB-6 from the USS *Enterprise*.

Also, the Dauntless's wings did not fold. To make space in the hangar deck, the Dauntless was hoisted and hung from overhead cables. Each Dauntless was manufactured with cables for this purpose.

Like all new combat aircraft produced after 1941, the Dauntless was manufactured with a drab finish after the military abandoned the colorful paint schemes of the 1930s for dull, low-visibility coverings or camouflage.

These early SBDs saw the greatest highs and lows. An SBD-2 from the USS *Enterprise* was the first American World War II aircraft to sink an enemy ship, foreshadowing its formidable ability to hobble the Japanese navy. Yet, before that first victory, the SBDs at Pearl Harbor took a beating during the Japanese surprise attack.

Starting delivery in 1941, the SBD-3 had increased armor plate, a bullet-proof windshield, and self-sealing fuel tanks. The rear gunner was provided with a second .30-caliber machine gun to match the pilot's dual guns. Readily available in 1942, the -3 variant (585 were built) was the one that earned the SBD its reputation in the Pacific Theater.

The Battle of the Coral Sea was the first major sea confrontation between the United States and Japan after Pearl Harbor and the American entry into the war. It was the first time in history when warring hostile ships could not see each other. The entire encounter occurred on the wings of carrier-based aircraft. The Dauntless was one of the aircraft that participated in the Coral Sea attack against the Japanese aircraft carrier *Shoho*.

Only one month after the Coral Sea confrontation, during the Battle of Midway, SBDs sunk a heavy cruiser plus four vital Japanese aircraft carriers—the *Akagi*, *Hiryu*, *Kaga*, and *Soryu*—that were used in the Pearl Harbor attack. The Battle of Midway is known as the turning point of the war in the Pacific. The Japanese fleet was never able to recover from the loss of equipment and experienced personnel.

The Dauntless was also instrumental in the U.S. Marines's first major fight to gain possession of the Pacific island of Guadalcanal.

The SBD-4 improved on the -3 variant; 780 were ordered. It had a Hamilton Standard constant-speed variable propeller, an improved 24-volt electrical system, and real-life combat experience to draw upon. The SBD-5 was the variant produced in the greatest quantity. Similar to the -4, almost 3,000 (2,965), were built. SBD-5s began equipping squadrons in 1943. The -5 could carry up to a 1,000-pound bomb, plus two 100-pound bombs for

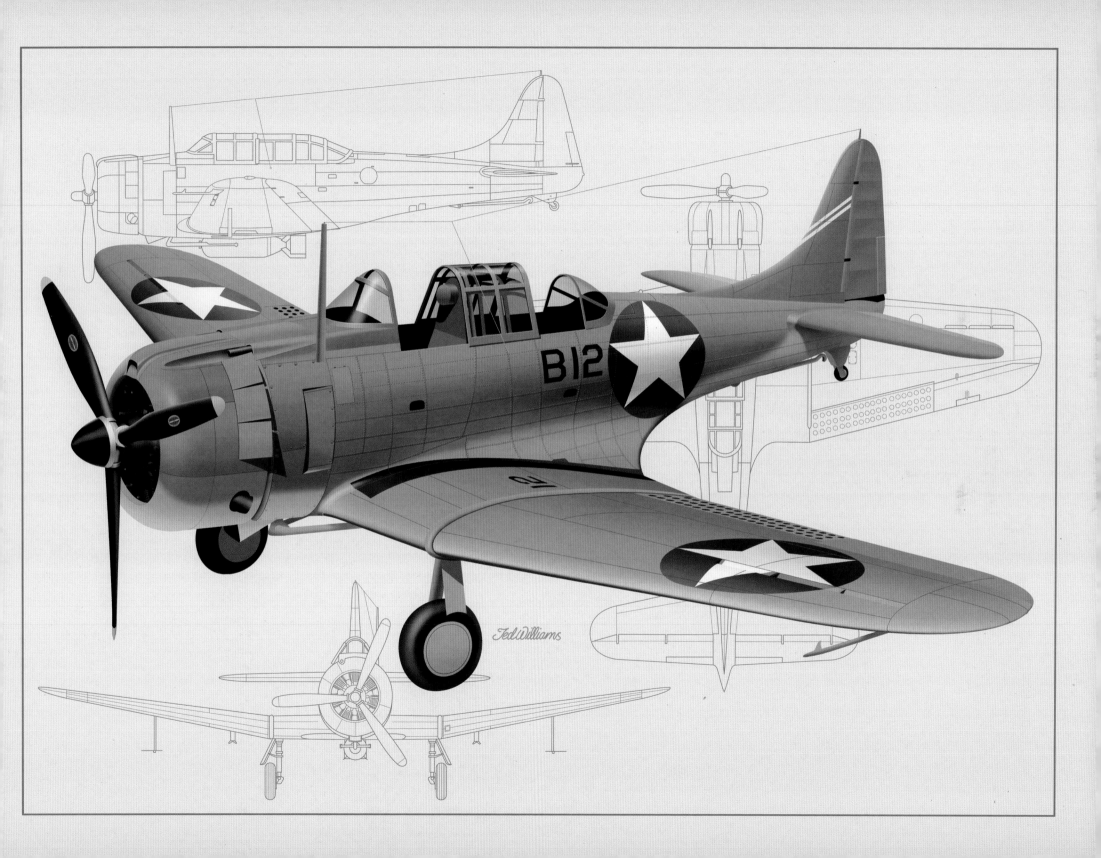

Ted Williams

LEFT: These SBDs at the Douglas plant in El Segundo, California, are painted in the naval three-color camouflage paint job. The red surround on the national insignia was only used from June 1943 through August 1943.

ABOVE: The Dauntless's rear gunner used twin .30-caliber guns on a flexible mount. The gun mount was equipped with an interrupter mechanism that would not allow the guns to fire when the muzzles passed by the vertical stabilizer.

dive-bombing. The last variant was the -6. Of the 450 that were built, most were used as training aircraft.

The SBD was the navy's principal dive-bombing aircraft until 1944, when the Curtiss SB2C Helldiver replaced it. The Helldiver was never as well-liked as the SBD Dauntless. For one, unlike the larger Helldiver, the SBD could operate from the smaller decks of escort carriers.

The U.S. Army also operated the SBD. Designated as the A-24 Banshee, the army purchased seventy-eight in 1940 and another ninety in 1942. The army wanted the capability to perform dive-bombing; however, it never developed the specialization. New Zealand, Great Britain, and France also received Dauntlesses, but only in small quantities.

Some SBDs saw activity over the Atlantic for antisubmarine missions, but, by far, its career was made in the Pacific Theater. Sometimes called "slow but deadly," it had a slow rate of climb and a maximum top speed of only 255 miles an hour, but it was tough and reliable. A comparison can be made to the B-17—the Dauntless was known for withstanding serious damage, but still managing to get its crew back home. On record as the carrier aircraft with the least war losses, the Douglas SBD Dauntless was, as its name implied, indeed fearless.

THIS PAGE: These SBD-5 Dauntlesses from the USS *Yorktown* are en route to a raid on Wake Island during the first week of October 1943. Navy pilots became adept at navigating across the wide expanse of the Pacific Ocean.

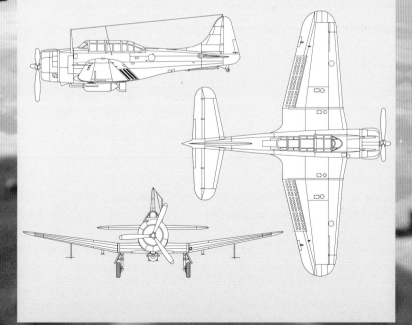

Douglas SBD-3 Specifications

Type: Scout bomber
Crew: Two
Power plant: One 1,000-horsepower Wright Cyclone R-1820-52 air-cooled radial engine
Performance: Maximum speed, 250 miles per hour; service ceiling, 427,100 feet; maximum range, 1,345 miles
Weight: Empty, 6,404 pounds; maximum takeoff weight, 10,700 pounds
Dimensions: Span, 41, feet 6 inches; length, 32 feet, 8 inches; height, 13 feet, 7 inches; wing area, 325 square feet
Armament: Two .50-cal and two .30-cal machine guns and 1,200 pounds of bombs

Grumman TBF/TBM Avenger

Grumman is best known for its series of U.S. Navy "Fighting Cats," felines such as the iconic Wildcat, Hellcat, Bearcat, and Tomcat. More recently, Grumman is known for its role in the United States's space program; however, Grumman also designed one of the most useful bombers of the Second World War.

Shortly after the stock market crash of 1929, Leroy "Roy" Grumman gathered his assets and the resources of several financial backers to form the Grumman Engineering Corporation, Bethpage, New York. Trained as a machinist by the military during World War I and educated as a mechanical engineer at Cornell University, Grumman gained his practical business experience working at the Loening Aircraft Engineering Company. When Grumman struck out on his own, several former Loening employees joined him. In particular, Leon A. "Jake" Swirbul, was a perfect administrative foil to Grumman's keen creativity. Together they made Grumman a respected name in aviation.

Throughout the 1930s Grumman provided the navy with some of the finest pursuit aircraft of the era: the FF-1 (the first naval fighter with retractable landing gear), the pugnacious F3F, and the F4F Wildcat. In 1939 the U.S. Navy was looking for a torpedo bomber with a top speed of 300 miles per hour, a range of 1,000 miles, and the capacity for a 2,000-pound bomb load to replace the Douglas TBD Devastator. Grumman was a natural choice. While Vought and Grumman both supplied proposals for the navy's consideration, the Grumman design proved to have better performance than the Vought, and, perhaps most importantly, Grumman was able to guarantee a speedy production of its new design. By 1940 Vought was engrossed with its F4U Corsair; it could not take on another large project. Timing was crucial. The surprise attack on Pearl Harbor changed the United States's attitude toward the situation in the Pacific. America was at war.

The Grumman XTBF-1 was a sturdy airplane, as were all of the aircraft that originated in the famous Grumman Iron Works. It was a three-place bomber with a single engine, the 1,700-horsepower Wright R-2600 Cyclone, and accommodations for a pilot, turret gunner, and radioman/bombardier/gunner. Its wings, a space-saving innovation from the Wildcat, swiveled to fold flat against the fuselage, so more aircraft could be parked side by side onboard a carrier.

The XTBF-1 had a Grumman-designed powered rear turret that was upgraded to use a .50-caliber machine gun, along with another fixed forward-firing .50 caliber machine gun mounted in the engine cowling, and a ventral

RIGHT: Aboard a carrier in the South Pacific, a hangar deck crew prepares a deadly aerial torpedo for loading into the Grumman TBF's torpedo bay. The aircraft was considered the best torpedo-bomber in the Pacific Theater. Avengers were credited with the sinking of three of Japan's largest and best battleships.

OPPOSITE: When Grumman could no longer keep up with demand for the new F6F Hellcats, the manufacture of the TBF Avengers was turned over to General Motors. Designated TBMs, these aircraft were virtually indistinguishable from the Grumman produced Avengers. This TBM-1C carries the three-color camouflage paint scheme and markings of VT-51 flown by Lt. George H.W. Bush serving aboard the USS *San Jacinto* in 1944.

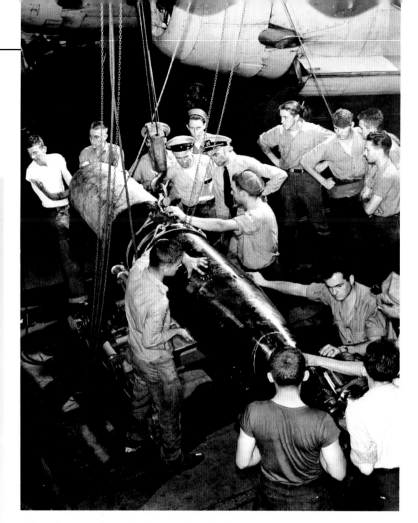

.30-caliber tunnel gun. It also premiered a large internal bomb bay that could conceal a 2,000-pound torpedo, four 500-pound bombs, or an extra tank for fuel. The navy ordered 286 production models only two weeks after the Japanese attacked Hawaii. The XBTF-1 was given the name "Avenger" because it went into mass production to avenge the events at Pearl Harbor.

The first production TBF Avengers were put to use at the Battle of Midway, but they did not fare well. In a true trial by fire, six brand-new Avengers were unable to get onboard the USS *Hornet* before it sailed from Pearl Harbor; instead the six flew directly to Midway Island. Only one survived the battle. Still, the navy needed the new bomber as the Devastator was clearly outclassed by its Japanese rivals.

By 1943 wartime production was frenzied. Grumman was building F4F Wildcats and TBF Avengers by the dozen, as well as engineering and producing the F6F Hellcat. To meet the navy's insatiable need for aircraft of all kinds, Grumman enlisted the help of the Eastern Aircraft Division of General Motors. As a result, in addition to the 2,290 TBFs from Grumman, GM would build

Grumman TBM-1C Specifications

Type: Torpedo bomber

Crew: Three

Power plant: One 1,700-horsepower Wright Cyclone R-2600-8 air-cooled radial engine

Performance: Maximum speed, 271 miles per hour at 12,000 feet; service ceiling, 22,400 feet; maximum range, 1,215 miles

Weight: Empty, 10,080 pounds; maximum takeoff weight, 15,905 pounds

Dimensions: Span, 54 feet, 2 inches; length, 40 feet; height, 16 feet, 5 inches; wing area, 490 square feet

Armament: Three .50-cal machine guns, one .30-cal machine gun, and 2,000 pounds of bombs, torpedo or extra fuel

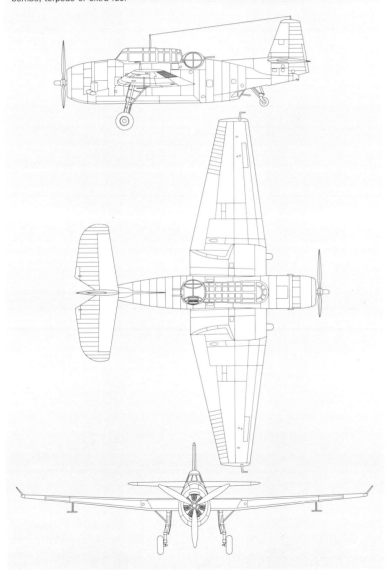

ABOVE: An Avenger is being refueled onboard an aircraft carrier. A deck crewman stands by with a fire extinguisher. Leroy Grumman invented the hinge mechanism that folds the wing rearward; he used two paper clips and an eraser to puzzle-out the unique pivoting motion. The Grumman folding wing was also used on the Wildcat and Hellcat.

7,546 Avengers for the war effort. Identified as TBM, they were identical to the TBF.

The Avenger earned a reputation for neutralizing large Japanese warships. In 1942 twenty-four Avengers were credited with sinking the Japanese aircraft carrier *Ryujo*. Next, during the battles for Guadalcanal, Avengers worked together to take out the Japanese battleship *Hiei*. Two of the largest battleships of the World War II, the Japanese *Yamato* and *Musashi*, also fell to the tenacity of the Avenger.

Former President George H.W. Bush flew the TBF Avenger. He was awarded the Distinguished Flying Cross in September 1944 for his heroic actions under fire during a mission near the Bonin Islands. As his Avenger received antiaircraft fire, Lieutenant Bush delivered his bombs on target before bailing out.

TBF and TBM variants received upgrades and improvements over the course of the program. Grumman concentrated on the TBF-1 and TBF-1C, which were both altered to carry two .50-caliber guns mounted in the wings instead of the nose-mounted gun and wing tanks for additional fuel. Grumman also produced 395 of the TBF-1Bs for lend-lease export to Great Britain. Grumman continued to develop Avenger prototypes to test emerging technologies.

GM's Eastern Division built 2,882 of the TBM-1 and 4,664 TBM-3s with the larger engine. Nearly one thousand of these served with the RAF. Wartime Avenger production continued through 1944. The TBM-3E and TBM-3H were fitted with radar equipment that continued to be used after the war for antisubmarine patrols. Used for bombing, ground support, and reconnaissance during the war, some Avengers, including newly devised postwar variants, saw service through 1954. A versatile performer, the Avenger was used for night operations, target training, and transport operations. The aircraft was also adept at Carrier Onboard Delivery (COD). One of the largest carrier aircraft during the war, it could easily ferry goods and personnel to and from the carriers.

BELOW: Avengers from Composite Squadron Six (VC-6) warm up on the USS *Tripoli*'s flight deck, June 18, 1944. They feature a unique paint scheme specifically created for antisubmarine warfare in the North Atlantic—the top color is dark dull grey, side and tail insignia white, and bottom glossy insignia white.

The Grumman Avenger was rugged. It had large thick wings (a Grumman trademark that made the aircraft easy to handle), an impressive range, and reliable radio communication. A workhorse in the Pacific Theater, the Avenger was also embroiled in one of popular culture's most famous legends: the Bermuda Triangle. When five Avengers went down during a training flight in 1945, the mysterious Bermuda Triangle was cited as a possible reason. People still speculate the cause for this unexplained tragedy.

Sensationalism aside, the Grumman Avenger was an American asset during the air war in the Pacific Theater. While it never could exceed 276 miles an hour, it worked hard and protected its men. After the war, many surplus Avengers were adapted for the fire service.

Martin B-26 Marauder

Like the Martin B-10 before it, the Martin B-26 was a standout medium bomber. Some would say it was the best American medium bomber to go to war; others would call it a widow maker.

In 1939 the U.S. Army Air Corps was looking for a medium bomber that could reach 350 miles per hour and haul a 4,000-pound payload. This request yielded the North American B-25 Mitchell and the Martin B-26 Marauder.

The B-26 derived from the Martin Model 179 designed by Peyton Magruder, a young designer with experience at the Naval Aircraft Factory. The Model 179 was built around two big Pratt & Whitney radials with four-bladed propellers and a modern, streamlined cylindrical fuselage. The Model 179 had cantilevered shoulder-mounted wings, a streamlined Plexiglas nose, retractable tricycle-style landing gear, and a very short wingspan with high-wing loading, an unusual design choice for an aircraft of its size. This design not only looked elegant, but it helped the aircraft achieve great speeds. However, as Marauder crews would soon learn, high performance came at a price: high stall speeds. To overcome instability at low speeds, the B-26 required takeoff and landing speeds that were uncommonly fast for the time. (Today, however, commercial jets routinely take off and land at speeds in excess of 100 miles per hour.)

The U.S Army ordered 201 production models, designated B-26, from the proposal plans, because a prototype was not requested. War was brewing; the United States military needed capable aircraft quickly. Instead, the first four to come off the line underwent three months of flight evaluations in late-1940; deliveries began in February 1941.

The B-26 had Pratt & Whitney R-2800 Double Wasp radial engines, each with 1,850 horsepower. It was armed with one .30-caliber machine gun in the nose and tail, plus a powered dorsal turret containing two .50-caliber machine guns. Operated by a crew of seven men—a pilot, copilot, nose gunner/bombardier, navigator, gunner/radio operator, turret gunner, tail gunner—the first B-26s could carry up to 4,800 pounds of bombs in internal bomb bays. Armor plate and self-sealing fuel tanks soon became part of the production package as war experience provided feedback.

The B-26 was met with approval despite some early, correctable teething problems, such as an inaccurate weight distribution that had been causing the nose wheel to fail. The RAF ordered fifty-two of the B-26A, a slightly improved variant with provisions for an extra fuel tank and .50-caliber machine guns

RIGHT: The streamlined nose of the B-26 did not leave much room for the bombardier. Peyton Magruder's concept for the Marauder was at the leading edge of aerodynamics. All of the aircraft's structures were designed to offer little aerodynamic resistance.

OPPOSITE: The B-26 marauder was a "hot" plane for its time. Pilots, who were not used to its high landing speed, could find themselves running out of runway on touchdown. Early in the program, there were so many accidents at MacDill Field, Florida, the phrase "one a day in Tampa Bay" was coined. However, in the end, the Marauder had the lowest loss rate of any U.S. bomber during World War II. This B-26B is from the 394th Bomb Group, 584th Bomb Squadron, 1944.

standard for all armament. The British gave it the name the "Marauder;" another 139 were delivered to American units.

In February 1941 the 22d Bombardment Group at Langley Field in Virginia was the first to receive the B-26. The Marauder started its combat career in the Pacific Theater and at Midway. It was soon reassigned to Europe and Africa where it was better suited, but the aircraft's early reputation was plagued by negative press. Bombardment groups were trained at McDill Field in Tampa, Florida. The 130-mile-per-hour landings were very challenging for the novice pilots and crews. This led to numerous accidents ("one a day in Tampa Bay"), the nickname "Widow Maker," and an investigation into war profiteering by the Truman Committee. However, in the hands of a trained pilot, the Marauder was an incomparable war machine.

The B-26B was the first variant to be built in large numbers; 1,883 were built in "production blocks." Each block had production upgrades and changes based on material availability and wartime needs. Starting with the B variant, the Marauder's tail was made taller and the wingspan lengthened to reduce landing speeds. As a result, the training accidents in Tampa Bay decreased.

The B-26C was also mass produced in quantity; 1,210 were built in Martin's new government-sponsored Omaha, Nebraska, factory. The -C was nearly identical to the B-26B: The B-26B and -C could boast two machine guns in the tail, new waist gun stations, and increased firepower in the nose for use during strafing maneuvers. Later B-26Bs could be outfitted with as many as twelve machine guns. External racks for torpedoes and new communications equipment were also included. Some B-26Bs were fitted for an oxygen system, and up to a total of 5,200 pounds of bombs could be carried in the aircraft's two separate internal bomb bays and external racks.

Three hundred B-26Fs were built with an increased wing angle, called "twisted wing," to further slow the high takeoff and landing speeds. The only other variant produced in quantity was the B-26G. Almost nine hundred (893) were built in the -G configuration. The -G was the last production version of the Marauder. By the end of the war, Martin's Maryland and Nebraska facilities, which were painted in camouflage paint schemes to help conceal them from enemy air attacks, each could complete 120 aircraft per month. In all, over

BELOW: Fuel trucks line up to refuel a squadron of Martin B-26 Marauders. Parked next to the B-24 in the foreground is "Lady Katy," a B-26B, of the 319th Bomb Group, 437th Bomb Squadron.

five thousand Marauders were built. By 1948 all Marauders were removed from active service.

Without a prototype cycle, it took pilots and Marauder crews—often called "Marauder Men"—time to understand and harness the aircraft's speed and operational quirks; yet the once-beleaguered medium bomber from Martin matured into a superhero with a laudable safety record. It was the American World War II bomber with the fewest losses. Statistically, a Marauder crew had a greater chance of surviving its tour of duty than the men in any other Allied bomber, and each individual aircraft went on to fly more missions than its compatriots. For instance, by April 17, 1945, the legendary Marauder named "Flak Bait" endured more than two hundred missions and 725 combat hours over Europe. Flak Bait saw more hostile action than any other World War II bomber. Today, Flak Bait's nose and front fuselage are kept at the preservation facility of the Smithsonian National Air and Space Museum. The National Museum of the USAF also has a B-26B in its collection.

Today, few Marauders exist. Most were scrapped. Only a few museums have parts, while even fewer have an entire aircraft.

Martin B-26C Specifications

Type: Medium Bomber

Crew: Seven

Power plant: Two 2,000-horsepower Pratt & Whitney Double Wasp R-2800-43 air-cooled radial engines

Performance: Maximum speed, 282 miles per hour at 15,000 feet; service ceiling, 21,700 feet; maximum range, 2,850 miles

Weight: Empty, 25,300 pounds; maximum takeoff weight, 38,200 pounds

Dimensions: Span, 71 feet; length, 58 feet, 3 inches; height, 21 feet, 6 inches; wing area, 713 square feet

Armament: Eight or twelve .50-cal machine guns and 5,200 pounds of bombs

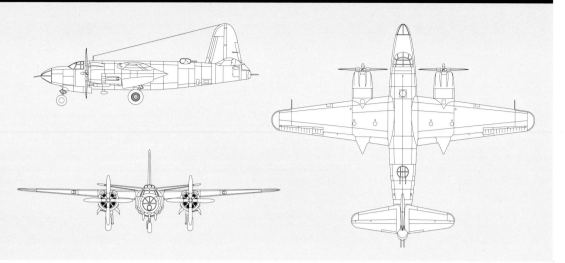

BELOW LEFT: Crewmembers of the B-26 "Jinx" pose for the photographer prior to a mission.

BELOW RIGHT: The B-26's high-speed thin airfoil and short wingspan helped give the Marauder its reputation as the "Widow Maker." Despite its initial reputation, the Marauder finished the war with the least combat losses—crews were safer in a B-26 than in all other Allied bombers of the war.

Curtiss SB2C Helldiver

The Curtiss SB2C Helldiver was the most-produced scout bomber of World War II. It was also the last American naval bomber created specifically for dive-bombing. Built in great quantity, production delays and undesirable handling characteristics (partially due to unreasonable specification requirements) tarnish its historical significance; however, once delivered to frontline carriers in the Pacific it acquitted itself as a capable aircraft—it was just too late, and out of step with progress.

In 1938 the U.S. Navy sought a new scout bomber that could replace the Douglas SBD Dauntless. With another world war imminent, the United States military was actively engaged in a rearmament campaign to improve and expand its military capabilities, as well as augment the availability of equipment for its allies. The leading candidates for the navy's 1938 appeal for a two-place, long-range dive-bomber with an internal bomb bay were the Curtiss SB2C Helldiver and the Brewster SB2A Buccaneer.

The Helldiver was designed by Curtiss engineer Raymond C. Blaylock and his team, who performed much of their work in a barn on the Ohio State University fairgrounds because the new Curtiss factory in Columbus, Ohio, was still under construction and all other Curtiss locations were dedicated to producing P-40s and P-36/Hawk 75s for the ensuing war effort. The Helldiver project was forced to seek alternate accommodations until the new building was ready.

Blaylock's design, designated as the XSB2C-1, was a low-wing monoplane with its origins in the earlier Curtiss SBC Helldiver, the navy's last biplane bomber. While the new Helldiver may have borrowed attributes from its namesake, the similarities were few. The XSB2C-1 was a thoroughly modern all-metal aircraft with folding wings, a retractable undercarriage, wing flaps designed to be used as dive brakes, and a Wright R-2600 Cyclone engine. The Helldiver prototype was armed with four forward-firing .50-caliber machine guns and another two .30-caliber machine guns in the rear that fired out of the collapsible turtledeck.

The pilot and radio operator/gunner were positioned under a tandem greenhouse canopy in unusually close quarters. As requested, the aircraft was designed to the navy's precise size specifications. The navy stipulated that two Helldivers must fit on a carrier elevator at one time. Ironically, the desire to speed up shipboard handling of aircraft during routine exercises, and especially during battle conditions, was the Helldiver's undoing. The

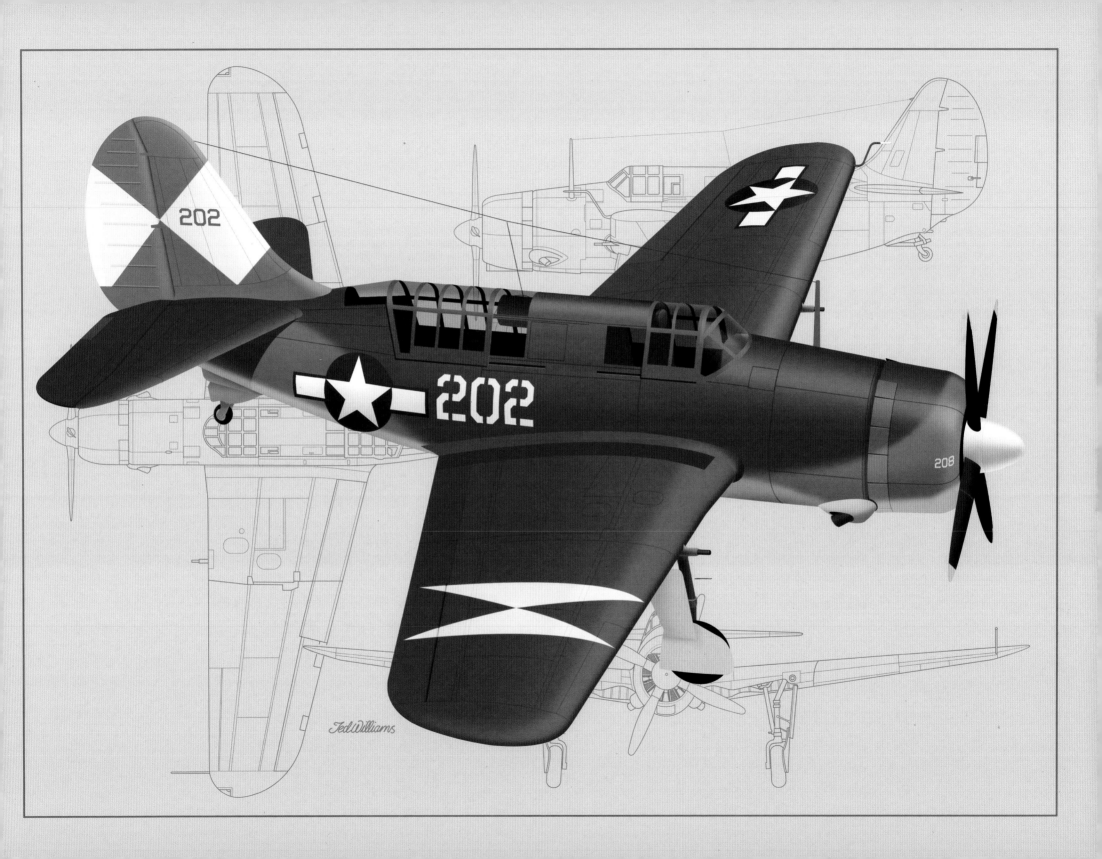

Ted Williams

exacting 40×48-foot elevator inhibited the Helldiver's development. Physical size limitations aboard ship overrode aerodynamic considerations. Preliminary wind tunnel tests of early scale models verified that the Helldiver's stubby, foreshortened fuselage would prove to be an engineering challenge.

The XSB2C-1 prototype flew on December 18, 1940, without praise; it crashed two months later. Rebuilt with many changes to improve the aircraft's airworthiness, it flew again in October 1941 only to experience a catastrophic failure in flight on December 21, 1941. But by then America was embroiled in the Second World War, and delivery of military equipment was paramount. The navy had already placed a production order for the Helldiver

BELOW: Two Helldivers from Air Group 1 stationed aboard the USS *Yorktown* fly on patrol near Guam, May 1944. By June 1944, SB2C-1Cs equipped the USS *Yorktown*, *Hornet*, *Bunker Hill*, *Wasp*, and *Essex*.

based on the revisions made to the technical drawings, and now the navy had no alternative but to proceed with building the aircraft. The new Columbus factory was staffed and ready to manufacture the new dive-bomber. Curtiss's reputation as an esteemed aircraft provider to the military was enough to keep the program alive.

The first production SB2C-1 did not fly until June 1942. Numerous delays in the factory, coupled with continued corrections to improve failings and to add armor and self-sealing fuel tanks, slowed progress and added weight to the already beleaguered aircraft. SBC2C-1s with four .50-caliber guns in the wings finally began arriving on fleet carriers in December 1942, but persistent flight instability and structural integrity issues barred them from use in combat situations until 1943. In total, only 200 SB2Cs were built and they were mostly used for training. Another 900 had been built without naval equipment for the U.S. Army as the A-25A Shrike. The army variants did not see active combat, and nearly 700 were given to the navy (270) and the Marine Corps (410).

Curtiss SB2C-3 Specifications

Type: Scout bomber
Crew: Two
Power plant: One 1,900-horsepower Wright Cyclone R-2600-20 air-cooled radial engine
Performance: Maximum speed, 295 miles per hour; service ceiling, 26,700 feet; maximum range, 1,200 miles
Weight: Empty, 10,495 pounds; maximum takeoff weight, 16,750 pounds
Dimensions: Span, 49 feet, 9 inches; length, 36 feet, 8 inches; height, 14 feet, 9 inches; wing area, 422 square feet
Armament: Two 20-mm cannons, two .30-cal machine guns, and up to 2,000 pounds of bombs

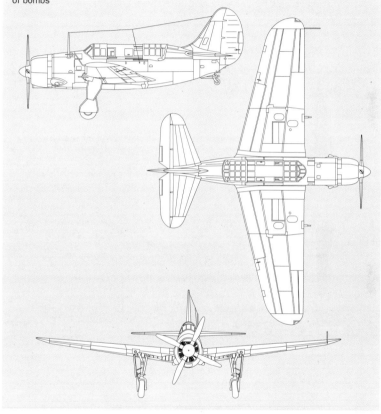

By now the Curtiss company, the program, and the aircraft's reputation were in trouble. The crews who had to maintain and fly the unruly aircraft called it the "Beast," among other even more derogatory nicknames. Compared to the beloved SBD Dauntless it was assigned to replace, the Helldiver was coming up a poor second.

The next production variant produced in quantity was the SB2C-1C; 778 were completed and sent to combat squadrons. The SB2C-1C featured two 20-mm cannons in the wings and extra fuel storage. It was the first SB2C to see combat. Helldivers from the USS *Bunker Hill* participated in the actions at Rabaul and Tarawa in the Pacific. The Helldiver was finally able to perform the job it was designed to do.

In 1944 the revised SB2C-3 became available. It had a more powerful Wright R-2600-20 Cyclone engine, which helped tame the previous handling issues; 1,112 were built. The Helldiver was now a credible dive-bomber that was finally able to supplant the Dauntless. Next, more than 2,000 SB2C-4s were built. They were improved to include under-wing racks to carry rockets or another 1,000 pounds of bombs, and perforations were added to the dive brakes to eliminate buffeting.

In 1945 an additional 970 SB2C-5s were built to carry more fuel for extended range. After the war, this final Helldiver variant became the U.S.

ABOVE: A photograph of the Helldiver prototype in its original configuration with the small vertical tail. The XSB2C-1 was revised with a larger tail for better lateral control; it was destroyed on December 21, 1941.

Navy's premier dive-bomber, but dive-bombing tactics would soon become obsolete as newer, faster aircraft and air-to-ground rockets were developed.

Like a diamond in the rough, the Curtiss SB2C Helldiver overcame engineering obstacles to meet expectations, though it took longer than anticipated. By 1945 more than 7,000 Helldivers had been built—the bulk by Curtiss, 2,000 by Canadian manufacturers—but the Helldiver's operational life was nearly over: The end of the war, plus changes in technology, put an end to the dive-bomber. Yet after such a difficult development, the Helldiver evolved into one of the U.S Navy's most effective dive-bombers.

Douglas A-26 Invader

The Douglas A-26 Invader was the last U.S. Army aircraft designated as an attack bomber. When it was delivered to the European front in 1944, the A-26 served well but had little time to impact the course of World War II; however, the Invader was a very successful aircraft with a remarkably long service life. It was used in two more conflicts after World War II (it was the only American bomber to participate in World War II, Korea, and Vietnam) and it also enjoyed an extensive civilian and commercial career well into the 1970s.

Ed Heinemann began designing the Invader in 1940. A big job, the new aircraft was to be the successor to the Douglas A-20 Havoc, as well as the North American B-25 Mitchell and Martin B-26 Marauder. It was also an opportunity for Heinemann to improve upon deficiencies already built into the A-20, namely inadequate armament, a reliance on longer runways due to its weight, an unimpressive top speed, and insufficient structural tolerances that limited maneuverability. Plus, the army specified additional modifications. In particular, the army wanted the option to mount a 75-mm cannon into the new design.

In 1941 Heinemann's design team submitted plans for two versions: a three-place, light attack bomber with a clear nose, and a night-fighting variant for a crew of two with radar equipment in a solid nose. They were both designed to use a new aluminum alloy and featured, as standard, tricycle-style landing gear. Already the aircraft was lighter and stronger than its predecessors. The new design also called for mid-mounted (shoulder) wings with an optimized laminar-flow airfoil that would help the aircraft achieve substantial performance gains. Two 2,000-horsepower Pratt & Whitney R-2800-27 Double Wasp radials, which were housed in unusually long nacelles, were selected to provide robust power. The new design had all the makings of a faster, modern attack bomber.

To bomb, the aircraft was designed to carry up to 4,000 pounds in an internal bomb bay with additional ordnance able to be suspended from external wing racks. To attack, it had two remote-controlled turrets fitted with twin .50-caliber machine guns.

Douglas, from the start, engineered the aircraft to be built in quantity. Design considerations were tuned to offer production efficiencies, and wind tunnel testing of wooden scale models was used to save money during the early evaluation and drafting phases. In April 1941 the army moved forward

OPPOSITE: The Douglas A-26 Invader is the only U.S. combat aircraft to serve in three wars: World War II, the Korean conflict, and Vietnam. Not just a stable weapons platform, the Invader also had the speed and maneuverability of a fighter-bomber and the strength to absorb punishment and still bring its crew home. This B-26B flew with 319th Bomb Group, 437th Bomb Squadron during the China offensive in 1945.

with the requisition of three prototypes: the XA-26, XA-26A, and XA-26B (the B was modified to carry the 75-mm cannon).

Negotiations between Douglas and the U.S. Army continued as the costs, manufacturing locations, and production quantities were debated. Ultimately, delays and indecision marred the program and its initial effectiveness, despite attempts at efficiency. A blame game ensued, the two factions accusing each other of protracting the process. To add to the mix, the Douglas company was also concurrently providing A-20 Havocs and C-47 transports to the army at a hectic wartime pace.

Despite the struggle, the first prototype—the three-place light bomber version with transparent nose—flew successfully and with merit on July 10, 1942. Its only easily correctable flight issue was the overheating caused by the large propeller spinners that blocked the flow of air into the engines. The next prototype, the XA-26A night version, also passed its evaluation, but it was rendered redundant by the Northrop P-61 Black Widow.

The last prototype was designed for low-altitude attack and strafing missions. It developed into the A-26B. Several combinations of armament were considered. Most production models had either six or eight .50-caliber machine guns in the solid nose, as the cannon originally intended proved to be too slow to fire and likely to jam. The A-26B (1,355 were built) was a potent weapon with up to fourteen forward-firing .50-caliber machine guns in the nose and wing-mounted gun pods. Other modifications occurred, such as canopy and cockpit alterations, to provide the pilot better visibility. The A-26B participated in conflict with the 13th Bomb Squadron in New Guinea in 1944. It also saw action in Europe with the Ninth Air Force.

Nearly eleven hundred (1,091) A-26Cs were built with a transparent nose for bombing activities. Both the A-26B and A-26C were redesignated as "B" in 1948 when the U.S. Air Force discontinued using a designation for attack. Thus they became known as the B-26A and B-26B, which today causes confusion with the B-26 Marauder, although at the time the Marauder had already been retired.

With the Second World War ending at the time of the Invader's introduction, its combat contribution was more significant during the Korean War, when Invaders flew more than fifty-five documented missions, and during the Vietnam War flying counter-insurgency missions.

The Invader was removed from combat duty in 1964, but was revived in 1966 when forty World War II A-26s were refitted as B-26Ks with larger

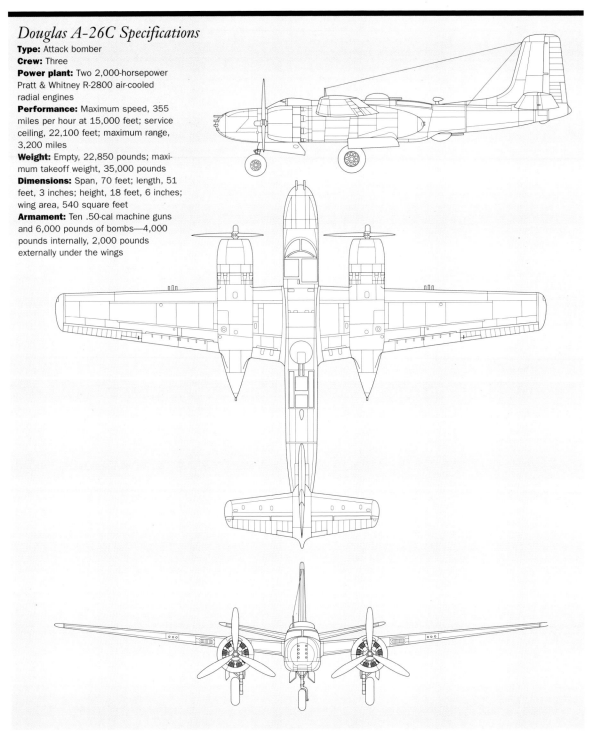

Douglas A-26C Specifications

Type: Attack bomber
Crew: Three
Power plant: Two 2,000-horsepower Pratt & Whitney R-2800 air-cooled radial engines
Performance: Maximum speed, 355 miles per hour at 15,000 feet; service ceiling, 22,100 feet; maximum range, 3,200 miles
Weight: Empty, 22,850 pounds; maximum takeoff weight, 35,000 pounds
Dimensions: Span, 70 feet; length, 51 feet, 3 inches; height, 18 feet, 6 inches; wing area, 540 square feet
Armament: Ten .50-cal machine guns and 6,000 pounds of bombs—4,000 pounds internally, 2,000 pounds externally under the wings

RIGHT: A mix of A-26B and A-26C Invaders during final assembly. The A-26B had a solid gun nose mounting six .50-cal machine guns, while the A-26C had a clear Plexiglas nose for the bombardier's position.

OPPOSITE TOP: This A-26B has the later 8-gun noise installation. It is flying with its bomb bay door open. Note the streamlined rear underbelly dorsal turret. During the Battle of the Bulge, A-26 Invaders were used for low-level strafing and bombing attacks against the advancing German army.

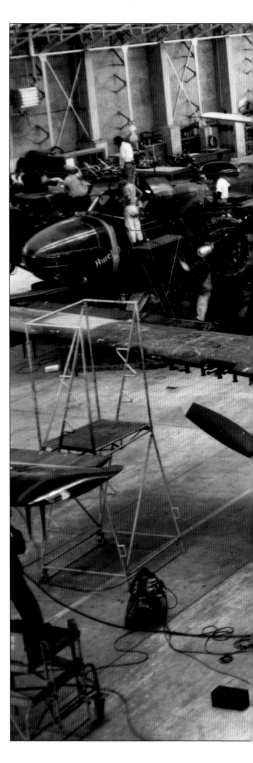

and newer Pratt & Whitney engines, greater fuel capacity, and other modifications. Called Counter Invaders, they were stationed at an air base in Thailand and used for training. It is a testament to the quality of the design and manufacture of Heinemann's creation that the aircraft's usefulness spanned from World War II through to the Cold War. The Air National Guard flew the Invader until 1972.

Invaders were exported around the world, including Great Britain, France, Brazil, Chile, Guatemala, and Portugal, among others. Surplus Invaders were refitted and used as commercial transports and luxury executive airliners for six to twelve passengers. Other decommissioned Invaders found work with the fire service. One Invader flew to fame as the "Reynolds Bombshell." Purchased by Milton Reynolds, a wealthy manufacturer of writing instruments, it was flown around the world by Bill Odom to beat Howard Hughes's time. The Reynolds Bombshell went on to break two more flight records, proving the Invader was built for longevity.

Lockheed PV-1 Ventura

Necessity can indeed be the mother of invention. During the critical early years of World War II, the United States needed bombers, and quickly. Lockheed offered an ingenious solution—the militarization of its successful air transport design that was already in use commercially. During a time when the manufacturing programs for other brand-new bomber designs, such as the Curtiss SB2C Helldiver and Douglas A-26 Invader, were experiencing production delays and teething problems, Lockheed could provide the United States military with a known quantity: airworthy high-altitude aircraft with the attributes of a bomber hidden beneath a civilian exterior.

Brothers Allan and Malcolm Loughead built their first airplane, a seaplane, in 1913. After a few lean years, the brothers earned enough money flying fee-paying thrill-seekers at the 1916 Panama-Pacific International Exposition in San Francisco to finance the start of their own aviation company, the Loughead Aircraft Manufacturing Company. After an unsuccessful run, Malcolm turned to the automotive industry, while Allan remained in aviation. In 1926 Allan teamed with Jack Northrop to form another aviation venture, the Lockheed Aircraft Corporation. Over time, both Loughead men evolved their Scottish surname and the names of their aviation and automotive companies from "Loughead" to a phonetic spelling that more accurately represented the pronunciation of their name, ergo "Lockheed."

The RAF first modified a Lockheed transport for military use. Known as the Lockheed Hudson, the aircraft was developed from the Lockheed Model 14 commercial airliner in 1938. Originally used by the British for bombing and reconnaissance, the Hudson gained a reputation for being able to sustain grave battle damage as it held its own against the best of the German Luftwaffe. The British deployed the Hudson around the world, and a Hudson squadron is credited with contributing to the events that led to the sinking of Germany's prized battleship, the *Bismarck*.

By 1941, because of the of the Hudson's accomplishments with the RAF, the U.S. Army and Navy also looked to Lockheed for their own specialized versions of the aircraft. The American militarized version of a Lockheed transport was designed by the engineering geniuses Hall L. Hibbard and Clarence "Kelly" Johnson, the forces behind the unconventional twin-tailed fighter plane, the Lockheed P-38 Lightning.

The new bomber was developed from the Model 14 Super Electra, which was the latest model in a line of stable Lockheed transports that were marketed

Fleet Air Wing 4

OPPOSITE: Like the Douglas B-18, the Lockheed PV-1 Ventura was an adaptation of a commercial airliner design. With payload capacity and relatively long range, the Ventura was perfectly adapted to its mission. Serving with the "Empire Express" in the Aleutian Islands, the Ventura endured harsh arctic conditions while attacking Japan's northern home islands. This PV-1 carries the paint scheme and markings of VB-135 stationed at Casco Field, Attu, Alaska, in 1943.

as an alternative to the Douglas DC transports, and an improvement to Lockheed Models 10 and 12. The Model 14 was a twin-engine low-wing monoplane that introduced technology like multidirectional Fowler flaps and feathering propellers. Commercially, the Model 14 was flown domestically in limited quantities by Northwest Airlines and Continental Airlines. Outside the United States, the Model 14 was purchased by KLM, British Airways, and Trans-Canada—even Japan relied on the aircraft.

The U.S. Army flew a military Model 14 under many designations, including the A-28 and A-29, while the navy called their variant the PBO-1. Overall, for both branches, it proved to be a versatile platform for reconnaissance, antisubmarine patrolling, and training.

As the Second World War continued to heat up, and actual combat experience began to influence aircraft development, another variant was developed. Based on the Lockheed Model 18 Lodestar, the militarized Ventura was a bigger version of the Model 14. It was powered by two Pratt & Whitney R-2800 Double Wasp engines that turned large three-bladed propellers. Lockheed assigned the production of the new bomber to the Vega Aircraft Corporation, a Lockheed subsidiary located in Burbank, California.

In total, Lockheed oversaw the production of more than 3,000 Venturas for the United States military and its allies. The U.S Army designated the Ventura as the B-34, and approximately 320 were built in this configuration. Great Britain, New Zealand, and Australia also received the Ventura. Another improved army version, called the B-37, was designed, but only eighteen were built because the U.S. Army stepped aside so the navy could acquire a sizable inventory of the newer bomber. Between 1942 and 1944 the navy purchased 1,600 of the aircraft, calling it the PV-1. The PV-1 could carry more fuel than the army's version for longer ocean-sweeping flights seeking enemy ships and submarines. The PV-1 had a top speed of 322 miles per hour at 13,800 feet.

The navy's PV-1 armament consisted of two forward-firing .50-caliber machine guns, a dorsal turret with .50-caliber machine guns, and two flexible .30-caliber machine guns that were aimed out of the belly of the bomber. Later versions also had an assortment of machine guns in the nose as well as under-wing mounts for additional machine guns or rocket launchers. The PV-1 could carry up to 3,000 pounds of bombs, torpedoes or depth charges in its internal bomb bay, and some naval Venturas had radar equipment installed for night operations.

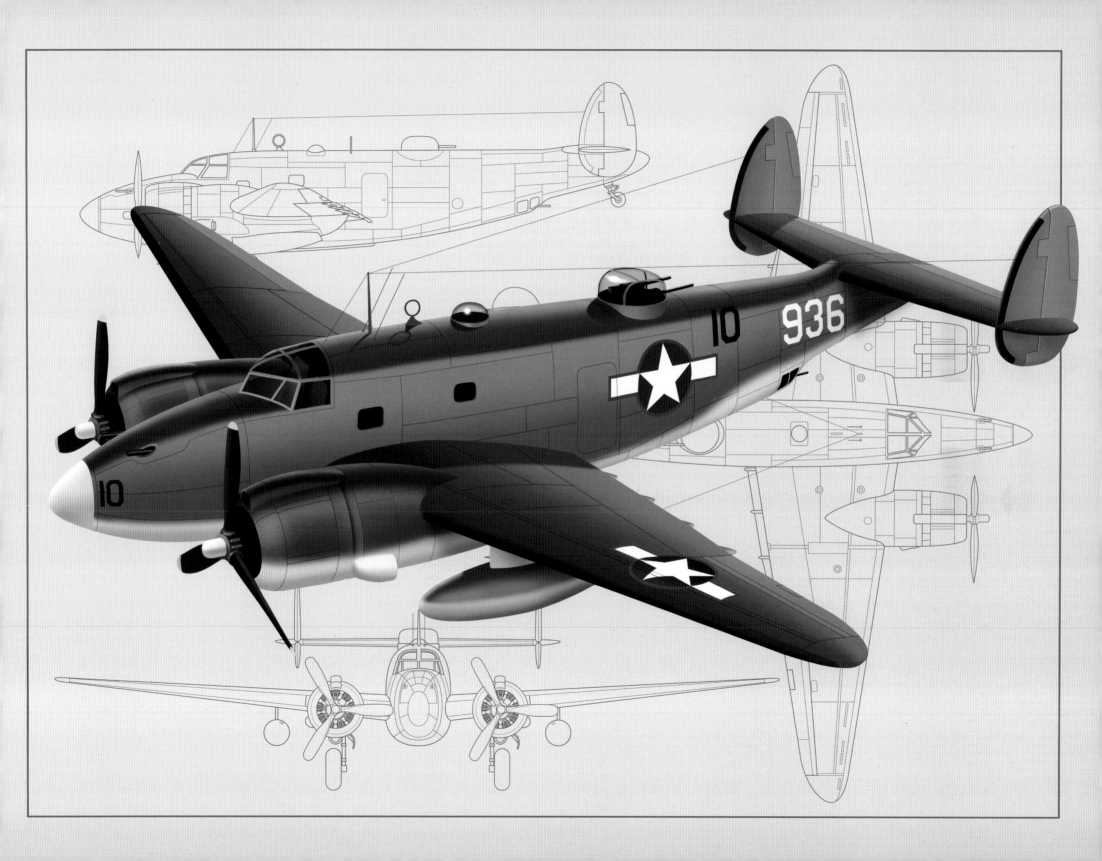

ABOVE: In June 1943, the navy ordered a version of the PV-1 Ventura that was modified to carry out long-range patrol missions. It was called the PV-2 Harpoon.

Lockheed PV-1 Specifications

Type: Patrol bomber
Crew: Five
Power plant: Two 2,000-horsepower Pratt & Whitney R-2800-31 air-cooled radial engines
Performance: Maximum speed, 322 miles per hour at 13,800 feet (296 mph at sea level); service ceiling, 26,300 feet; maximum range, 1,600 miles
Weight: Empty, 20,197 pounds; maximum takeoff weight, 34,000 pounds
Dimensions: Span, 65 feet, 6 inches; length, 51 feet, 9 inches; height, 11 feet, 11 inches; wing area, 551 square feet
Armament: Four .50-cal, two .30-cal machine guns, and 3,000 pounds of bombs, depth charges or torpedoes

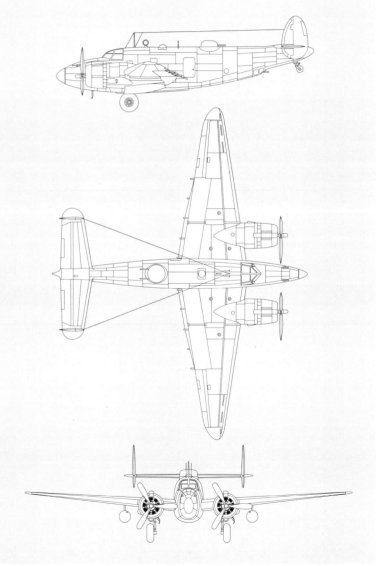

The next naval variant, the PV-2 Harpoon had a longer wingspan and other changes that altered the aircraft's size and shape. In total, 522 were produced. Nearly all of these aircraft were used in the Aleutian Islands campaign to protect the Alaskan region from Japanese domination.

Based on the success and longevity of these World War II military aircraft that were derived from a line of transports, as well as the stories from notable warbirds, including the P-38 Lightning and later jet fighters such as the P-80 Shooting Star and F-104 Starfighter, the Lockheed name remains respected in the aviation industry. In 1995 Lockheed merged with Martin to form Lockheed Martin, bringing together two names from the earliest days of flight.

RIGHT: Three PV-1s from VB-135 are parked in a revetment at Casco Field in Attu, Alaska—the western-most Aleutian island suitable for aircraft, May 1944. The PV squadrons that flew aerial strikes against the Japanese Kuriles were known as the "Empire Express" because their mission was to take the war directly to the Northern end of the Japanese Empire.

BELOW: Early version of a PV-1 Ventura with a glazed nose, identified as flying with Bombing Squadron 135 (VB-135) stationed at Adak, Alaska, April 1943.

Boeing B-29 Superfortress

In 1940 the U.S. Army Air Corps circulated a request for a bomber that could carry 2,000 pounds for 5,000 miles at 400 miles per hour. Long range was deemed vital. If Great Britain fell to Germany, the United States would lose proximity to its European enemy. America was gearing up for transatlantic warfare. Lockheed, Douglas, Consolidated, and Boeing submitted proposals.

Well aware of the B-17's 1930s-era limitations amid a changing international landscape, the engineers at Boeing had already taken the initiative to prepare a new, large long-range bomber that could replace its B-17 Flying Fortress. Built with experience from earlier experimental programs, such as the XB-15, the initial Boeing submission for the 1940 specification was the Model 341. This model was quickly updated to meet the increasingly demanding combat challenges being described by the British. Changes for self-sealing fuel tanks, more substantial armor, and increased armament led to the 105,000-pound Model 345. The army ordered three prototypes of the 345, all designated XB-29.

Based on the promise of the design alone, fourteen evaluation (YB-29) and an eventual total of 500 production models (B-29) were ordered—before the prototypes were finished or flying. When the first prototype did take to the air on September 21, 1942, it was not a rousing success. More despairingly, the second prototype caught fire and crashed into a building on August 18, 1943, killing its entire test crew and eighteen bystanders. The B-29 needed some work before it could take its place in history as the most advanced heavy bomber of World War II.

At the same time, Consolidated was instructed to go ahead with its design for the XB-32. An understudy to the B-29, approximately 115 B-32 Dominators were built. Two variants were produced, many exclusively for training purposes.

Boeing was known for its big bombers, but the B-29 was undeniably its largest yet. Powered by four Wright R-3350-13 Cyclone radial engines, the huge aircraft had an astounding 141 feet of wing. A structure of this size required special considerations. Boeing engineered a unique wing shape, called Boeing 117. It employed special flaps to help maintain lift while reducing airspeed, thereby improving the giant bomber's handling and maneuverability.

The YB-29 spearheaded slight alterations that would be introduced into the production models, including improvements to the propellers and engine.

RIGHT: During the first stage of construction, a B-29's wing was mated to the fuselage center section. This subassembly was then moved to a larger construction area for final production.

OPPOSITE: Everything about the Boeing B-29 was revolutionary. From its performance as a strategic bomber to the way it was manufactured required new methods and procedures never before attempted in the aviation industry. Many of these innovative ideas incorporated into the Superfortress are still in use today. The B-29 "Dina Might" has the markings of the 504th Bomb Group, 421st Bomb Squadron stationed on Tinian's North Field, 1945.

The production B-29s followed in September 1943, just two months after the first flight of a YB-29. The B-29 could lift itself plus 20,000 pounds of bombs. In total, 2,513 were built in the B-29 configuration by Boeing (1,620), Martin (536), and Bell (357).

Many other technological advancements were engineered into the aircraft. The B-29's crew was contained in pressurized cabins, creating a more comfortable environment for the typical crew of ten men who flew as many as eighteen hours at a time at high altitude where the temperature is well below freezing. To enable the bomb bay to function while the rest of the aircraft underwent pressurization, the rear personnel area was connected to the central and front cabins via a 40-foot pressurized tunnel. As a result, the crew felt they were flying at a more comfortable altitude, while actually traveling as high as 30,000 feet.

Another technological innovation was the B-29's remote-controlled guns designed by General Electric. A series of turrets and computer-operated sights allowed the gunners to fire more than one gun at a time. The guns were most often the .50-caliber machine gun; a 20-mm cannon could also be used. Radar was also standard equipment on the B-29.

The next variant was the B-29A; 1,119 were built with a slightly longer wing and increased forward armament. Many of the B-29As were not built

Boeing B-29A Specifications

Type: Heavy bomber
Crew: Ten
Power plant: Four 2,200-horsepower Wright Cyclone R-3350 air-cooled radial engines
Performance: Maximum speed, 357 miles per hour at 25,000 feet; service ceiling, 33,600 feet; maximum range, 6,000 miles
Weight: Empty, 71,360 pounds; maximum takeoff weight, 133,500 pounds
Dimensions: Span, 142 feet, 2 inches; length, 99 feet; height, 27 feet, 9 inches; wing area, 1,736 square feet
Armament: Twelve .50-cal machine guns, one 20-mm cannon, and 20,000 pounds of bombs

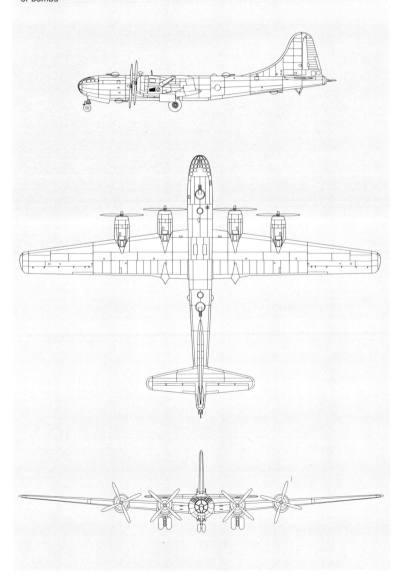

OPPOSITE: The B-29 was a marvel of modular construction. This photograph was taken to demonstrate how the different subassemblies came together. The development and production of the B-29 was one of the most expensive programs of World War II, second only to the Manhattan Project.

BELOW: "Dauntless Dotty," from the 869th Bombardment Squadron, led the first B-29 raid on Tokyo in November 1944. In the foreground, ordnance men prepare 500-pound bombs for loading.

until after the end of World War II, thus they served in Korea from 1950 to 1953, although at a disadvantage against jet aircraft.

Another 311 of a B-29B variant were built in 1945 for use as a low-level bomber in the Pacific Theater. They were lighter than the -A. Other variants were discussed or built in single quantities to test new ideas and technologies. A B-29D would become the B-50, one of the last American propeller and piston-engine heavy bombers to be used by the U.S. Air Force. Before all Superfortress production ended in 1946, almost 4,000 were built. Most were used for bombing Japanese cities in the Pacific Theater.

The most famous B-29 is the Enola Gay, the first aircraft to transport and drop the nuclear bomb. On August 6, 1945, the Enola Gay of the 509th Composite Group, which was specifically trained for the delivery of nuclear weapons, dropped the atomic bomb on Hiroshima, Japan. A second B-29, Bock's Car, dropped another atomic bomb on Nagasaki three days later. Japan surrendered soon after, ending World War II. Today the Enola Gay has been restored and is in the collection of the Smithsonian National Air and Space Museum.

Post-World War II, the Superfortress was used militarily through to September 1960. It was well-suited to carry fuel for the in-flight refueling required by jets, and for reconnaissance and patrol missions.

First the Flying Fortress, then the Superfortress; Boeing served the United States admirably throughout the entire Second World War with its sturdy bombers of brute strength and size. Looking to the future, Boeing had still another fortress up its sleeve.

Douglas Skyraider

The Douglas SBD Dauntless was the U.S. Navy's reigning diving attack bomber for most of World War II, but it was obsolete almost as soon as it took to the skies. While beloved and of sound engineering, it was underpowered and technologically outclassed as early as 1941. It is purely the mark of its maker—Douglas—that the Dauntless was able to serve so well for so long. By 1944 it was imperative that the navy procure its successor.

Throughout the war, several aircraft had been developed to replace the SBD. The closest contender was the Curtiss SB2C Helldiver, but the Helldiver could never completely take the place of the Dauntless. Its development period was a painfully long, drawn-out affair that was unable to produce a credible aircraft until much too late in the war.

Another attempt, the Douglas BTD Destroyer, was also an unsuccessful runner-up. Designed by a team led by top Douglas engineer Ed Heinemann, the Destroyer was a heavily armed two-place model with many advanced features, including tricycle-style landing gear and a distinctive gull wing that allowed for an enlarged internal bomb bay. Nonetheless, the radical Destroyer was never able to achieve its promise; its design team smartly abandoned the soon-to-be cancelled project in favor of an all-new design.

In 1944 the U.S. Navy moved forward with the post-Destroyer design from Douglas. This time, Heinemann was joined by aerodynamic specialist Gene Root and designer Leo Devlin. Together they created a carrier-based multi-role attack bomber that was designed around an eighteen-cylinder Wright 2,500-horsepower R-3350-24W Cyclone engine. Like the SBD, it was a dive-bomber equipped with dive brakes. For the new design, the folding and tapered straight wings were mounted low and the undercarriage, tail wheel, and arrestor hook were retractable.

Designated XBT2D-1, it did not have a crew, only a pilot. The entire aircraft, including its shape and lack of an internal cavity for a bomb bay, was optimized to support a heavy load on external racks located under the fuselage and wing. Nor was it armed as heavily as the Destroyer. America had claimed air superiority over the Pacific; guns were now a secondary concern. The war had shown the navy that versatility was even more important than firepower. A bomber with the ability to carry a changeable array of ordnance was incredibly useful for the current conditions in the Pacific Theater. With that ideal in mind, the XBT2D-1 was designed to lift up to 8,000 pounds of bombs, torpedoes, or rockets. Twenty-five evaluation models were built and tested.

VA-65 Attack Sixty-Five

OPPOSITE: The Douglas Skyraider was a big, strong single-engine aircraft that could carry a heavy weapons load. This aircraft is decorated in the green-and-white markings of VA-65 Tigers. The Skyraider was the backbone of U.S. Navy and Marine Corps attack squadrons aboard many different carriers for twenty-one years, from 1947 to 1968. In Korea, VA-65 logged 1,645 combat missions in their ADs.

The first XBT2D-1 flew on March 18, 1945. The navy ordered 548 production models based on the XBT2D-1's evaluation period. The new aircraft was to be designated AD; however, only 277 were completed once the war and the accompanying production frenzy ceased. The AD-1 prototype was originally called the Dauntless II, but in 1946 the AD acquired the name "Skyraider."

Of the 242 AD-1 Skyraiders built between 1945 and 1949, the first twenty production models were determined to have structural issues that were corrected and changed on all subsequent models. The next production variant, the AD-1Q, was modified to carry electronic countermeasures (ECM) radar equipment. The AD-1Q also had an additional seat for the ECM operator. Thirty-five were built.

The next two production variants, the -2 and -3, were both delivered in 1948. The AD-2 had a redesigned cockpit area and greater fuel stores; 156 were built, plus an additional twenty-one with ECM equipment. The AD-2 had two fixed forward-firing cannons. The AD-3 encompassed four versions: 124 AD-3s with increased structural strength, thirty-one AD-3Ws with airborne early warning (AEW) radar, twenty-three AD-3Qs with ECM equipment, and fifteen AD-3Ns with provisions for night operations.

In 1949 the AD-4 was introduced. It was the most-produced variant of the entire program. Again, Douglas produced a variety of production models: 372 AD-4s, 307 AD-4Ns for night operations, 168 AD-4Ws with AEW radar, 165 AD-4Bs with the ability to deliver tactical nuclear weapons, and thirty-nine AD-4Qs with ECM equipment. Later, some of the basic AD-4s and night versions were tailored for other specialized functions. By 1950 the -4 was the standard in-service Skyraider.

Introduced too late to be used in World War II, the Skyraider found work during the Korean War. Flown by the U.S. Navy and Marine Corps, the Skyraider proved to perform close support most effectively, and it was well-suited to carry a combination of bombs, torpedoes, rockets, napalm, depth charges, or mines. The Skyraider was so valuable to the conflict in Korea, another variant was produced. The two-seat AD-5 incorporated many changes. It was longer and wider and standardized to have four 20-mm cannons mounted in the wing. The AD-5 had the full complement of radar equipment, same as the models before it. The aircraft could also use conversion kits aboard ship to configure the -5 for use as an ambulance and twelve-seat or cargo transport. In total, 665 were delivered. Another 713 of a single-seat AD-6 were built.

NAVY
VA-65

201

RIGHT: The AD-4B Skyraider's airframe was strengthened so it could carry and deliver nuclear weapons. These aircraft are from Air Development Squadron 5 (VX-5) stationed at China Lake, California.

The -6 was used for low-level bombing. AD-7, another low-level bomber with structural enhancements was the last variant. Seventy-two were built.

Between 1945 and 1957, a total of 3,180 Skyraiders were built. In 1964 the Skyraider returned to combat duty. Redesignated as the A-1 in 1962, the U.S. Navy employed the Skyraider in Vietnam through to 1972 where it protected downed airmen as it held its own against the much more modern Soviet MiG-17 jet fighter.

An aircraft with many nicknames, whether known as the Able Dog, Sandy, or Spad, the Douglas AD/A-1 Skyraider has gone down in history as one of the best American military attack aircraft. Finally, a worthy contender to carry on the legend of the SBD Dauntless.

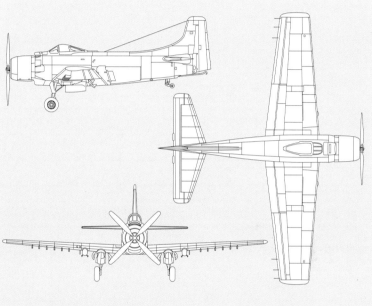

Douglas AD-4 Specifications

Type: Attack bomber
Crew: One
Power plant: One 2,700-horsepower Wright R-3350-26 air-cooled radial engine
Performance: Maximum speed, 320 miles per hour; service ceiling, 23,800 feet; maximum range, 900 miles
Weight: Empty, 11,783 pounds; maximum takeoff weight, 24,221 pounds
Dimensions: Span, 50 feet; length, 39 feet, 3 inches; height, 15 feet, 9 inches; wing area, 400 square feet
Armament: Two 20-mm canons and up to 6,000 pounds of bombs, torpedoes, or extra fuel internally, another 500 pounds externally

TOP LEFT: A pilot cranks up the big Pratt & Whitney R-3350 of this Skyraider from Composite Squadron 33 (VC-33) stationed at the Naval Air Station in Atlantic City, New Jersey.

BOTTOM LEFT: A formation of AD-6 (A-1H) Skyraiders from the USS *Independence*, Attack Squadron 75 (VA-75), which was known as "The Sunday Punchers."

Convair B-36 Peacemaker

Conceived as a result of the same fearful projections that prompted the Boeing Superfortress, the Convair B-36 Peacemaker was introduced as a remedy should the United States need to deliver bombs to the European Theater from a great distance. Had Hitler taken possession of Great Britain, the United States would have lost its toehold in Europe. All raids against Germany would have needed to be staged thousands of miles away from American bases. When the Allies were able to turn the tide of the war in their favor, a transatlantic situation was never realized. Instead, the Peacemaker was relegated to lesser tasks, but it was still a fantastically large aircraft built to serve a specific purpose.

In 1941 the U.S. Army Air Corps issued a specification for a bomber that could reach 300 to 400 miles per hour while carrying 10,000 pounds of bombs to a target 5,000 miles out and back, or while carrying 72,000 pounds for fewer miles. Douglas submitted an unsuccessful proposal, asserting that the requirements were unobtainable. Northrop also supplied a design—the "Flying Wing"—which did not suit the competition, but it was investigated separately. Consolidated's design for the Model 35 was the only one to meet the prerequisites set by the 1941 specification. The army moved forward with an order for two prototypes.

Once an order was secured, Consolidated faced a daunting task. The prototype, designated XB-36, would become the largest piston-engine bomber ever produced. New manufacturing techniques and material such as aluminum alloys, magnesium, and plastics were introduced because controlling weight was paramount. Typically, an aircraft design would get heavier as it moved along the production line. The XB-36 needed to cut excess weight and avoid bloat in every area of development to keep the fuel-distance-weight equation in check. The engineers were often reminded how any extra pound of aircraft equaled two additional pounds of fuel.

Under the guidance of Isaac Laddon (the designer of the B-24 Liberator), the XB-36 featured many new technologies. To save weight, fuel was stored in internal cavities without unnecessary and heavy bladder containment; the systems to move flaps and control surfaces were optimized to require smaller mechanical systems; and power was provided by an alternating current (AC) system that employed smaller, lighter motors. As a result, the prototype's maximum gross weight was kept to 265,000 pounds.

While the XB-36 was undergoing prototype development, in March 1943 the Consolidated and Vultee aircraft companies merged to form the Consolidated

Vultee Aircraft Corporation, which was more commonly known as Convair. Upheld as a valued aircraft supplier throughout World War II, Consolidated and the Convair name are recognized for the thousands of aircraft it built for the burgeoning war effort. Today, Convair has been folded into General Dynamics.

The XB-36 prototype was designed to be powered by six 3,000-horsepower Pratt & Whitney R-4360-25 Wasp Major radials with pusher propellers. It was 162 feet long with a 230-foot wingspan. By comparison, the Boeing B-29 Superfortress was 99 feet long with a 141-foot wingspan. The only airplane with a longer wingspan was Howard Hughes's flying boat, "Hercules." Amazingly, a crew of just fifteen men was needed to fly the giant XB-36.

The first XB-36 flew on August 8, 1946. The program had weathered delays and stoppages as wartime production quotas took precedence and conditions in the European Theater evolved. The validity of such a large aircraft was questioned.

The second aircraft, the YB-36, flew on December 4, 1947. It was similar to the prototype except for a raised greenhouse-style cockpit and changes to the landing gear. The prototype was originally supplied with a tricycle-style landing gear, but the two single main gear tires proved to be insufficient and the design was changed to incorporate four tires for better weight distribution. The tires were specially produced by Goodyear. Each tire weighed 1,320 pounds and had a diameter of 110 inches. Only three runways in the United States had the 22-inch depth of concrete able to withstand the forces generated by the huge aircraft at takeoff and landing, and a tire malfunction could prove deadly— another reason the number of tires was increased to four.

The first production variant was the B-36A. Twenty-two were built, but none were equipped with armament, although the aircraft had provisions for five cannons and ten .50-caliber machine guns. The next variant was the B-36B; seventy-three were produced. The B-36B had armament (sixteen 20-mm cannons) and sixty-four were converted to mount four General Electric J47-GE-19 turbojets in separate nacelles to augment the six 3,500-horsepower Pratt & Whitney R-4360 Wasp Major radial engines. Hence the expression: "six turning and four burning." The jet engines, while in use, could raise the top speed to 406 miles per hour (cruising was 225 miles per hour). Another twenty-two were built as the B-36D.

Later all B-36As were converted to the RB-36E for reconnaissance. The RB-36E also included jet engines. Thirty-four improved B-36D were built with

Convair B-36D Specifications

Type: Strategic heavy bomber
Crew: Fifteen
Power plant: Six 3,500-horsepower Pratt & Whitney R-4360-41 air-cooled radial engines and four General Electric J47-GE-19 turbojets with 5,200 pounds of thrust
Performance: Maximum speed, 406 miles per hour at 36,000 feet; service ceiling, 45,200 feet; maximum range, 7,500 miles
Weight: Empty, 161,371 pounds; maximum takeoff weight, 370,000 pounds
Dimensions: Span, 230 feet; length, 162 feet, 1 inch; height, 46 feet, 8 inches; wing area, 4,772 square feet
Armament: Sixteen 20-mm canons and 72,000 pounds of bombs

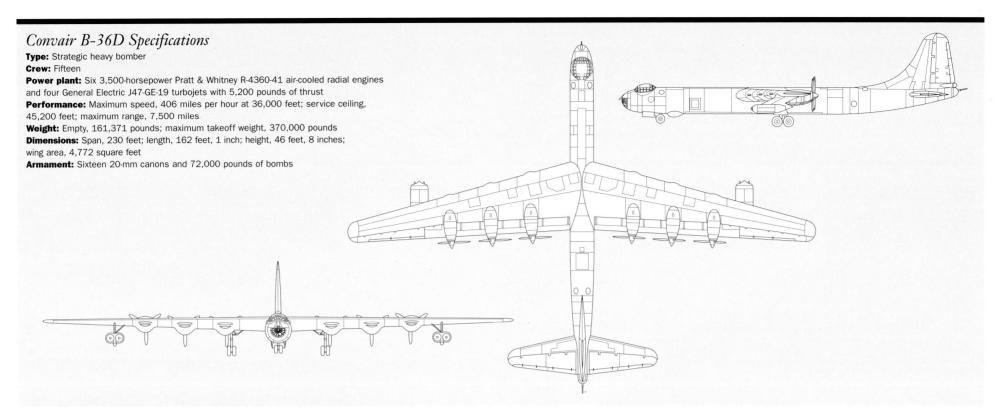

LEFT: A flight engineer at his station on a B-36. From this position he can monitor and control the performance of all ten engines—six reciprocating and four jet turbines.

OPPOSITE TOP RIGHT: A bombardier leans over the bombsight on a practice run during one of the many Cold War training exercises. The B-36 offered ample room for the bombardier's position.

OPPOSITE BOTTOM RIGHT: A crewman pulls himself through the pressurized tube that traverses the bomb bays connecting the forward and rear crew compartments.

radar equipment and bigger Pratt & Whitney engines; they were designated as the B-36F. Another twenty-four were built for reconnaissance. Eighty-three B-36Hs were built. They were a continuation and improvement to the B-36F. The B-36H became available in 1952. Seventy-three reconnaissance models were produced as RB-36H. A program with longevity, the final variant of the aircraft was the B-36J. Thirty-three were built.

Over the course of the program, the B-36 was a cause of consternation and debate. Post–World War II military procurement was scrutinized and every large government expenditure examined. Being such a big aircraft, the hubbub surrounding it seemed that much bigger, too.

The B-36 Peacemaker was designed during World War II, but did not fly until 1946. The first intercontinental bomber, it could fly from the United States to any continent, without needing to refuel. In its ten years of active duty the B-36 never saw combat, but it certainly was a deterrent during the Cold War. Its unofficial name "Peacemaker" is a fitting moniker indeed, as was its nickname "Aluminum Overcast." To this day, the Convair B-36 Peacemaker remains the largest piston-engine bomber ever produced by the United States military. There is a surviving B-36 on display at the National Museum of the United States Air Force.

ABOVE: A completed B-36D on the production line at Fort Worth, Texas. The large bomb bay doors on the Peacemaker were designed to open and close in two seconds.

North American AJ Savage

The end of World War II paved the way for three key evolutionary factors in military aviation: jet engines, nuclear weapons, and the Cold War. After World War II, the world was ready for peace. Yet the recently affirmed post–World War II superpowers were locked in a tenuous situation. For forty-five years, the United States and the then Soviet Union participated in a head-to-head but passive ideological conflict in the form of the Cold War. The threat of nuclear weapons fueled the fear that one false move by either group could bring on world annihilation. Both the United States and the Soviet Union had nuclear weapons. The delivery of these weapons was fundamental; in this new political climate, fast jet-powered aircraft would be the four horsemen.

In 1945 the U.S. Navy initiated a search for a carrier-based strategic bomber/attack aircraft that could carry a 10,000-pound bomb load. It was only days after the delivery of two atomic bombs to Japan by the U.S. Army Air Forces. The U.S. Navy quickly recognized that the way war was waged was changing. The navy was looking to introduce an aircraft into the fleet with accommodations for a nuclear weapon.

North American Aviation was a likely candidate to design the aircraft. From the late 1930s until 1945, North American supplied the United States war effort with the most aircraft, more than all other providers in the United States. The North American aircraft proposal to the navy's bid featured traditional wing-mounted air-cooled radials, in this case Pratt & Whitney R-2800 Double Wasps. In the rear of the aircraft, however, a General Electric J33 turbojet offered a performance gain unachievable by radial engines alone.

In the mid-1940s, jet propulsion was new, but not completely unknown. In 1939 Germany designed the Messerschmitt Me 262; it was the first jet to participate in combat during World War II. Among the Allies, Frank Whittle, an RAF officer, was one of the first to develop jet-engine technology. It was understood that a piston-engine aircraft could not exceed speeds much above 500 miles per hour. At 500 miles per hour and higher, the tips of spinning propeller blades approach the speed of sound. At such high speeds, the propeller loses its ability to produce thrust. Additionally, the nature of the internal-combustion reciprocating engine held speeds below 500 miles per hour. American companies, like North American, were just starting to experiment with jet propulsion because it required different structural elements, such as air intakes and exhausts, which were new to aircraft design.

In June 1946 the U.S. Navy ordered three prototypes, designated as XAJ-1. The aircraft had an interesting landing gear that was designed around the jet's

RIGHT: Fuselage of an AJ Savage under construction. The Savage was the first naval multi-engine attack bomber. A large fuselage was required to enclose the aircraft's Allison-built GE turbojet engine and a 10,000-pound nuclear bomb.

OPPOSITE: The AJ Savage was designed to deliver a thermonuclear weapon while deployed aboard an aircraft carrier. To make the Savage capable of carrier operation, it was designed to use three power plants— two Pratt & Whitney R-2800 radial engines and an Allison J-33 turbojet in the rear fuselage. Both the radials and the turbojet burned the same fuel.

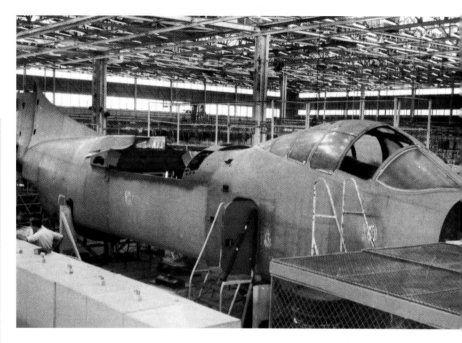

extensive plumbing. First a dozen, then another twenty-eight production versions were ordered, even before the June 1948 flight of the prototype.

In 1947 the U.S. Air Force became its own service independent from the army, but the newly created U.S. Air Force and the U.S. Navy were at odds regarding the delivery of nuclear firepower. The U.S. Air Force claimed dominion because of its aircraft such as the Convair B-36 Peacemaker; at the same time, the U.S. Navy was unwilling to relinquish nuclear capability. It was decided that the U.S. Air Force would have the training and equipment for nuclear weapons delivery; however, the U.S. Navy could continue to stay current in nuclear weapons deployment: The North American program was a go.

In all, three versions of the North American AJ were developed, and 140 aircraft were produced. They were all given the name "Savage." While the prototype was a two-place aircraft, the first production variant, the AJ-1, had a crew of three. Also, many structural updates occurred to the production models, including the development of a new sealed-canopy design that required the crew to use an exit door in the fuselage's right side. Plus, now, the wings folded for easier carrier stowage. Fifty-five AJ-1s were built, and deliveries began in September 1949. The next production model was a recon-naissance version with photography and radar equipment; it was called the AJ-2P. Twenty-three were built. The first AJ-2Ps flew with three crewmen, but later aircraft had an additional seat for a mission-specific crew member.

The last and most widely used version was the AJ-2. Fifty-five were built in 1951, after forty-two AJ-1s were modified to the AJ-2 standard in

LEFT: The modern jet aircraft ushered in an era of equally modern production facilities. Here, the AJ wings in the foreground have their engine nacelles in place. Soon, these wing assemblies will receive flaps and more sheet metal. The Savage's one-piece shoulder-mounted wing was exceptionally strong.

BELOW: Deckcrew on the USS *Randolph* (CVA-15) assess this Savage's damaged wing panels, 1957.

1950. To assist this variant's crew of three, the cockpit controls were placed within reach of all. Also, the tail design was altered. The last variant had two 2,300-horsepower radials and an Allison-built General Electric turbojet with 4,600 pounds of static thrust. Its maximum speed was 471 miles per hour. Since its top speed was so great, the Savage was not equipped with defensive armament. The aircraft would simply outfly attackers.

A fourth variant to make the aircraft smaller for easier carrier handling was considered by the U.S. Navy but was never initiated.

Despite the controversy at its inception, the Savage was never called to deliver nuclear weapons. In fact it never saw any combat. And although it was a pioneer in the jet age, it still relied on its two radial engines. Soon real jets, including the Douglas A-3 Skywarrior, pushed aside the Savage. The internal bomb bays on some Savages were refitted to carry fuel and the aircraft repurposed as in-flight refueling tankers. All Savages were inactive by 1960. After its military career, this tanker modification also proved to be useful for carrying water to fight forest fires.

In its day, the North American AJ Savage was the largest carrier-based attack aircraft. It paved the way for even larger aircraft, such as the Douglas A-3 Skywarrior, and it helped introduce the navy to the jet age, the nuclear age—and "diplomatic relations" with the U.S. Air Force.

North American AJ-2 Specifications

Type: Attack bomber

Crew: Three

Power plant: Two 2,300-horsepower Pratt & Whitney R-2800-48 air-cooled radial engines and one Allison J33-A-10 turbojet with 4,600 pounds of thrust

Performance: Maximum speed, 471 miles per hour; service ceiling, 41,500 feet; maximum range, 2,475 miles

Weight: Empty, 30,800 pounds; maximum takeoff weight, 55,000 pounds

Dimensions: Span, 75 feet, 2 inches; length, 63 feet, 1 inch; height, 21 feet, 5 inches; wing area, 836 square feet

Armament: 12,000 pounds of bombs, nuclear weapons, or extra fuel

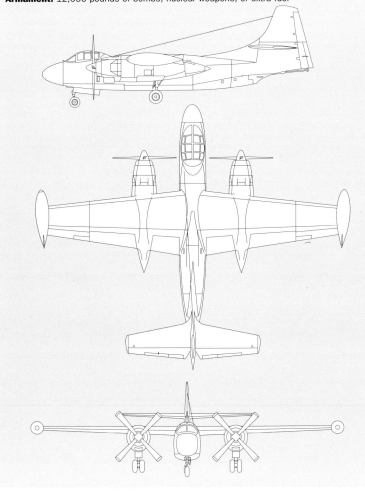

RIGHT: Engine maintenance has been completed on this AJ Savage. It is being brought up from the hangar deck to the flight deck for engine run up.

Lockheed P2V Neptune

Developed from the Lockheed PV-2 Harpoon, the final variant of the Lockheed PV-1 Ventura, the Lockheed P2V Neptune was designed to be a land-based patrol bomber with reconnaissance capabilities. A 1941 concept, the Neptune's design goals were for increased payload and range. Lockheed had worked on the idea for this aircraft for several years; however, the wartime production demands for existing aircraft delayed progress with the new design.

In 1944 Lockheed finally had something to sell to the U.S. Navy. Up until that point, most naval squadrons operated flying boats; the navy was intrigued by the idea of adding a reliable long-range land-based aircraft to its patrol squadrons. The navy ordered two prototypes and fifteen production models of the new design, but the Neptune was completed too late to serve in World War II.

The first prototype, the XP2V-1, flew on May 17, 1945. It was a twin-engine aircraft with two 3,500-horsepower Wright R-3350 Cyclone radial engines. It had a mid-wing design and a large internal bomb bay for 8,000 pounds of bombs, torpedoes, or depth charges; armament included three power-operated gun turrets (nose, dorsal, and rear) with two .50-caliber machine guns in each turret. It also had onboard radar equipment. The XP2V-1 was handled by a crew of seven, although later variants could accommodate eight to ten men. Initial evaluations were positive and flight characteristics were judged favorable.

The P2V-1, developed from the prototype, commenced active duty in 1947. Before that, a modified P2V-1, from the first production run of fifteen, set a world record in 1946. The "Truculent Turtle," as it was named, flew 11,235 nonstop miles from Perth, Australia, to Columbus, Ohio. Flight time totaled 55 hours and 17 minutes; a record that was not bested until 1962, when it was finally broken by a B-52 Stratofortress. Today, the Truculent Turtle is in the collection of the National Naval Aviation Museum in Pensacola, Florida.

The next production variant was the P2V-2. Eighty-one were built, and all were active by July 1948. They had larger Wright R-3350-24W Cyclone engines with 2,500 horsepower and Hamilton Standard three-bladed propellers. The machine guns were replaced with 20-mm cannons, and attachment points for jet-assisted takeoff (JATO) rockets were added. After all these improvements, the P2V-2's top speed was 320 miles per hour, and its range was just less than 4,000 miles. Also notable were the P2V-2's wings, which were

VP-65 Tridents

RIGHT: This Lockheed P2V Neptune gets a boost from its externally mounted jet-assisted takeoff (JATO) bottles, January 1951.

OPPOSITE: The P2V Neptune, with its high aspect ratio wing, large fuel capacity, and a pair of Wright R-3350 turbo-compound engines, put the seaplane out of business as a maritime patrol bomber. Now a land plane could perform long-distance missions without the need for ship tenders. In 1946, a Neptune set a distance record of 11,235 miles flying non-stop from Columbus, Ohio to Perth, Australia. This P2V-7 flew with VP-65 from Point Mugu, California, 1973.

designed to keep the aircraft afloat long enough for the crew to escape in the event of an emergency landing at sea.

By 1950 the United States was involved with the Korean War. This accelerated the need for aircraft. The P2V-3, like the variant before it, had more powerful engines and could fly at faster speeds. Several models were built from the -3 platform, totaling eighty-three aircraft. In addition to the basic configuration, there was an armed transport version and a model with a specialized JATO system to allow the land-based aircraft to take off from an aircraft carrier. Another version was fitted with airborne early-warning equipment and another was built with the ASB-1 low-level radar bombing system. These specially modified Neptunes could only take off from, not land on, a carrier deck.

Next, fifty-two P2V-4s were built. Introduced to the fleet in 1949, they had even larger, turbo-compound Wright engines, antisubmarine equipment,

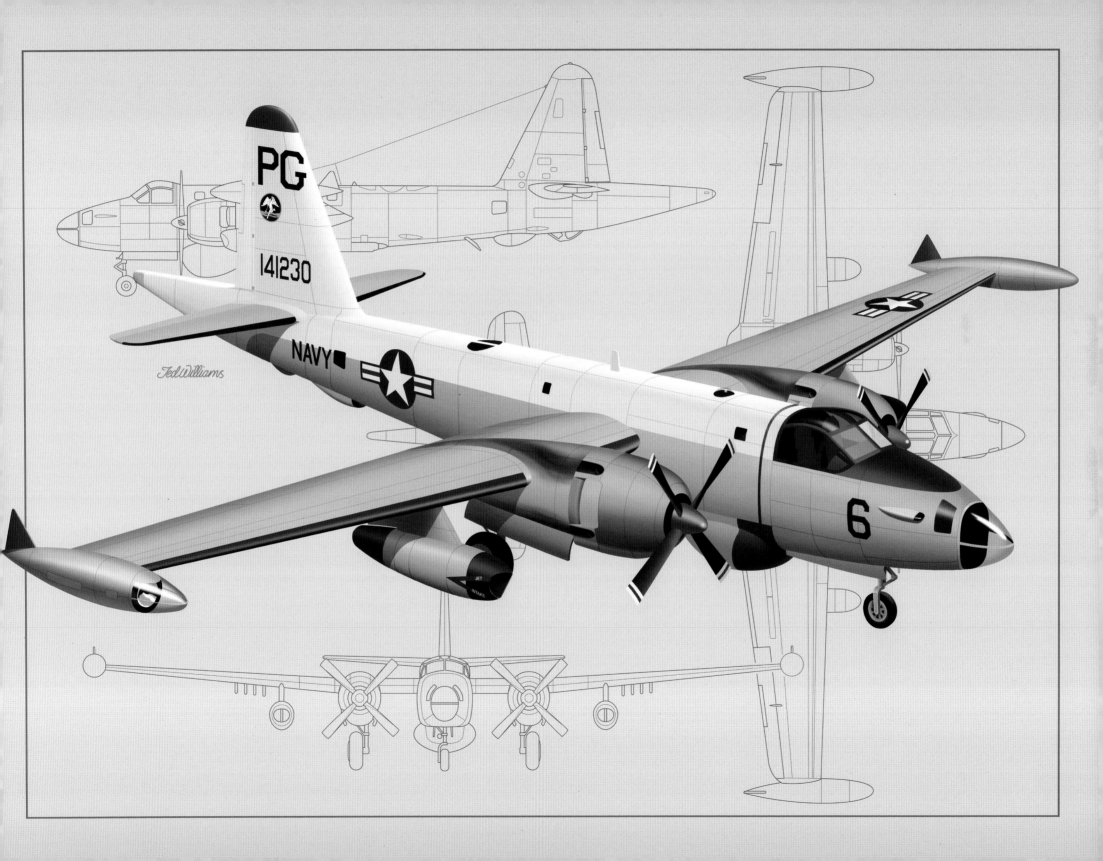

and auxiliary fuel tanks. The -4 was followed by the P2V-5—the most produced variant. By 1950 a total of 424 P2V-5s had left Lockheed's factory.
Similar to the -4, they had new electronic countermeasures and specialized
antisubmarine warfare (ASW) equipment. The -5 also introduced two additional Westinghouse J34 turbojets with 3,400 pounds of static thrust.

Eighty-three P2V-6s followed. These were surpassed by the P2V-7, which
was the last variant produced in quantity; 359 were built. The -6 was used for
training and antisubmarine patrols, while in 1962, the -7 was redesignated as
the P-2. To speed production, the Neptune was constructed in a series of subassemblies. This made manufacturing the aircraft quicker, and maintenance
and refittings in the field easier.

Overall, between 1945 and 1962, more than 1,000 Neptunes were built for
the U.S. Navy and Air Force, and for export. The aircraft was quite adaptable,
and many changes occurred throughout the course of the program: For
instance, an upgrade to carry nuclear weapons was developed and an export
version called the P-2J was used by Japan.

During the Korean War, the Neptune found a niche in rescue operations,
a role previously held by flying boats such as the Consolidated PBY Catalina.

**OPPOSITE: Four P2V-7 Neptunes are
shown on the moving production line at
the Lockheed Burbank, California, plant.
After work is completed at each station,
the entire aircraft is moved forward to
the next station for additional assembly.**

**BELOW: These P2V-5s from Patrol
Squadron Four (VP-4) are on a routine
reconnaissance flight over Okinawa,
November 1959. With its high aspect
ratio wing and large fuel capacity, the
Neptune was well suited for long-range
reconnaissance patrols.**

Versatile, the Neptune performed day- and night-bombing runs and ground
attacks, could be used as a transport, and proved to be a valuable patrol aircraft
when it was used during the Vietnam War for antisubmarine activities. It was
the last naval bomber to use radial engines.

Ultimately, the Neptune was replaced by another Lockheed design, the
P3 Orion. Like many other bombers, after its military career was over, surplus
Neptunes were used for fighting forest fires.

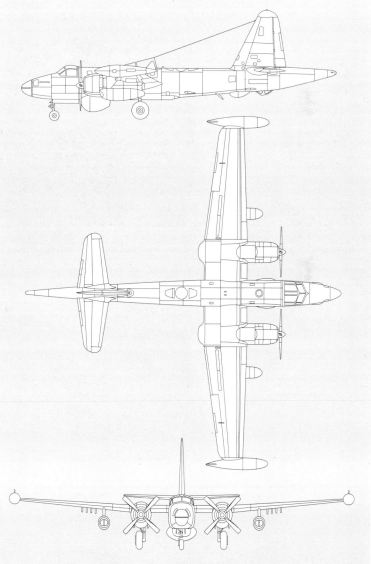

Lockheed P2V-7 Specifications

Type: Patrol bomber

Crew: Seven to ten

Power plant: Two 3,500-horsepower Wright R-3350-32W air-cooled radial engines, two Westinghouse J34 turbojets with 3,400 pounds of thrust

Performance: Maximum speed, 364 miles per hour; service ceiling, 22,400 feet; maximum range, 4,300 miles

Weight: Empty, 43,010 pounds; maximum takeoff weight, 80,000 pounds

Dimensions: Span, 103 feet, 10 inches; length, 91 feet, 8 inches; height, 28 feet, 1 inch; wing area, 1,000 square feet

Armament: 8,000 pounds of torpedoes, depth charges, or mines

North American B-45 Tornado

Only 140 North American B-45 Tornados were built for the U.S. Air Force, but this short-run aircraft's mark on bomber development far exceeds its limited production numbers. The Tornado was the U.S. Air Force's first operational jet bomber.

In 1944 the U.S. Army Air Force issued a request for a bomber aircraft that could reach 500 miles per hour. To reach this extraordinary speed, the specification stipulated that the newly perfected General Electric J35 turbojet engine was to be incorporated into all proposals. At 500 miles per hour, a bomber approaches the speed of sound. Near 500 miles per hour, the blade tips of its rotating propeller arrive at their maximum thrust capability—all energy is expended and no additional forward velocity is possible. Since a jet engine takes in, compresses, then expels air to create thrust without external moving parts, a jet engine can power an aircraft past the 500-mile-per-hour threshold.

The Boeing, Consolidated Vultee (Convair), Martin, and North American aircraft companies all responded with proposals for jet bombers. The United States knew that Germany had already pioneered jet capabilities, and the U.S. Army Air Force was in a rush to have its own jet-powered aircraft, lest it risk losing air superiority and, possibly, the Second World War.

The J35 was an improved version of the General Electric J33 turbojet engine. North American Aviation had an advantage. It had experience incorporating the J33 engine into another bomber that it had already designed for the U.S. Navy, although the J33 was not that aircraft's sole method of power. The North American AJ Savage still utilized two air-cooled Pratt & Whitney R-2800 Double Wasp radial engines.

The J33 closely resembled Frank Whittle's original engine, the one that he used in the Gloster Whittle E 28/39, the British test aircraft his team built and successfully flew in 1941 to demonstrate Whittle's concept. One year later, in 1942, Frank Whittle traveled to the United States to assist General Electric with the development of the J33. In Great Britain, the first jet engine led to the Gloster Meteor. In the United States, the J33 was used several aircraft including the Lockheed P-80 Shooting Star and the North American AJ Savage. General Electric continued to improve upon the design; this led to the J35, and later to the even more powerful J47.

To make it easier to produce its new bomber quickly, North American proposed an airframe that was mostly conventional, except for the installation

OPPOSITE: The B-45 Tornado was the U.S. Air Force's first operational all-jet bomber and the first four jet aircraft to fly in the United States. The B-45 first flew on March 17, 1947 but it wasn't until the Korean War that this jet-bomber came of age. While the United States was embroiled in the conflict, Tornados flew missions as a nuclear deterrent to keep the Soviet Union at bay. This B-45 is in the markings of the 47th Bomb Wing.

of four J35 turbojet engines in two under-wing nacelles, positioned two in two. The army wanted its new jet bombers to be available for combat in the European Theater as soon as possible. State-of-the-art airframe construction would aid manufacturing. Seemingly pedestrian in design, the North American entrant was a wolf in sheep's clothing. The unassuming aircraft would go down in history as the world's first multiengine jet bomber—a feat not wholly unexpected coming from Dutch Kindelberger's North American.

The army ordered three XB-45s from North American in March 1945. Ultimately all four of the 1944 contenders' designs were granted an evaluation; however, only the North American and Boeing models would progress to mass production. North American's XB-45 prototype was manned by a crew of four, including a pilot, bombardier/navigator, radio operator, and a rear gunner who operated a powered turret with two .50-caliber machine guns. Just like its sister jet, the Boeing B-47 Stratojet, it was equipped only with rear guns since the jet aircraft was deemed so fast it would, of course, outpace any enemy interceptors. The aircraft could carry one long 12,000-pound bomb or one large 22,000-pound bomb—called a "Tall Boy" and "Grand Slam," respectively.

The XB-45 was evaluated against the Convair XB-46. After flight tests, the North American design was determined to have more favorable characteristics than the XB-46. As a result, ninety-seven production models were ordered and built with the improved J47-GE-7 turbojet engine. The Consolidated Vultee program was discontinued by 1952. First flown in February 1948, the resulting B-45As were the first jet bombers to serve the U.S. Air Force.

Prior to the first flight of the B-45A, the U.S. Air Force became an independent organization separate from the U.S. Army. This was brought about by the National Security Act of 1947. This act, signed into law by President Harry S. Truman, created the Department of Defense with a distinct service for the U.S. Army, Air Force, and Navy. However, because of the nature of the U.S. Navy and Marine Corps and the unique challenges inherent to sea operations, the U.S. Navy continued to maintain its naval aviation program.

The next production variant of the Tornado was the B-45C, which was fitted with auxiliary drop tanks to hold more fuel for extended range. It also had a redesigned cockpit that was more structurally sound. Only ten were built. Another thirty-three were built and refitted for reconnaissance and surveillance use. In lieu of a bombardier's quarters in the nose, cameras

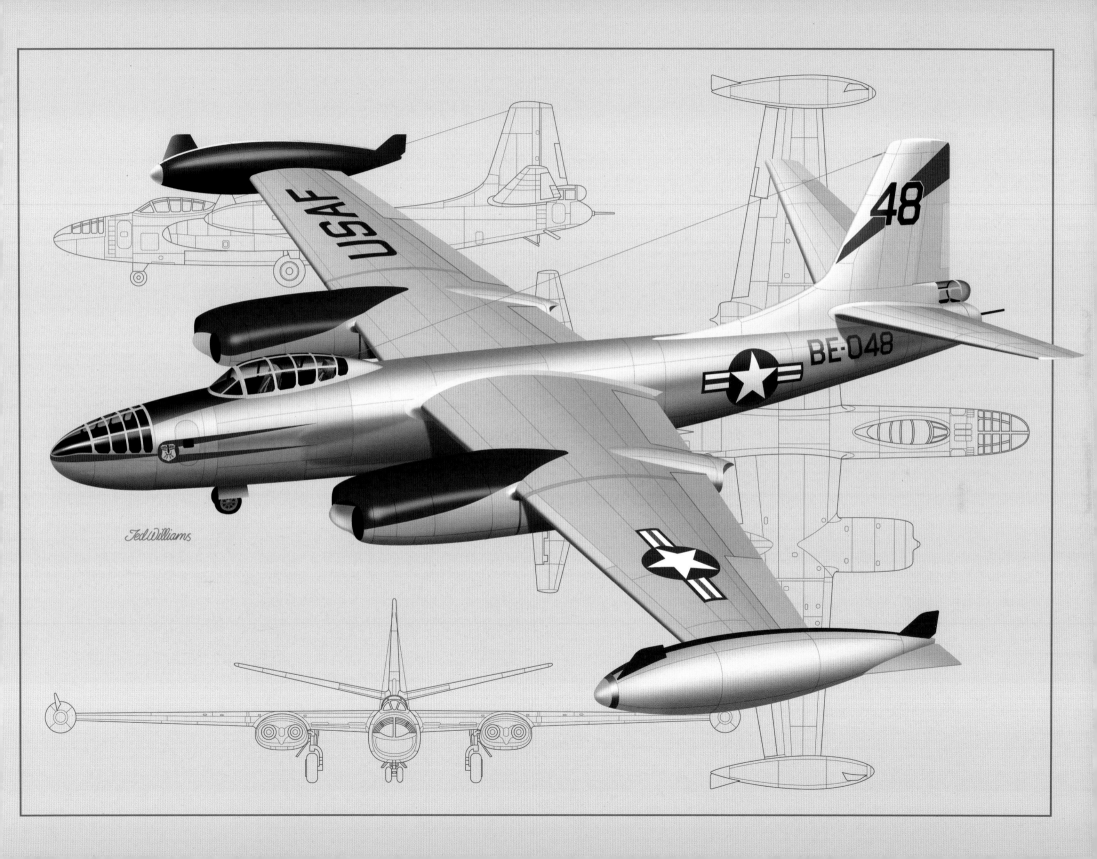

were installed in the thirty-three RB-45Cs. More cameras were mounted in the bomb bay. When not capturing vital photographic intelligence, some RB-45Cs could also be used for in-flight refueling.

Completed too late for World War II, the B-45 was pressed into service during the Korean War. Not a top performer, its active service life was short. When the Boeing B-47 Stratojet proved to be a better aircraft, both in principle and practice, the production of the B-45 slowed, and then stopped.

Branded an "interim" aircraft, the North American B-45 Tornado's reputation precedes its production record. It was the first American air force jet bomber. Conceived at a troubled time, during a world war, it was tested over Korea and administered just as the U.S. Army was relinquishing control over the air service. Still, the North American B-45 Tornado managed to leave a historic legacy.

North American B-45A Specifications

Type: Heavy bomber

Crew: Four

Power plant: Four General Electric J47 turbojet engines with either 5,820 or 6,000 pounds of thrust

Performance: Maximum speed, 575 miles per hour; service ceiling, 46,400 feet; maximum range, 2,170 miles

Weight: Empty, 45,694 pounds; maximum takeoff weight, 82,600 pounds

Dimensions: Span, 89 feet; length, 75 feet, 4 inches; height, 25 feet, 2 inches; wing area, 1,175 square feet

Armament: Two .50-cal machine guns and up to 22,000 pounds of bombs

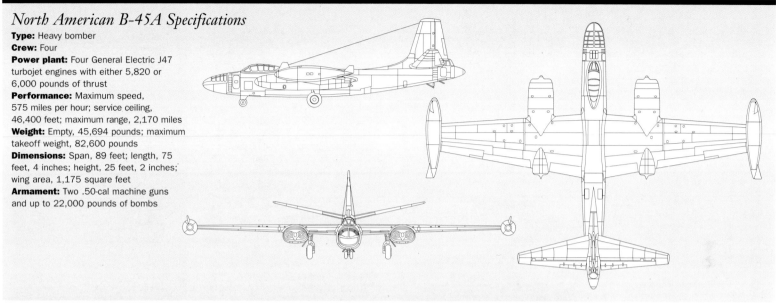

OPPOSITE FAR LEFT: The tail gun position of a North American B-45 Tornado. From this position, the gunner operated a remote control gun site and firing mechanism that was originally developed for the Boeing B-29 Superfortress.

OPPOSITE LEFT: The first aircraft from the 142 B-45s ordered by the U.S. Air Force come down the production line in 1948. Most Tornados were produced at a facility in Long Beach, California.

LEFT: After the aircraft left the paint shop, to maximize the space inside the factory, final installation of the Tornado's avionics and engine systems was completed outdoors in the bright California sun. Temporary sun shades were erected to protect the technicians working inside the cockpit.

Boeing B-47 Stratojet

The same 1944 U.S. Army Air Force competition that that gave birth to the North American B-45 Tornado also brought about the Boeing B-47 Stratojet. It was almost halfway through the 1940s and the Second World War was entering its final phase, due in part to the abundance and superiority of American fighting war materiel. A victorious end was in sight—as long as the United States could maintain its position as a leading military power. But the U.S. Army knew how unpredictable the tides of war could be. Germany had already introduced the world's first jet fighter. It was imperative the United States gain its own jet aircraft capabilities. To speed development, four jet bomber proposals from the 1944 request were granted an evaluation.

The initial Boeing Stratojet featured the same General Electric J35 turbojet with 4,000 pounds of static thrust as used on the B-45; however, Boeing upped the jet equation to six. It had only been nine months since the Tornado amazed a crowd with the first flight of a multiengine jet bomber, now the Stratojet was doing it again. The J35 was the United States' first axial-flow compressor engine. Developed by General Electric in 1943, the propulsion device was derived from RAF officer Frank Whittle's revolutionary design. The manufacture of the J35 was undertaken by the General Motors' Allison Division, which built more than fourteen thousand between 1947 and 1955. The power plant was used in several bombers, as well as in several prominent fighter aircraft.

Boeing's original concept for the 1944 design competition was to use the already proven B-29 Superfortress airframe as the test bed for the new jet engines, but an emerging engineering principle ushered in a new era of aerodynamic thinking—the swept-back wing. The Boeing engineers redesigned their bomber to employ high-mounted wings that swept back thirty-five degrees, a configuration quite common today. The idea of a rearward angled wing was a German innovation that offered many performance advantages. Coupled with the six jet engines (housed in under-wing nacelles mounted on pylons), the Boeing swept-wing proposal was sure to surpass the army's desired speed of 500 miles an hour.

The Model 450, as it was called in the Boeing plant, also implemented an inventive landing gear arrangement. To help decrease the runway length required for takeoff, the front wheel apparatus was taller than the rear, giving the aircraft an exaggerated angle of attack. Also, the rear gear wheels were

RIGHT: The B-47 Stratojet had a unique "bicycle" landing gear configuration. The gear was mounted on the centerline of the fuselage to support the weight of the aircraft. Additional smaller dolly-like wheel assemblies extended from the inboard engine nacelles to offer lateral stability.

OPPOSITE: The Boeing B-47 was the first jet-bomber to introduce swept-back wings. The Stratojet was a pilot's airplane. It flew higher and faster than any previous U.S.A.F. bomber and had the speed and maneuverability of contemporary fighter interceptors. Although it could only deliver a bomb load within a medium range, it made up for this by its deployment at forward bases in Europe, North Africa, and Alaska. This B-47 carries the Strategic Air Command insignia.

situated in tandem for strength. Additional wheels were installed inside the outermost engine nacelles to help the big aircraft taxi. All of the gear retracted.

The army ordered two prototypes, as XB-47, in 1946. The first one flew in December 1947. In addition to the six J35 turbojet engines, equipment for jet-assisted takeoff (JATO) was onboard to assist the jet engines; later, in 1948, the second prototype flew with even more powerful next-generation J47 turbojet engines with 5,000 pounds of static thrust and electrically regulated afterburners. The J45 was also the first jet engine approved for commercial use.

The XB-47 was intended to be operated by a three-man crew that included a pilot, radio operator/gunner, and navigator/bombardier. Though no longer a facsimile of the Superfortress, the XB-47 was still a large aircraft. It could carry 22,000 pounds of bombs. Because of its top speed of 578 miles per hour, the aircraft was only equipped with two rear-facing .50-caliber machine guns. The popular belief was that its slower enemies could only chase it, so why arm the nose?

An initial array of ten production models was ordered from the second prototype in September 1948. Called the B-47A, all ten were used for training and continuing evaluation. A jet aircraft has different characteristics from a propeller-driven aircraft. At jet speeds, whatever could go wrong would go wrong. Parachutes deployed on landing roll to help slow the aircraft. Meanwhile, engineers needed to learn how to tame the scalding-hot, exhaust-spewing jet engines. The late-1940s through to the 1950s was a transitional time; much like the changeover from biplane to monoplane, the move from propellers and piston engines to jets required retooling.

BELOW: To help a fully loaded 100-ton B-47 get airborne, it relied on eighteen solid fuel rockets that were mounted in the rear fuselage. Later models used more powerful jet engines, which made the jet assisted takeoff unnecessary.

The B-47B was the first mass-produced variant; 399 were built by Boeing, with a handful by Lockheed (eight) and Douglas (ten). With the United States' increasing involvement in the Korean War came the need for aircraft. In 1950, at the start of the Korean conflict, the United States resurrected many World War II aircraft but newer technology bombers and fighters were required to survive engagement with the more-advanced Soviet designs.

The B-47B was updated with external drop tanks and the capability for in-flight refueling. The tail guns were upgraded to 20-mm cannons, and the bomb capacity could include a nuclear payload. Plus, by 1956, other new

BELOW: Test pilots at the control of the XB-47 Stratojet prototype. Covered by a bubble-type Plexiglas canopy, the cockpit is completely pressurized and temperature controlled. A refrigeration unit is used to lower the high temperatures caused by the friction of air on the outside skin at high speeds.

innovations like ejection seats and avionics were becoming the norm. When all was said and done, the B-47B's top speed was increased to 630 miles per hour. Several B-47Bs were modified to perform roles such as reconnaissance and training. An improved B-47C was discussed but cancelled.

The next production variant of note was the X-47E; 1,591 were built by Boeing (931), Lockheed (386), and Douglas (274). The E version was basically an improvement of the B variant. It had the upgraded J47-GE-25 engine with 7,200 pounds of static thrust. Another 240 reconnaissance models were built from the XB-47E.

In addition, numerous evaluation aircraft were developed from the B-47E to test advanced radar and reconnaissance techniques, as well as refueling and engine options. The XB-47E was active until 1960, with some evaluation models operational through to 1969. The Stratojet also served in the Vietnam War.

The Boeing B-47 Stratojet was one of the first American jet bombers. In hindsight it can be criticized for its light payload and short range; however, the B-47 helped to introduce many innovations—including swept-back wings and jet engines—to the bombing category. Along with the B-45, the B-47 paved the way for other even more modern jet bombers.

BELOW: A row of B-47 tandem engine pods with pylon assemblies. This particular engine pod and pylon mounting design was pioneered by Boeing to help decrease the drag on the thin swept-back wing.

Boeing B-47E Specifications

Type: Heavy bomber
Crew: Three
Power plant: Six General Electric J47-GE-25 turbojet engines; 7,200 pounds of thrust each
Performance: Maximum speed, 610 miles per hour; service ceiling, 39,300 feet; maximum range, 3,500 miles
Weight: Empty, 80,758 pounds; maximum takeoff weight, 226,000 pounds
Dimensions: Span, 116 feet; length, 107 feet, 1 inch; height, 28 feet; wing area, 1,428 square feet
Armament: Two 20-mm cannons and 22,000 pounds of conventional or nuclear bombs

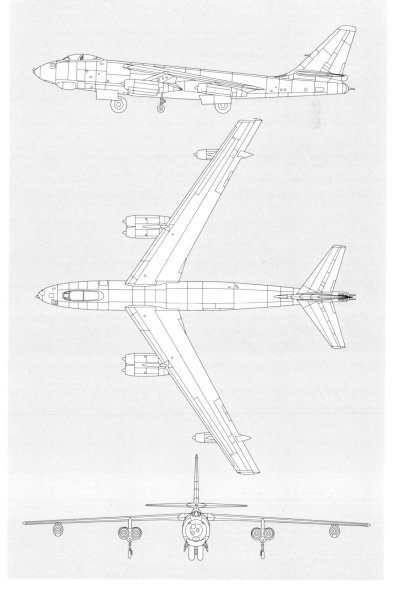

Boeing B-52 Stratofortress

Originally designed to be a high-altitude, long-range strategic bomber, the B-52's role has grown to encompass many additional and varied missions as need and technology dictated. The competition that spawned the development of the Stratofortress was initiated by the U.S. Army Air Forces in 1946. It was the same request that led to the Convair B-36 Peacemaker. The army wanted a bomber that could deliver 10,000 pounds of bombs an intercontinental distance of 5,000 miles, while traveling at a constant 300 miles per hour.

By 1946, Boeing had more than earned its reputation as a respected military supplier, with renowned experience pushing the envelope with its heavy bombers. To try to meet the army's demands, the initial Boeing proposal was for a large straight-wing aircraft that was similar to the B-29 Superfortress. The plan was to have six Wright T35 turboprop engines mounted under the wings. A turboprop uses a jet engine to turn specially designed propellers.

In 1947 Boeing received a contract from the newly independent U.S. Air Force to build two prototypes; however, the XB-52 that resulted four years later was markedly different from the first proposal. In 1948 the design was fine-tuned to incorporate newer jet engines, 35-degree swept-back wings, and a longer fuselage.

The first evaluation model to fly was the YB-52. It took to the air in April 1951, with the XB-52 joining it later that same year. They both had eight Pratt &Whitney J57 turbojet engines, each with 8,700 pounds of static thrust. Both prototypes could attain 610 miles per hour, and had a demonstrated range of 7,000 miles. Operated by a crew of only five, the aircraft could carry 25,000 pounds of bombs, and were armed with two .50-caliber machine guns in a rear turret.

Only three of the first production variant, the B-52A, were built. The B-52B was similar to the A. Twenty-three were built, with another twenty-seven B-52Bs fitted for reconnaissance. In June 1955 the B-52B was the first variant to be used by an active bomb group, the 93d Bomb Wing at Castle Air Force Base. The B-52C went active in 1956; thirty-five left the factory as the -C variant. With each variant came improvements to the systems used to navigate and bomb, as well as slight cosmetic changes for better heat deflection and the addition of larger auxiliary fuel tanks.

One major design change that affected all production B-52s was initiated by General Curtis Emerson LeMay, then commanding general of the Strategic Air Command (SAC), who, along with the U.S. Air Force, demanded a

RIGHT: An Air Force crew sits at the radar and navigation stations within a B-52 Stratofortress. A red light illuminates the instrument panel.

OPPOSITE: A testament to the B-52's effectiveness as a strategic bomber is its longevity. The Stratofortress has been on active duty since 1955. In that time it has seen constant use as the Strategic Air Command's deterrent in the Cold War, as a strategic bomber in the Vietnam War, in the Gulf War, and in Iraq and Afghanistan. It is the U.S. Air Force's intention to keep the big B-52 in service until at least 2040. This B-52D is shown in the Cold War bare aluminum-and-white paint scheme adopted by SAC during the late 1950s.

reconfiguration to the design of the aircraft's cockpit. As a result, the tandem seating for the pilot and copilot under a bubble canopy, as introduced on the prototypes, was changed to a conventional cockpit with side-by-side seating for all production B-52s.

The B-52D was the next variant to follow; 170 were built. The Stratofortress now had a top speed of 638 miles per hour and a crew of six: a pilot, copilot, bombardier, navigator, electronic warfare officer, and a tail gunner. The B-52D was used extensively throughout the Vietnam War. There were no longer any provisions for reconnaissance; the B-52D was pure warship with the capability to carry 60,000 pounds of bombs. The B-52D participated in many large-scale bombing campaigns over Southeast Asia, including Operation Arc Light and Rolling Thunder. The B-52D remained operational until 1983, and many C variants were updated to D standards.

One hundred B-52Es were available by October 1957. The B-52E was equipped with two under-wing mounts to carry the new AGM-28. The AGM-28 was a nuclear missile designed by North American. The "Hound Dog," as it was known, could be launched 600 miles away from its target, which was more typically a ground location.

The B-52F continued the E's mission, but with larger Pratt & Whitney J57 turbojet engines. This J57 could generate up to 13,750 pounds of static thrust. The B-52F was used in Vietnam and for Cold War patrols up until 1978.

A G version was modified to reduce the aircraft's weight; 193 were built before 1958. Still in service in 1991, the B-52G saw combat during Operation

Ted Williams

U.S. AIR FORCE

USAF

Desert Storm. The final variant was the B-52H; 102 were completed between 1961 and 1962. Throughout the years, frequent "modernizations" have occurred to keep the B-52E in current operational condition. These updates and field refittings have kept the B-52 at pace with technology, the advent of electronic countermeasures systems, and abreast of changing military directives.

The B-52 can boast an illustrious career. In 1957 three B-52Bs were the first aircraft to fly around the world without stopping. Another well-known historic mission of the B-52 was an airborne readiness initiative that was improved by in-flight refueling. After a testing period, in 1958 the B-52 participated in the first Airborne Alert program. For four months, the 92d Bombardment Wing maintained at least five B-52s loaded with a nuclear payload airborne around the clock. Then, between 1960 and 1968, the B-52 was used to perform continuous airborne patrols. This tactic, although expensive and grueling on its crews, is credited with helping to deter the Cuban missile crisis. During this time period, other B-52s were also kept ready on the runway, able to leap in to action in under fifteen minutes.

In the 1960s, during Vietnam, the B-52 was modified with a "Big Belly" for tactical bombing operations. And now, with the reduction of the Cold War tensions, the B-52 has been called to serve in military actions in Iraq and Afghanistan.

Reinvention and usefulness may be the key reasons why the B-52 is still, despite its age, one of the U.S. Air Force's frontline heavy bombers. Its good engineering and even better bloodline have worked together to keep the B-52 versatile and active—and a potent protector for many decades. The Boeing B-52 Stratofortress is the perfect embodiment of Boeing's entire line of airborne fortresses.

OPPOSITE TOP: This B-52 was equipped with eight Pratt & Whitney Turbofan jet engines. It was flown as a test bed while the B-52H production line was being set up.

OPPOSITE BOTTOM: Bomber crew from the 22nd Bombardment Wing scrambles to their aircraft, a B-52D, during a Strategic Air Command (SAC) training alert.

RIGHT: The 193rd and last B-52G built. Shown here as it moved into final assembly at Boeing's manufacturing facility in Wichita, Kansas. It rolled out on September 23, 1960; the first B-52H rolled out seven days later.

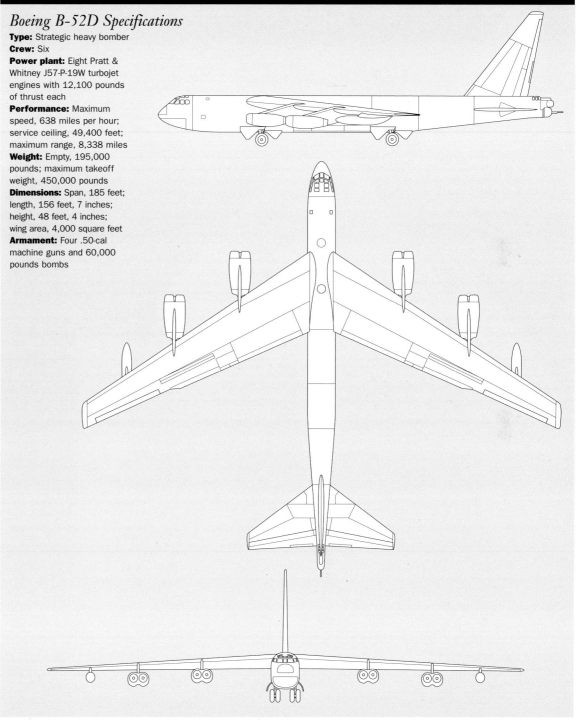

Boeing B-52D Specifications

Type: Strategic heavy bomber

Crew: Six

Power plant: Eight Pratt & Whitney J57-P-19W turbojet engines with 12,100 pounds of thrust each

Performance: Maximum speed, 638 miles per hour; service ceiling, 49,400 feet; maximum range, 8,338 miles

Weight: Empty, 195,000 pounds; maximum takeoff weight, 450,000 pounds

Dimensions: Span, 185 feet; length, 156 feet, 7 inches; height, 48 feet, 4 inches; wing area, 4,000 square feet

Armament: Four .50-cal machine guns and 60,000 pounds bombs

Convair B-58 Hustler

Looking at the Convair B-58 Hustler is like looking at the future. It was all new, and all dangerous, at a time when aircraft designers were just beginning to step out of the mold of World War II-era design principles. For starters, the B-58 was the world's first supersonic (Mach 2) bomber, and it was built around four jet engines and a delta wing.

After World War II, the U.S. Air Force was reviewing its options. It wanted a jet-powered strategic bomber that could, in time, replace the Boeing B-52 Stratofortress. In particular, the U.S. Air Force wanted an aircraft that could fly at a constant 500 miles per hour, travel 2,500 miles, and weigh 170,000 pounds. To that aim, the air force tested the Boeing design for the XB-55, and reviewed proposals from several other American aircraft companies, including North American, Martin, Douglas, Curtiss, and Consolidated Vultee, which was also known as Convair.

In 1946 the U.S. Army Air Forces was using a series of advanced bomber studies, called GEBO (Generalized Bomber), to evaluate design considerations for its first supersonic bomber. The GEBO program was a way to test aircraft designs and newer engineering principles without the expense and risk associated with building and flying a full-scale prototype; it was first used to assess the Boeing XB-55, a larger update to the Boeing B-47. The XB-55, with its turboprop engines, was determined to be deficient. None were built.

GEBO II was conducted in 1949. Convair used this evaluation program to develop and perfect design elements that it would put to use in the B-58 Hustler. During the GEBO review, the "parasite" concept was contemplated. In this scenario, to save fuel, Hustlers would be attached to the underside of B-36s and ferried to their locations, but the idea was ultimately rejected.

The XB-58 was designed to have a delta wing. Convair also used the delta wing in its fighter aircraft development of the time. The delta wing was invented by Alexander M. Lippisch, an aeronautical engineer from Germany. The United States acquired his research after World War II. In 1946 the United States Department of Defense brought Lippisch to Wright Field in Dayton, Ohio, through Operation Paperclip, a covert intelligence operation created to bring German scientists out of post-war Germany and into the United States.

The delta wing, while offering numerous performance gains, was also a challenge. Inefficient at low altitudes, a delta-wing aircraft required a long runway for takeoff; however, the wing provided plenty of internal

RIGHT: This B-58 Hustler takes on fuel from a KC-135 at the midway point of a record setting Los Angeles-to-New York flight. The roundtrip run was completed in fewer than five hours in March 1962. The B-58 set over nineteen performance records.

OPPOSITE: Looking at the B-58 Hustler today, it is hard to believe it made its first flight in 1956. The Hustler was the U.S. Air Force's first supersonic bomber that could attain Mach 2. Entering this realm of speed and performance presented Convair engineers with many problems that had to be solved, from overcoming the heat generated by the aircraft traveling at such speeds to ejecting crewmembers at Mach 2 and protecting sensitive electronic systems. This illustration shows off the Hustler's revolutionary delta wing planform.

space to store fuel and it allowed for supersonic speeds during straight, high-altitude flights.

In 1953 the U.S. Air Force ordered two prototypes, an XB-58 and XRB-58 for reconnaissance. Also in 1953 Convair was purchased by General Dynamics.

The prototypes were powered by four General Electric J79 turbojet engines with 15,000 pounds of thrust with afterburner that were mounted on pylons underneath a delta wing that swept back 60 degrees. The "wet" wing could hold 9,000 gallons of fuel. The fuselage had a nipped-in, or "wasp waist." This design feature helped the aircraft perform more efficiently at supersonic speeds. This concept became known as the Whitcomb Area Rule, named for Richard T. Whitcomb, the National Advisory Committee for Aeronautics (NACA) engineer responsible for its development.

The prototype flew on November 11, 1956. It had a crew of three: a pilot, a bomber/navigator, and an operator for the defensive systems who was responsible for the electronic countermeasures system (ECM). Each crewman sat in a separate cockpit with a clamshell cover. At a time when the Stratofortress had a cruising speed of 610 miles per hour, a number on par with the current best of the best top speeds, the XB-58's top speed was 1,325 per miles hour—twice the speed of sound.

Convair B-58A Specifications

Type: Supersonic high-altitude bomber
Crew: Three
Power plant: Four General Electric J79 turbojet engines with 15,600 pounds of thrust each
Performance: Maximum speed, 1,325 miles per hour; service ceiling, 64,800 feet; maximum range, 4,400 miles
Weight: Empty, 55,560 pounds; maximum takeoff weight, 163,000 pounds
Dimensions: Span, 56 feet, 10 inches; length, 96 feet, 9 inches; height, 29 feet, 11 inches; wing area, 1,542 square feet
Armament: One 20-mm cannon and 19,450 pounds of conventional bombs, nuclear weapons, or equipment

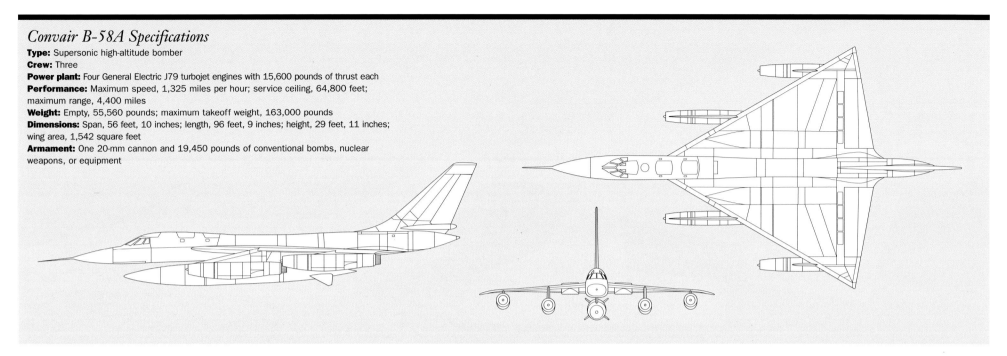

The second prototype flew in 1957 as another XB-58; not as a XRB-58 for it never fulfilled the reconnaissance role. Eleven YB-58As were built from the first prototype. Another seventeen YB-58As were delivered as RB-58A for reconnaissance.

The XB-58 and YB-58 carried a pod underneath the aircraft since the slender fuselage and delta wing were not suited for internal bomb stowage. The pod could contain additional fuel, equipment, or a nuclear weapon. As a result, the aircraft's tricycle landing gear was unusually tall to support the aircraft, plus its engines and pod, above the ground. This gave the B-58 an ungainly appearance on the tarmac.

The only production variant was the B-58A. Eighty-six were built at the General Dynamics Forth Worth, Texas, factory. The majority of the structure was covered in an innovative new laminated-aluminum honeycomb skin designed to dissipate heat. The B-58 was armed with a 20-mm cannon in the tail and radar equipment in the nose. A refit in 1962 introduced an escape capsule. To survive ejection at such high speeds, the crewmen needed the protection of a pressurized airtight container. Before ejection, a crewman would activate the clamshell enclosure, locking himself into the capsule device. The capsule could be ejected from the aircraft at Mach 2, safely delivering its occupant to the ground. The capsule had its own parachute and it could float.

Two other variants were suggested, a B and C with structural improvements and bigger engines, but they never left the drawing board.

OPPOSITE: A B-58 Hustler is shown moving along the production line at Convair's Fort Worth, Texas, plant. The aircraft were transported on rails. At the end of the assembly line hydraulically operated built-in platforms lowered the aircraft to the factory floor. Although the B-58 represented significant advances in aviation technology, the program's $3 billion price tag attracted constant criticism from Capitol Hill.

The B-58 Hustler was operational with the United States Strategic Air Command (SAC) from 1960 to 1970. It ushered in an era that saw many speed records shattered, winning the Bleriot, Mackay, and Harmon Trophies in 1961 and a Bendix Trophy in 1962, as well as several other high-profile competitions. In all, the B-58 set nineteen world speed records.

Yet, speed has its price. The U.S. Air Force was just beginning to experiment at Mach speeds. Today the Hustler is recognized as one of the most dangerous U.S. Air Force aircraft of all time. It had an abysmal safety record and the highest fatality rate of any aircraft in the U.S. Air Force. Over its operational career, twenty percent of all Hustlers met a harrowing end. It quickly became apparent that Hustler crews needed extensive training. Eight TB-58A were built specifically to train pilots, and maintenance was also an issue. The U.S. Air Force would learn that there is no margin for error at 1,325 miles an hour. Low speeds were equally challenging. The Hustler excelled at straight-line, high-altitude flight. At lower altitudes it did not perform as well, and the delta wing made maneuverability difficult.

It was a machine built for speed, but another fast-moving technology was also coming to the fore: the missile. The U.S. Air Force needed to decide if a supersonic Mach 2 bomber like the B-58 Hustler was really needed when a missile could be launched and reach the same target, while keeping the aircraft away from harm. Unfortunately, for the Hustler, the answer would be no.

Douglas A3D Skywarrior

As the Cold War ramped up, the U.S. Air Force and Navy were in disagreement over which branch of the armed services was better equipped to oversee nuclear warfare. The air force believed the best way to deliver a nuclear strike was from an intercontinental bomber like its B-36. The navy, on the other side of the argument, was moving forward with the development of its first supercarrier, the USS *United States*.

In 1947 the U.S. Navy's Bureau of Aeronautics issued a request for a jet-powered bomber expressly for use on a supercarrier. A combat radius of 4,000 miles and the ability to carry a 10,000-pound nuclear device were both essential requirements, and because the new aircraft was to be used on a ship, albeit a supership, the weight still had to be kept below 100,000 pounds. The weight restriction and the need to arm a nuclear device in flight were immutable factors that made designing the navy's first twin-engine strategic jet bomber challenging.

Douglas answered the call, as did North American and Curtiss. The design team at Douglas was guided by master engineers Ed Heinemann and Leo Devlin, creators of the Douglas AD Skyraider. Keen to the design challenges, the team decided on a 36-degree swept-back-wing aircraft with a crew of three (pilot, bombardier/navigator, gunner). The wing was mounted high on the fuselage to allow for a large bomb bay that was easily accessed from the crew's cockpit area. Heinemann, sensitive to the decisions being made about nuclear deployment, encouraged the design team to keep the weight lower than the 100,000-pound allowance, correctly suspecting that the supercarrier class would never materialize.

In March 1949 the navy ordered two prototypes from Douglas, plus an additional airframe for wind tunnel and static tests. The prototype aircraft were designed to weigh 68,000 pounds—well below the navy's weight specification. This meant the aircraft could comfortably operate from the deck of a Midway-class carrier. True to speculation, the USS *United States* and the supercarrier idea were both dead in the water by April 1949.

After several years of development, the first prototype flew on October 28, 1952. Designated XA3D-1, many decisions had been made to maintain the aircraft's weight. Still, at the time it was the largest naval aircraft to operate on an aircraft carrier. Once on deck, it would earn the nickname the "Whale." Flight evaluations quickly showed how underpowered the Westinghouse J40 engines were. As a result, both prototypes were upgraded to Pratt & Whitney J57s. Flight evaluation continued.

The first production variant was the A3D-1. Forty-nine were built. After 1962 it would be called A-3A under the newly unified designation system. The Pratt & Whitney J57 jet engine had 10,000 pounds of static thrust times two. Additional jet-assisted takeoff (JATO) rockets offered another several pounds of thrust. An A3D-1 Skywarrior could take off from a smaller Essex-class carrier. The aircraft had a tall swept-vertical tail that folded for storage, two 20-mm cannons in the tail that were operated by a radar-controlled firing mechanism, and an internal bomb bay that could hold 12,000 pounds. Five were refitted for reconnaissance.

The next variant was the most produced version; 164 were built. Of these, 123 had more powerful engines, a redesigned bomb bay, and structural adjustments for added strength; twenty were equipped to provide in-flight fuel; another twenty-one were identifiable by a redesigned tail and radome. Over time, many A3D-2s, designated A-3B after 1962, were updated to include newer electronic countermeasures equipment or in-flight refueling provisions.

Over the course of the program, 282 Skywarriors were built to a specific purpose, including electronic countermeasures, photographic reconnaissance, and as training aircraft. The Skywarrior was used in Vietnam for bombing and, more importantly, as an aerial refueling tanker—a role that is credited with assisting hundreds of aircraft.

The Skywarrior served until 1991. Some surplus Skywarriors continued to be flown long after 1991. Its weight was the secret to its success. Had it

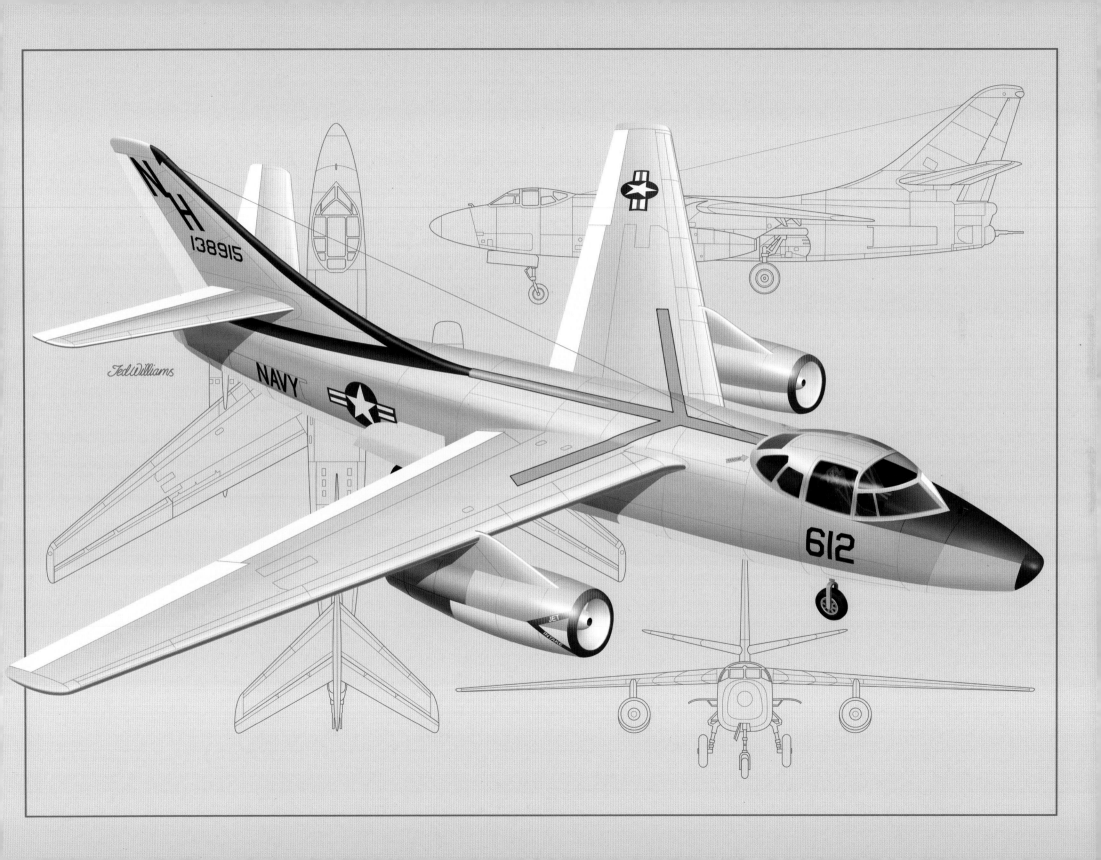

ABOVE: A Douglas B-66 Destroyer takes
on fuel from a Boeing KB-50 Tanker.
The B-66 was developed from the
Skywarrior for the U.S. Air Force.
It was the first air force bomber that
was capable of in-flight refueling.

Douglas A3D-1 Specifications

Type: Attack bomber
Crew: Three
Power plant: Two Pratt & Whitney J57-P-10
engines with 12,400 pounds of thrust each
Performance: Maximum speed, 610 miles
per hour; service ceiling, 41,000 feet;
maximum range, 2,100 miles
Weight: Empty, 39,409 pounds; maximum
takeoff weight, 82,000 pounds
Dimensions: Span, 72 feet, 6 inches;
length, 76 feet, 4 inches; height, 22 feet,
9 inches; wing area, 812 square feet
Armament: Two 20-mm cannons and
12,000 pounds of bombs

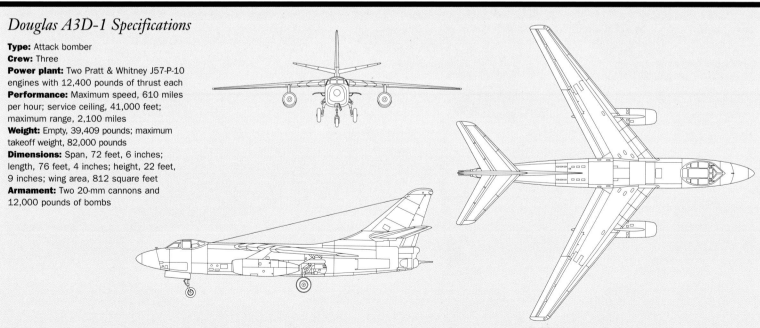

been as heavy as intended, it would have met the same fate as the USS *United States*. Yet keeping the Skywarrior light was also its downfall. The aircraft was not designed with an ejection system. To save weight, it was built with only an escape chute for the crew.

The Skywarrior was a crossover hit. The U.S. Air Force took the airframe and developed its own land-based bomber and reconnaissance versions called the B-66 Destroyer. It was a replacement for the Douglas A-26 Invader.

At first, only five RB-66As were built for reconnaissance. Another 145 of a day-and-night reconnaissance variant were built in 1953. Then, sixty-two B-66Bs were procured in 1956. It would be the U.S. Air Force's last tactical bomber. Between 1955 and 1957, thirty-six RB-66Cs and thirty-six WB-66Ds were delivered to perform all-weather reconnaissance. They were installed with specialized surveillance and radar equipment.

BELOW: An A3D-2 (A-3B) from Heavy Attack Squadron Eleven (VAH-11) lands aboard the USS *Independence* (CVA-62). A Landing Signal Officer (LSO) on the LSO platform helps the pilot set up his approach using colorful paddles to communicate the aircraft's glide slope and angle of attack.

The last Destroyer variant was the EB-66E. It had equipment for electronic countermeasures, including jamming equipment. The EB-66E was used in Vietnam; however, it was replaced by "Wild Weasel" aircraft. In all 294 Destroyers were built for the U.S. Air Force, but they had a shorter service life than the naval version.

No doubt about it, the Douglas A3D Skywarrior/B-66 Destroyer was a very successful aircraft. It is interesting to note that an aircraft built because the air force and navy couldn't get along came to have an operational career with both branches.

Douglas A4D Skyhawk

On the wings of the Skywarrior, Douglas continued its line of "Sky"-themed bombers. But unlike the whale-like Skywarrior, the Skyhawk was an unusually small, light attack bomber. Incredibly versatile, the Douglas A4D Skyhawk could accommodate a large and varied payload.

Ed Heinemann was an advocate for the development of lightweight, nimble bombers at a time when big was in. After World War II and into the 1950s, most new military aircraft designs were large; two noteworthy examples were the intercontinental B-36 and the B-52. Despite the Skywarrior's distinction as being one of the largest American carrier bombers, Ed Heinemann worked with his team to shave unnecessary weight from the big aircraft. As much a businessman as an engineer, Heinemann knew bigger aircraft were more expensive and had performance limitations. Heinemann envisioned a carrier-based attack bomber with the ability to deliver a nuclear device that weighed less than 30,000 pounds.

In 1952 Heinemann presented his idea to the Bureau of Aeronautics. The navy required 500 miles per hour, a 345-mile combat radius, and the ability to carry 2,000 pounds of bombs. Douglas delivered a proposal for a tiny aircraft of only 8,286 pounds that exceeded all requirements. To develop his "hot rod," as it became known, Heinemann urged the project team, led by Ben Collins, to consider weight-reducing solutions with every aspect of design.

For example, the wing was a delta wing with a span of only twenty-seven feet. Since the span was so short, the wing did not need to fold for carrier stowage; it was the first carrier aircraft since the Douglas SBD Dauntless without folding wings. The smaller delta wing and the absence of a folding mechanism saved weight, as did the redesigned ejection seat and power-generation systems. The designers also experimented with newer construction materials and technologies that were not as heavy.

The XA4D-1 prototype flew in June 1954. Nineteen evaluation models followed. The prototype was underpowered; as a result, subsequent models received the Wright J65 turbojet with 7,700 pounds of static thrust. Further flight-testing also led to slight alterations to improve airframe structures.

The first production model was the A4D-1; 165, including the evaluation examples, were built. All of them were delivered to naval and Marine Corps units by 1957. The A4D-1 could carry 5,000 pounds of nuclear weapons or three drop tanks with up to an additional 800 gallons of fuel on under-wing pylons. Armament included two 20-mm cannons. In 1955 a Skyhawk set a

VA-153 Blue Tail Flies

RIGHT: This Skyhawk carries two Bullpup A missiles at the outboard positions, 12 250-pound bombs on multiple racks mid wing, and six 500-pound bombs at the centerline. Scores of other combinations were possible. For its size, the Skyhawk could lift an impressive amount of ordnance.

OPPOSITE: The diminutive size of the A4D Skyhawk belies its capabilities as an effective attack aircraft. The brainchild of Douglas Aircraft designer Ed Heinemann, the A4D was a replacement for the Skyraider. The little delta wing aircraft could outperform the Sykraider in every category, especially in speed and heavy weapons load. This performance earned it the nickname "Heinemann's Hot Rod." This A-4C is shown in the markings of VA-153 Blue Tail Flies serving aboard the USS *Coral Sea*, 1961–1966.

new speed record of 695 miles per hour, surpassing the record previously held by the North American F-86 Sabre—a remarkable feat for an attack bomber.

There were 542 of an improved A4D-2 built with enhancements to the tail structure to reduce the vibration that occurred at higher speeds. Other changes included an improvement to the ejection seat, the inclusion of more sophisticated navigation and bombing systems, more powerful J65 turbojets, and equipment to accept or offer fuel in-flight.

The next variant was modified to function in all-weather and night conditions. Designated the A4D-2N, 638 were built with radar, autopilot, and a bombing system. All this equipment brought the Skyhawk's weight up to 9,146 pounds, which was still lower than the average attack bomber of its day.

The next variant built in quantity was the A4D-5, or A-4E. In 1962 the U.S. Navy adopted the unified designation system prescribed by the Department of Defense. All Skyhawks were reordered as A-4A (A4D-1), A-4B (A4D-2), and A-4C (A4D-2N). The A-4E, formerly the A4D-5, was powered by a Pratt & Whitney J52 with 8,500 pounds of static thrust. It was updated to carry conventional bombs. Five hundred were built. The last naval production Skyhawk for attack was the A-4F; 147 were built, many to replace equipment losses during the Vietnam War.

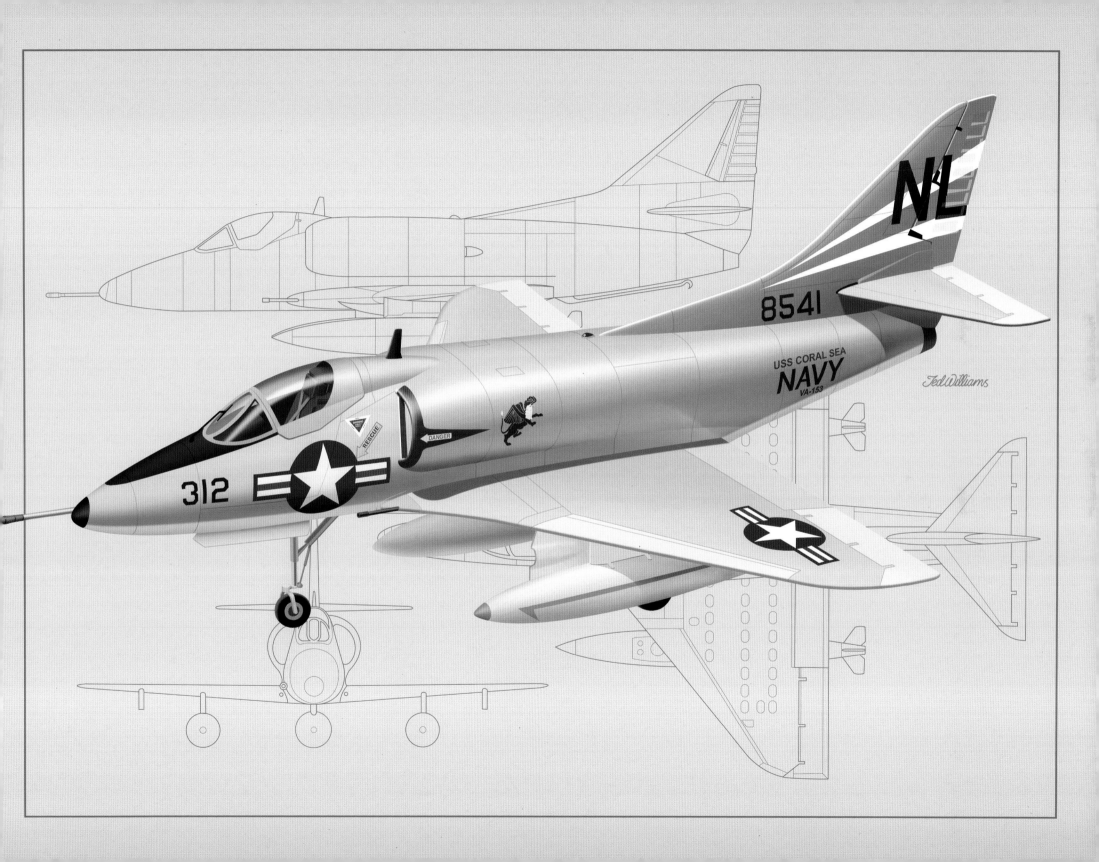

Other variants were tested and built. A two-seat version was attempted in 1964. Several additional variants were developed for specialized purposes such as electronic warfare, training, the U.S. Marine Corps, and for military export to Argentina, Australia, Israel, Kuwait, Malaysia, New Zealand, and Singapore. In all, between 1954 and 1979, 2,960 Skyhawks were built, in twenty-nine variants.

The Skyhawk was used extensively during the Vietnam War. It was used to destroy targets of tactical significance, such as enemy installations, power plants, and bridges, as well as for close ground support. Employed throughout the entire conflict, the Skyhawk was the most-used American aircraft in Southeast Asia. Senator John McCain, III, a Skyhawk pilot in 1967, became a prisoner of war after ejecting from a Skyhawk on his twenty-third mission.

BELOW: A formation of Skyhawks from Attack Squadron Seventy-Six (VA-76), known as the "Spirits," fly over the USS *Enterprise* (CVAN-65). During the Vietnam conflict, the Skyhawk was a versatile attack aircraft, flying more bombing missions than any other navy aircraft.

The Skyhawk was also used in other military conflicts around the world, including Operation Desert Storm in 1991.

A nontraditional attack bomber, the Skyhawk adapted well to assignments atypical for an attack bomber. From 1974 to 1986, the navy's Blue Angels' flight-demonstration team flew the A-4F Skyhawk II. Its maneuverability was also put to use with the navy's Top Gun program where it played the part of a Soviet MiG-21 in aerial exercises.

The Skyhawk was operational with the U.S. Navy until 2003. It is an amazing testament to Ed Heinemann's career and his foresight and deep understanding of how an attack-bombing aircraft should function. Using the events of the Korean War as a primer, he was able to engineer an aircraft that was useful, and able to keep pace with technology and the changing face of conflict, for more than fifty years.

LEFT: A Skyhawk, loaded with six 500-pound bombs, takes off for a bombing mission from the flight deck of the USS *Intrepid* on November 3, 1968.

BELOW: A ground crewman secures a bomb to an A-4 from Marine Air Group Twelve (MAG-12) at Chu Lai, Vietnam, December 1967. The Marines, who relied on the small but indispensable Skyhawk for ground support, called it the "Mighty Midget."

Douglas A-4C Specifications

Type: Attack bomber
Crew: One
Power plant: One Wright J65 engine with 8,400 pounds of thrust
Performance: Maximum speed, 649 miles per hour; service ceiling, 42,250 feet; maximum range, 1,140 miles
Weight: Empty, 9,146 pounds; maximum take-off weight, 22,500 pounds
Dimensions: Span, 27 feet, 6 inches; length, 39 feet, 4 inches; height, 15 feet; wing area, 260 square feet
Armament: Two 20-mm cannons and 8,000 pounds of bombs

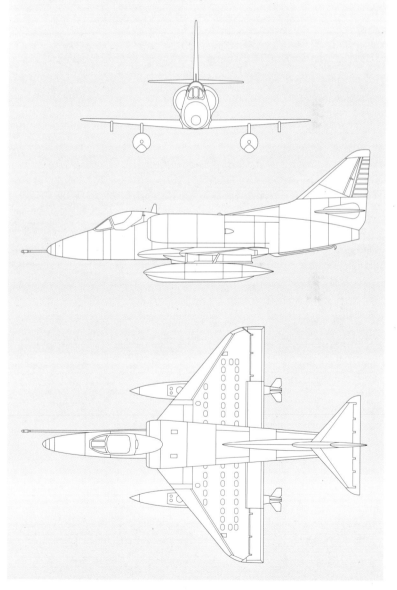

Grumman A-6 Intruder

The Grumman A-6 Intruder arose from a 1957 navy effort to find a replacement for the Douglas AD Skyraider. The competition was fierce: Vought, North American, Martin, Lockheed, Grumman, Douglas, Boeing, and Bell all applied. The U.S. Navy's requirements called for an all-weather day-and-night two-place bomber with a long range and aptitude at low-level attack.

The Grumman proposal ultimately won the bid. The design for the Intruder emphasized the ability to carry payloads versus raw speed—design thinking completely opposite from the Douglas Skyhawk, another naval attack bomber commencing production in the 1950s. Where the Skyhawk was compact, fast, and maneuverable, the Grumman was heavy, slower, and more conventional. Empty, the Grumman design had the weight of three A4Ds, but it would prove to be just as successful as it carved a niche in the activities over Southeast Asia.

In 1958 the Grumman design proceeded to a mock-up stage, during which changes and improvements were initiated. Eight evaluation models were ordered. By 1960 they began flight testing. The first to fly was powered by two Pratt & Whitney J52s, each with 8,500 pounds of static thrust that could take the aircraft to a comfortable cruising speed of 481 miles per hour.

The design of the aircraft was defined by mid-mounted 25-degree swept-back wings with a single-slotted flap the length of the entire trailing edge. The wings could fold to reduce the length of the 53-foot span for easier carrier stowage. The Intruder's crew, a pilot and bombardier/navigator, sat on ejection seats positioned side by side under a sliding canopy. The nose was reserved for the advanced radar equipment.

The Intruder was originally designed to have speed brakes, but they proved to be entirely too problematic. Many alterations were attempted, yet the best solution was the complete removal of any speed-brake mechanism from all later models.

The evaluation period was lengthy. The Intruder was designed to use the new digital integrated attack and navigation equipment (DIANE) avionics system. DIANE was created so crews could deliver ordnance without taking attention away from the cockpit, foreshadowing the more advanced heads-up display systems. Problems with the delivery of DIANE slowed the completion of the first production model, the A2F-1; however, the technical problems were eventually overcome and Intruders began entering the fleet in 1963. The advent of sophisticated electronic systems brought many advantages, as well as

VMA-242

RIGHT: An EA-6A Intruder stationed with Marine Composite Reconnaissance Squadron One (VMCJ-1) refuels in a revetment at Da Nang, South Vietnam, January 1970.

OPPOSITE: The Grumman A-6 Intruder became the U.S. Navy and Marine Corps's frontline all-weather/night attack aircraft. The Intruder's longer range, capability to carry heavy weapon loads, and its ability to fly in all weather conditions made it an important part of naval air tactics during the Vietnam War. The A-6 served in various roles for over thirty-five years with the last Intruders retiring in 1997. This Marine Corps A-6 shows the markings of All Weather Attack Squadron VMA-242, stationed at Da Nang, South Vietnam, 1966.

a more complex transitional period. Aircraft designers needed time to invent and incorporate the new systems, just as the pilots and crews needed to be trained how to operate them. New technology extended to more advanced weaponry, such as missiles and radar-seeking devices.

The A2F-1 was redesignated as the A-6A in 1962 to conform to the new numbering system; 488 were built and easily identifiable by the prominent, fixed refueling probe mounted in front of the cockpit. Between 1965 and 1970 a limited number of Intruders were modified to complement the A-6A. Nineteen A-6Bs were outfitted to detect and suppress surface-to-air missiles during daylight operations. These had specialized equipment onboard to track radar transmissions and a complex target identification and acquisition system (TIAS). The A-6B could carry the AGM-78 Standard ARM anti-radiation missile. Another twelve of the original A-6As were modified for night-only operations. This night version, the A-6C, was used during the Vietnam War along with the other Intruder variants.

The Intruder also converted easily to a refueling tanker. Designated KA-6D, ninety A-6As were modified to offer fuel midair. The tanker version acquired the nickname "Buddy." A versatile aircraft, the Marine Corps had another twenty-seven EA-6As developed to use electronic devices, such as radar-jamming equipment that could suppress enemy electronic activity and surveillance systems.

In 1970 the improved A-6E variant was introduced. It contained a host of new and updated electronic weapon-delivery systems including a sophisticated computer. The A-6E was powered by two uprated Pratt & Whitney J52 jet engines with 9,300 pounds of static thrust. It could carry up to 18,000 pounds of conventional, nuclear or missile ordnance on external hard points under the wing and fuselage. The Intruder was not equipped with cannons.

Over the course of its production, the A-6E received a multitude of upgrades to include emerging technologies such as carrier aircraft inertial navigation system (CAINS), target recognition attack multisensor (TRAM), and forward-looking infrared (FLIR) sensor. In 1988 most A-6Es were refitted with a wing made of an epoxy-and-graphite composite to relieve fatigue. A weapons systems improvement program was also instituted to continue the modernization of the Intruder's electronic systems. An A-6F Intruder II variant and A-6G variant were considered, but not accepted for production.

BELOW: Pre-flight check of an A-6 Intruder with Attack Squadron Eighty Five (VA-85), known as the "Black Falcons," aboard the USS *Kitty Hawk* (CVA-63) on station in the South China Sea, January, 1966. This Intruder has successfully completed fifty missions over Vietnam.

Another aircraft called the Grumman EA-6A Prowler was developed from an Intruder airframe that was strengthened and lengthened by five feet to carry more men and equipment. The Prowler was a four-place aircraft with equipment for advanced electronic weaponry systems. The crew was increased to include a pilot and three officers to operate the sophisticated systems. An EA-6B followed; it carried the High–speed Anti-Radiation (HARM) missile. The Prowler is still in service with the Marine Corps, with upgrades scheduled in the coming years.

The Intruder and its many variants distinguished itself as a workhorse in Vietnam. It also served in conflicts in Lebanon, Grenada, and Libya, as well as in Operation Desert Storm. The U.S. Navy retired the Grumman A-6 Intruder in 1997. The Marine Corps used the Intruder until 1993, when it was replaced by the F/A-18 Hornet.

The Grumman A-6 Intruder has been called ugly by some, but it served admirably for decades, adapting to changing technology over its long career.

TOP LEFT: This photograph displays the various types of ordnance carried by the A-6. During the Vietnam War, Intruders delivered more ordnance than B-52 heavy bombers.

TOP RIGHT: An Aviation Structural Mechanic lubricates the boarding platform of an EA-6B Prowler from Electronic Attack Squadron 136 (VAQ-136), known as the "Gauntlets," aboard the USS *Kitty Hawk* (CV-63), May 2008.

Grumman A-6A Intruder Specifications

Type: Attack bomber
Crew: Two
Power plant: Two Pratt & Whitney J52 engines with 9,300 pounds of thrust each
Performance: Maximum speed, 646 miles per hour; service ceiling, 40,250 feet; maximum range, 1,350 miles
Weight: Empty, 25,298 pounds; maximum takeoff weight, 53,700 pounds
Dimensions: Span, 53 feet; length, 54 feet, 9 inches; height, 16 feet, 2 inches; wing area, 529 square feet
Armament: 15,000 pounds of ordnance

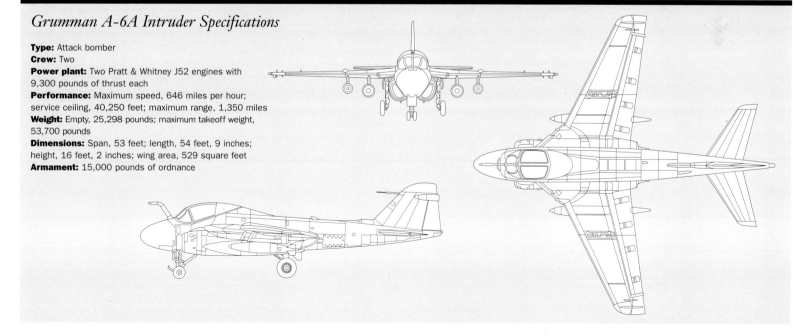

Lockheed S-3A Viking

In 1966 the U.S. Navy solicited the aviation manufacturing community for a new aircraft to replace the Grumman S-2 Tracker, which was a well-used, but outdated, propeller-driven search-and-attack antisubmarine aircraft. By the 1960s the Soviet navy had propagated the use of nuclear submarines. The equipment on the Tracker was quickly rendered insufficient; it could not locate the new, stealthy submarines, and its performance was below the standards set by the jet age. To oppose the threat presented by the Cold War, the U.S. Navy needed a new antisubmarine aircraft that was jet-powered with support for newer surveillance and tracking equipment that could detect nuclear vessels.

In 1969 a proposal from the design team of Lockheed, the Vought division of LTV (Ling-Temco-Vought), and the Univac Federal Systems Division of Sperry Rand Corporation was selected to provide a next-generation search-and-attack antisubmarine aircraft to the U.S. Navy. It was an engineering dream team, each company supplying its best work: from Lockheed, a sturdy airframe and seamless project management; from LTV, carrier-rated landing gear and accessories; and from Univac, its state-of-the art electronics systems. North American Rockwell, McDonnell Douglas, Grumman, and General Dynamics also participated in the selection process, but to no avail.

The first prototype from the Lockheed team, the YS-3A, flew in January 1972. The wings were optimized for lift, which also improved the aircraft's low-speed behavior. Overall, the aircraft was specifically designed to carry a heavy load, forsaking top-end performance. The wings were mounted high (as a shoulder wing) with a 15-degree sweep. The tail also had a swept configuration. The wings folded hydraulically into an overlapping crossed configuration for maximum space savings—the sixty-eight-foot wingspan reduced to twenty-nine feet, and the top of the vertical tail folded down.

Given the name "Viking," the aircraft was manned by a pilot, copilot, and two crewmen—a TACCO (tactical coordinator) and a SENSO (sensor operator)—who operated the sophisticated avionic systems sitting in pairs side-by-side in a pressurized cockpit. Ejection seats were standard. The crew boarded the aircraft through a small hatch built into the side of the fuselage. In an emergency evacuation situation, the crew would need to remove the windows on each side of the cockpit to facilitate an escape since the entry door was small. Retractable tricycle landing gear and a refueling probe completed the design's obvious characteristics.

VSB-21 Vikings

OPPOSITE: The Lockheed Viking was originally designed to search-and-destroy enemy submarines. In 1996 the Viking's mission had changed to surface warfare and aerial refueling. It also deployed as an electronic warfare and surface surveillance platform for the carrier group. The S-3B saw combat in Operation Iraqi Freedom while making missile attacks at the port city of Basra. This Lockheed Viking served with VS-21 Vikings aboard the USS *Constellation*.

The YS-3A's innovations included two new fuel-efficient General Electric TF34 turbofan engines with 9,275 pounds of static thrust. Each turbofan engine was mounted in an under-wing pod designed by LTV. The YS-3A also contained a complex, feature-rich avionics system made up of a Univac digital processing computer, radar, and sensors that incorporated a magnetic anomaly detector (MAD), electronic support measures (ESM), and forward-looking infrared (FLIR) for advanced electronics warfare. Navigational aids included Doppler radar, UHF radios and an internal navigation system (INS). Eight YS-3As were built for evaluation, flight testing, and carrier trials.

The evaluation models tested well. The Viking was able to carry 4,000 pounds of bombs internally with another 3,000 pounds suspended on external under-wing hard points. Ordnance could consist of torpedoes, depth charges, and mines or pods containing additional countermeasures gear, rockets, and/or external tanks for 300 gallons of fuel. The aircraft was not delivered with defensive armament, such as machine guns or cannons.

The Viking demonstrated a greater range than the Grumman S-2 Tracker it had been designed to replace. The new Lockheed aircraft could easily cover more than 2,000 miles on one sortie, a valuable asset for a search-and-attack antisubmarine aircraft. Internally, the fuel needed to enable this range was stored inside the wings in a space located inboard from the hinge point for the fold.

Based on its evaluations, 179 production S-3As were ordered, in addition to the first eight YS-3As. By 1978 fourteen squadrons were equipped with the Viking. The aircraft was a pilot's airplane, quite maneuverable and tolerant.

The S-3A was capable in a variety of roles. It served in the antisubmarine warfare (ASW) role as its avionics system was purposely tuned to locate the radiation signature of nuclear submarines. Other S-3As were modified to support the fleet as carrier onboard delivery (COD) aircraft which were refitted to carry cargo or up to five passengers to and from aircraft carriers. The Viking also proved to be a reliable fuel tanker for midair refueling. The ES-3 Shadow variant was developed for electronic reconnaissance. Sixteen Vikings were converted to the Shadow configuration.

In 1987 a weapons systems improvement program to upgrade the Viking was initiated. As a result, 119 in-service S-3As were improved with newer technology avionics and missile delivery systems, such as the AGM-84A Harpoon antiship cruise missile. Updated models were called S-3B.

In 1991 the S-3B was used in Operation Desert Storm, and again in 2003 for Operation Iraqi Freedom where it introduced the aircraft launching of the laser-guided Maverick missile. Also in 2003 President George W. Bush flew in an S-3B Viking from the Naval Air Station North Island in San Diego, California, to the USS *Abraham Lincoln*, which was at sea in the Pacific Ocean. He was the first United States president to experience a landing on the deck of an aircraft carrier. (Most presidential carrier visits are via a helicopter.)

By 2006 more than thirty of the S-3Bs conceived during the 1960s were still on active duty. In 2009 all remaining Vikings will be obsolete, removed from service, and replaced by the Boeing F/A-18 Super Hornet strike fighter. In service since the early-1970s, the Viking has more than earned the right to retire.

ABOVE: An S-3B Viking from Sea Control Squadron 41 (VS-41), known as the "Shamrocks," is moments away from its catapult launch from the USS *John C. Stennis* (CVN-74).

RIGHT: An S-3 Viking from the Sea Control Squadron 22 (VS-22), known as the "Checkmates," refuels another Viking during routine flight operations aboard the Nimitz-class aircraft carrier USS *George Washington* (CVN-73).

Lockheed S-3A Specifications

Type: Anti-submarine bomber
Crew: Four
Power plant: Two General Electric TF34-GE-2 engines with 9,275 pounds of thrust each
Performance: Maximum speed, 506 miles per hour; service ceiling, 35,000 feet; range 2,302 miles
Weight: Empty, 26,554 pounds; maximum takeoff weight, 52,539 pounds
Dimensions: Span, 68 feet, 8 inches; length, 53 feet, 4 inches; height, 22 feet, 9 inches; wing area, 598 square feet
Armament: Varying combination of bombs, missiles, mines, and torpedoes

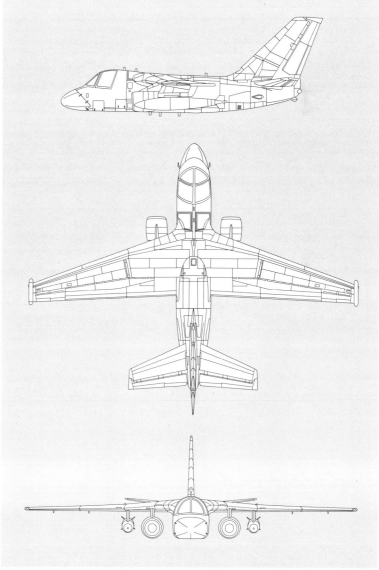

ABOVE: A crew chief of Sea Control Squadron 22 (VS-22) performs routine maintenance to an S-3B Viking on the flight deck of the Nimitz-class aircraft carrier USS *Harry S. Truman* (CVN-75).

LEFT: Ordnancemen load a Tactical Air Launched Decoy (TALD) onto an S-3B weapons pylon. The TALD is used as a target drone for the Sea Sparrow surface-to-air missile.

General Dynamics F-111 Aardvark

The General Dynamics F-111 Aardvark has a remarkable history. Depending on the account, the F-111 was either a miserable failure or a laudable success story.

In the 1950s the U.S. Air Force was looking for an all-weather fighter to replace the North American F-100 Super Sabre, McDonnell F-101 Voodoo, and Republic F-105 Thunderchief. For this new aircraft, the air force desired high technology, Mach 2 speeds, and vertical and short takeoff and landing (VSTOL) capabilities. When VSTOL was determined to be an unrealistic requirement, a revised specification was issued in 1960 for an attack aircraft with the range to cross the Atlantic Ocean and the ability to lift up to 30,000 pounds, in addition to another 1,000 pounds that were to be housed internally.

Around the same time, the U.S. Navy was seeking a new aircraft to replace its aging Vought F-8 Crusader and McDonnell F-4 Phantom. Unlike the air force's requirements, the navy wanted a two-place, carrier-based aircraft that was fitted with a missile delivery system and a large fuel capacity for extended patrolling.

In February 1961 United States Secretary of Defense Robert McNamara sent military procurement practices into an upheaval. McNamara, then a novice federal official and former business leader, determined that the best course of action for government coffers would be to develop a single aircraft to serve all branches of the United States military, including the air force, army, navy and Marine Corps. McNamara viewed his role as one of problem-solver and innovator. A career businessman not a politician, McNamara focused on finding cost savings and organizational efficiencies. To his mind, the similar aviation requests from the air force and navy were an unnecessary duplication.

The military was stunned. To complicate matters, the entire congressional procurement process was played out in the evening news, as reporters latched on to the drama fueling the controversial aircraft's development. After considerable negotiations and compromises, McNamara was persuaded to back down from the close support component required for use by the army and Marine Corps; however, he would not waver from his ideal of a single multi-role aircraft that could suit both the air force and navy's needs.

At first glance, the air force and navy requirements were poles apart. The air force's emphasis was for a fighter, while the navy wanted an aircraft that was smaller with a more rugged airframe that could withstand carrier duty. It was clear that the two branches needed to devise a way to build an

RIGHT: A look at the high-tech environment inside the cockpit of an F-111. The aircraft was not fitted with ejection seats. Instead, when the yellow-and-black ejection handle was pulled, the entire cockpit would eject from the aircraft. Parachutes would automatically deploy from the capsule, bringing the crew safely back to earth.

OPPOSITE: The F-111 was an interesting mix of mission capabilities. It was a tactical strike aircraft, a strategic bomber, a reconnaissance platform, and an electronic warfare aircraft. It was the first military aircraft to have variable geometry wings and terrain-following radar. The F-111 and its variants were in continuous service with the U.S. Air Force from 1967 to 1998. This F-111 is from the 48th Tactical Fighter Wing, 493rd Tactical Fighter Squadron known as the "Grim Reapers." This unit took part in Operation El Dorado Canyon, the 1986 attack on Libya.

aircraft they could agree upon; McNamara was firm about financing only one design.

The joint project was called TFX, Tactical Fighter Experimental. Both branches endorsed a variable geometry wing for the new aircraft, but could concur on little else. Also known as a "swing wing," the wing sweep could be repositioned to achieve optimum efficiency during varying flight conditions. It was a versatile solution for the first multi-role, multidiscipline aircraft; one that took into account each branch's operational specialty. In this case, the wings could be locked in a swept-forward position to control speeds and handling upon takeoff and landing, but switched to a swept-back configuration at higher speeds, a variable between 16 and 72.5 degrees.

Other design decisions proved to be more challenging. The air force wanted a longer, heavier aircraft than the navy could tolerate. The navy needed the TFX to comply with a set of rigid standards that included size and weight restrictions for carrier elevator dimensions plus reduced weight limitations for shorter catapult-assisted takeoffs. In addition, the air force and navy used discrete radar technology that was incompatible. To keep moving forward in the face of these obstacles, McNamara established that the air force's version of the TFX would become the F-111A, while the navy would get a slightly altered F-111B.

In September 1961 Republic, Northrop, North American, McDonnell, Lockheed, Grumman, General Dynamics, Douglas, and Boeing were offered the opportunity to supply designs for the TFX. Of the submissions, only the Boeing and General Dynamics proposals were granted further appraisal.

LN

AF
71 889

Ted Williams

General Dynamics F-111A Specifications

Type: Tactical/strategic strike aircraft

Crew: Two

Power plant: Two Pratt & Whitney TF30-P-3 engines with 18,500 pounds of thrust each

Performance: Maximum speed, 1,452 miles per hour; service ceiling, 57,000 feet; maximum range, 3,632 miles

Weight: Empty, 46,172 pounds; maximum takeoff weight, 92,657 pounds

Dimensions: Span, 32 feet swept; 63 feet extended; length, 73 feet, 6 inches; height, 17 feet, 2 inches; wing area, 525 square feet

Armament: One 20-mm cannon and up to 30,000 pounds of bombs, missiles, or extra fuel

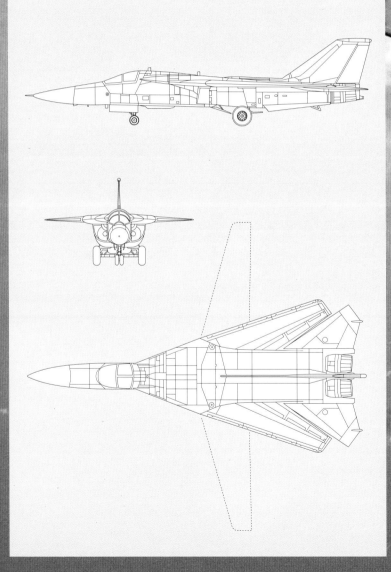

THIS PAGE: An F-111 spreads its wings to receive refuel in-flight from a KC-135R Stratotanker from the 912th Aerial Refueling Squadron. Despite its age, the aircraft performed admirably during Operation Desert Storm, flying more than 2,400 sorties against enemy targets.

OPPOSITE BOTTOM: The first public demonstration of the F-111's variable sweep wings was during its roll-out ceremony on October 15, 1964 at General Dynamics' Fort Forth facility. Here, the aircraft is shown with its wings fully extended.

RIGHT: Like all high-performance military aircraft, the F-111 could very quickly unload fuel through its aft fuel dump tube. The Aardvark could easily and safely ignite the escaping liquid. Pilots called it "dump and burn." The effect did not serve any tactical purpose, but it offered air show audiences a spectacular pyrotechnic display.

In 1962 the air force and the navy's judging bodies—the Air Force Logistics Command, the Air Force Council, and the Bureau of Naval Weapons—endorsed the Boeing design; however, Secretary McNamara and the Defense Department ultimately selected the proposal from General Dynamics, because it was less expensive. The TFX program was again a top news story as Boeing proponents unsuccessfully battled to reverse McNamara's decision to award General Dynamics the lucrative contract.

The winning General Dynamics design for the F-111A and B consisted of a uniform airframe with Pratt & Whitney turbofan TF30 engines. Both the A and B had a cockpit for two crewmen who sat beside each other (the configuration preferred by the navy), but the A was more than eight feet longer than the B version. The air force variant had General Electric and Texas Instruments radar systems, while the navy used Hughes pulse-Doppler radar, as well as Phoenix missiles from Hughes; but since General Dynamics was inexperienced with Navy requirements, it invited Grumman in to work on the navy's B version.

The first TFX to fly was an F-111A in 1964. Soon more followed. Interestingly, the per unit cost for each aircraft was more than $2 million above the estimate. As a result, significantly fewer aircraft were put into production than initially planned.

The first F-111B left the famous Bethpage Iron Works in May 1965. Evaluation models proved to be much too heavy, lacking power, and short on range. In 1968 after fruitless attempts to improve the aircraft failed, all work on the naval B variant ceased. Only seven F-111Bs were delivered.

Meanwhile, production F-111As began equipping air force squadrons in 1967. The A version went on to engender improved air force models. Of the 159 that were built, some saw service in Southeast Asia during Operation Linebacker II. Later, an improved F-111C was developed for export to Australia. In time, a D (ninety-six), E (ninety-four) and F (106) model were built, each with improvements to power plants and avionics. Both a G and H were also considered but not put into production. The F variant was used extensively in 1991 during Operation Desert Storm.

While the F-111 was originally conceived as a strategic strike aircraft/fighter bomber, it was most successful, and used most frequently, as a bomber. In addition, a series of FB-111s (fighter bombers) was also built.

The F-111 was removed from active duty in July 1996. That same year, the aircraft was conferred with the name Aardvark.

The F-111's soap-operatic upbringing was unlike anything experienced in military aviation. The concept was a tall order—building one aircraft for the air force and navy—so it's no wonder the F-111 could not make all of the people happy all of the time. The Aardvark was never able to serve the navy, but what developed, through cooperation on all levels, was a versatile aircraft that the air force used as an all-weather fighter bomber for nearly thirty years.

Republic A-10 Thunderbolt II

Named after the World War II P-47 Thunderbolt, a legendary close-support warbird, the A-10 Thunderbolt II was designed to excel in the same role as it namesake. It was also one of the first aircraft to carry the "A" for attack since 1947, when the identifier was abandoned by the air force. But most people simply know it by its popular nickname: "Warthog."

A warthog is a strong, resilient, wild beast that is characterized by its four tusks and lumpy exterior. It is easy to see the comparison to the A-10. The brawny animal's distinctive lumps offer protection during a brawl; likewise, the rugged A-10's unusually placed engine nacelles look odd but offer protection during battle. The engines are located atypically high on the fuselage and toward the rear of the aircraft. This nickname-earning characteristic protects the engines from ground fire.

Its distinctive engine placement is just one of the many reasons why the A-10 is such an effective attack bomber. The A-10 was developed around several innovative ideas and pioneering features that work together to significantly improve the aircraft's performance in the exceedingly hostile environment near ground action. All this thoughtful engineering also helps to increase the survivability of the pilot.

In 1970 the U.S. Air Force proceeded with a program called A-X (Attack Experimental) to develop an aircraft that could fly low and slow over enemy activity. In addition, the air force had a list of important criteria that included speed, maneuverability, and the ability to accurately deliver a payload and contain enough fuel to maximize loiter time over the battlefield. The new aircraft was to become the first purpose-built U.S. Air Force aircraft for close support. To meet these specific requirements, designs from Northrop and Republic were selected to compete for the contract from among the twelve submissions that came in as a response to the air force's request.

Testing of the Northrop A-9 and Republic A-10 commenced in 1972. Each company was asked to build two prototypes. In 1973 the air force awarded the A-X contract to Republic. The Republic design was judged to have better handling and greater weapon capabilities. The first six production variants, the A-10A, were available by 1975. These six underwent an intense development, test, and evaluation period to appraise and modify all aspects of the new aircraft. As a result of the exhaustive testing program, another 713 A-10s came to be built, albeit with slight modifications to extend the aircraft's capability.

BELOW: Air Force crew chiefs and jet engine mechanics from the 51st Maintenance Squadron perform a complete system overhaul on an A-10 during an inspection at Osan Air Base, Korea. The aging A-10s are routinely inspected for cracks, leaks and chafing.

OPPOSITE: The A-10 Thunderbolt II was named after the famous P-47 Thunderbolt fighter-bomber of World War II. Its ungainly appearance, however, has earned it the moniker "Warthog." Its ability to operate in rugged tactical airfields, its superior maneuverability at low speeds, and its ability to absorb punishment from ground fire explain the reason for the unconventional planform. Not to mention it mounts a humongous 30-mm rapid firing Gatling gun—the most powerful cannon ever flown. This A-10 is painted in modern non-specular gray paint with the markings of the 23rd Tactical Fighter Wing, 74th Tactical Fighter Squadron.

Republic Aviation was launched in 1939 when Alexander de Seversky, a Russian immigrant and the force behind the Seversky P-35, was thrown out of the company he founded in 1931. Seversky had been immersed in aviation since childhood; he was also responsible for recruiting Alexander Kartveli, who later achieved great success at Republic. While Seversky would go on to become a celebrated advisor on the topic of air superiority, the newly reorganized Republic Aviation began work on the P-47. The original P-47 Thunderbolt, the F-84 Thunderjet, and the F-105 Thunderchief were developed and credited to Republic and Kartveli's genius.

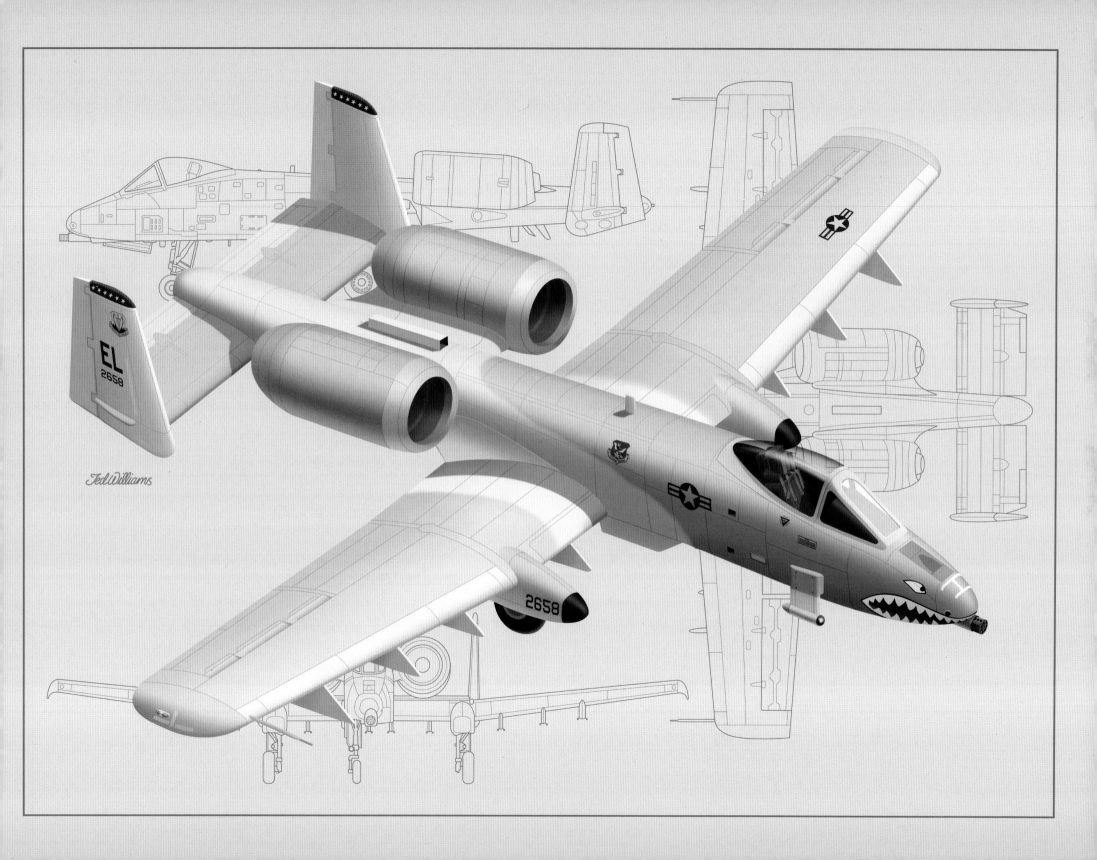

Ted Williams

In 1965 Republic surrendered control to Fairchild, becoming the Republic Aviation Division of Fairchild Hiller. The division became Fairchild Republic in 1973; it is the organization recognized for building the A-10.

Notable features of the A-10A include a Gatling gun in the nose, the high and wide engine placement, and an impenetrable titanium-plated cockpit for the pilot, plus the ability to take off and land on short or rough landing areas. Fuel is housed in self-sealing tanks with an advanced foam system, and the aircraft can continue to be flown with an incapacitated hydraulic system and a massive amount of battle damage—these are the design features that help the aircraft get near the front lines to perform its close air support duties, while safeguarding the pilot. Also, maintenance is streamlined, since many of the aircraft parts are interchangeable left or right, and field maintenance is enhanced by the accessibility to major components. In all, the A-10 is an incredibly adaptable warrior.

The A-10's primary weapon is the 30-mm Avenger Gatling gun with an 1,800-rounds-per-minute rate of fire. With the big gun's mix of armored piercing incendiary (API) that contains depleted uranium and high explosive incendiary (HEI) ammunition, it is capable of piercing enemy tanks. As equipped, the A-10 is an incomparable gun platform. It can also carry missiles and bombs, such as AIM-9 Sidewinder and AGM-65 Maverick missiles and Mk-82 and Mk-84 bombs, on pylons under the fuselage and wing. In all, up to a 16,000-pound payload is possible.

The A-10 is powered by twin General Electric TF-34-100/A turbofan engines with 9,000 pounds of static thrust each. The aircraft's structure employs aluminum alloys. The A-10 makes use of an avionic suite that includes a heads-up display (HUD) that provides the pilot with all pertinent flight conditions data, sophisticated navigation devices with a Global Positioning System (GPS), and electronic countermeasures equipment. It also has a night vision imaging system (NVIS) so the pilot can carry out night missions.

In 1991 the A-10 participated in Operation Desert Storm, as well as more recently in Operation Enduring Freedom and Operation Iraqi Freedom.

In 2007 the A-10 was selected to undergo an update for newer technologies. This version is known as the A-10C. The "Precision Engagement" upgrade entails the addition of a targeting system to allow the A-10 to deploy the JDAM, joint direct attack munitions, enhanced cockpit displays, as well improvements to many of the aircraft's computerized systems. Modifications continue. The U.S. Air Force is committed to keeping the A-10 combat ready through to 2028.

BELOW: The A-10 is a highly maneuverable, tactical, close air support aircraft capable of delivering rockets and bombs with pin-point accuracy.

OPPOSITE TOP: The GAU-8/A Avenger is the largest and most powerful cannon ever used on a U.S. combat aircraft; it is capable of firing 1,800 30-mm rounds per minute. The A-10 was specifically designed around this massive gun.

OPPOSITE BOTTOM: Ground crew members of the 354th Tactical Fighter Wing prepare to load 30-mm rounds using the high-speed ammunition loader.

Republic A-10A Specifications

Type: Ground attack bomber

Crew: One

Power plant: Two General Electric TF34-GE-100 engines with 9,000 pounds of thrust each

Performance: Maximum speed, 518 miles per hour; service ceiling, 44,200 feet; maximum range, 2,454 miles

Weight: Empty, 24,959 pounds; maximum takeoff weight, 50,000 pounds

Dimensions: Span, 57 feet, 6 inches extended; length, 53 feet, 4 inches; height, 17 feet, 8 inches; wing area, 506 square feet

Armament: One 30-mm Gatling gun and 16,000 pounds of bombs, mines, munitions, missiles, countermeasures, and equipment

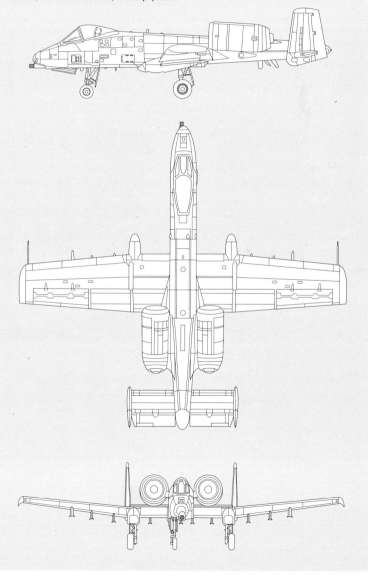

Rockwell B-1 Lancer

The B-1 is the last of the conventional heavy bombers and a well-tuned weapon delivery system. Still active, it has participated in several military operations and it is forecasted to be in service through 2030.

The B-1's story starts in the early 1960s. The air force wanted to replace the Boeing B-52 Stratofortress, which had its origins in World War II, with a new long-range strategic bomber. During this period of world history, the United States was embroiled in the Cold War with the Soviet Union. Both superpowers were locked in an arms race that included nuclear capabilities. To match the Soviet threat, the new U.S. Air Force bomber was charged with having the ability to deliver a nuclear weapon over Russian soil.

The air force approved the initial concept for the B-1 from North American Rockwell in 1970. The Rockwell-Standard Corporation got its toehold in the aviation industry in 1967 after a merger with North American, forming North American Rockwell, which later took the name Rockwell International. In 1996 Rockwell sold all of its aviation, space, and defense holdings to Boeing.

By 1974 the first completed B-1A prototype was ready for evaluation. Three more B-1As were delivered, but by 1977 the entire program was canceled, mostly due to the exorbitant $280 million price tag for each prototype and to changing political ideologies. Production B-1As were never built, however, in 1981 attention was refocused on the prototypes. In 1982 the air force placed an order for 100 of a new variant called B-1B.

Like the General Dynamics F-111 Aardvark, the B-1B has a swing wing to optimize the lift and drag required for different flight conditions at takeoff and landing, and for operation at supersonic speeds. The B-1B also introduced stealth technology, including radar absorbent material (RAM), electronic jamming equipment and design innovations that worked to minimize the aircraft's radar cross-section, and greater weapon stowage capacity. The additional payload increased the aircraft's total weight, in turn, bringing its speeds down. The B-1B could only achieve Mach 1.2, while the B-1A could exceed Mach 2. This concession was deemed acceptable in light of the bomber's priority role as a nuclear weapons delivery platform.

The B-1B was markedly improved from the earlier A variant—structurally and technologically, but it was still as expensive. The first B-1B was delivered in 1984 with the bulk of the order delivered between 1985 and 1988. The B-1B benefited from an improved avionic suite and radar system, but it experienced teething problems that were in contrast with the B-52's stalwart nature. Scores

RIGHT: A B-1 under construction at Air Force Plant 42 in Palmdale, California. The B-1 defied its critics, becoming a highly versatile multi-mission weapons system. The B-1 uses sophisticated avionics and navigation. In 2007, Boeing was awarded a contract to upgrade the aircraft to incorporate software enhancements, which will enable the B-1 to keep pace with technology.

OPPOSITE: The B-1B Lancer offers a most pleasing shape with its blended wing body and variable-sweep wing. It is hard to imagine that this graceful machine is an efficient weapon of war, but efficient it is. The Lancer's semi-stealthy airframe can deliver a variety of weapons, both nuclear and conventional, fly long intercontinental missions without refueling, while advanced electronic countermeasures enhance its survivability. The first B-1B "Star of Abilene" was delivered in 1985 and the 100th and final Lancer was delivered in 1988. The U.S. Air Force projects the useful service life of the B-1B Lancer through 2030.

of B-1Bs were often grounded with expensive maintenance concerns that were not completely overcome until upgrades and changes in the 1990s.

The B-1B is powered by four General Electric F101-GE-102 afterburning turbofan engines with 30,000 pounds of thrust each. It can travel intercontinental distances up to 7,500 miles without refueling. For longer missions, the bomber has the capability to refuel in flight.

In 1991 treaties between the United States and Russia barred the B-1B from carrying nuclear weapons. To preserve the B-1B fleet and to comply with the treaties, the air force instituted the Conventional Mission Upgrade Program to refit the nuclear bomber to carry conventional bombs and missiles. As a result, because of an inventive moveable bulkhead, a B-1B can actually carry a larger payload (75,000 pounds) than the Boeing B-52 Stratofortress, and it has the largest internal dimensions of all current American bombers. The B-1B's internal bomb bay is complemented by six external hard points capable of carrying another 59,000 pounds.

The Conventional Mission Upgrade Program continued into the mid-2000s. Other updates in 2004 and 2005 replaced aging systems with newer technologies to improve the B-1B's combat readiness.

The B-1B is officially named Lancer, but it is affectionately called "Bone" (for B-1 or B-one) by air force personnel who work with the aircraft. The aircrew of four includes an aircraft commander, pilot, and two weapon systems operators (an offensive systems operator and defensive systems operator) for the aircraft's many sophisticated computerized systems.

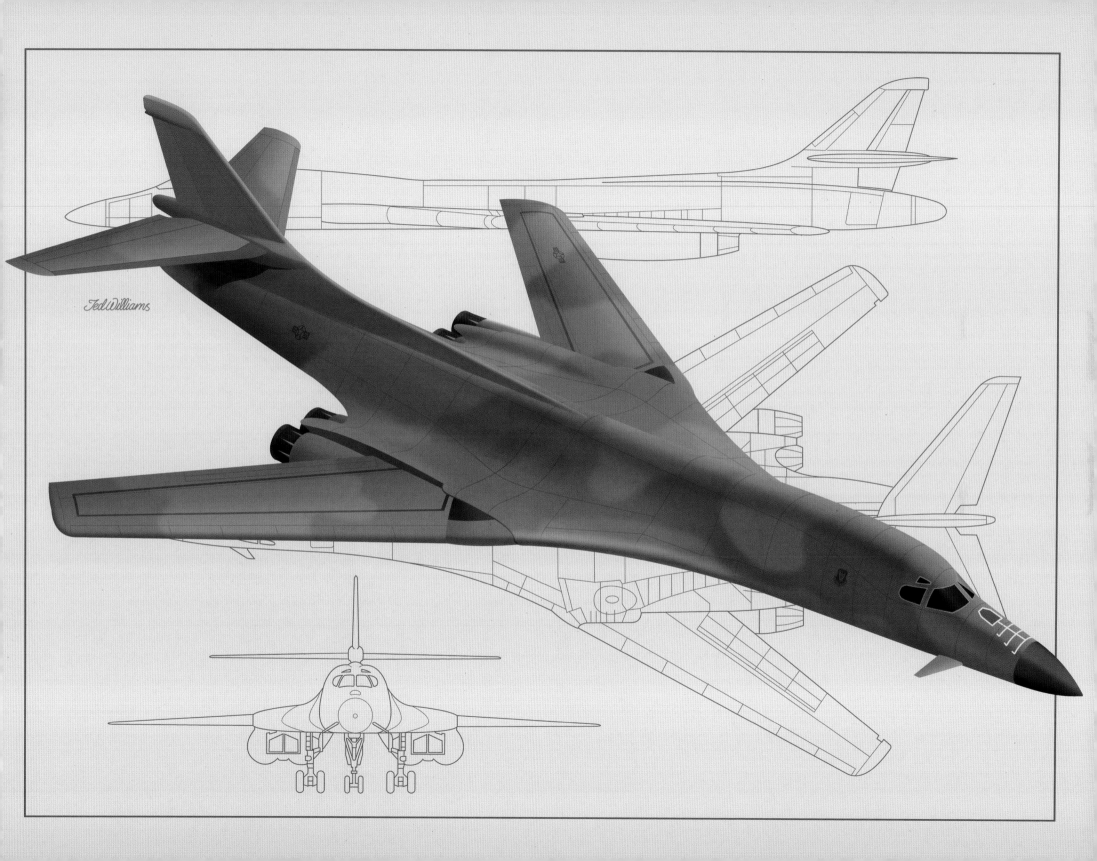

Ted Williams

Rockwell B-1B Specifications

Type: Strategic/multi-role heavy bomber

Crew: Four

Power plant: Four General Electric F101-GE-102 engines with 30,000 pounds of thrust each

Performance: Maximum speed, 900 miles per hour (Mach 1.2); service ceiling, 60,000 feet; maximum range, 7,500 miles

Weight: Empty, 192,000 pounds; maximum takeoff weight, 477,000 pounds

Dimensions: Span, 79 feet swept, 137 feet extended; length, 146 feet; height, 34 feet; wing area, 1,950 square feet

Armament: 133,800 pounds of conventional and nuclear weapons

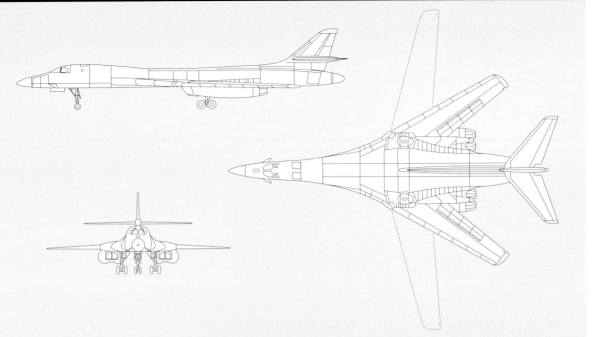

OPPOSITE: The B-1's blended wing body configuration not only makes the aircraft aerodynamically efficient, but it also adds to its stealth characteristics.

BELOW: A B-1 with its variable sweep wings fully extended. As of 2009, the B-1 Lancer is the only remaining U.S. military aircraft with variable sweep wings, outlasting the General Dynamics F-111 and Grumman F-14 Tomcat.

The modern B-1B bomber makes use of a satellite-aided GPS, Doppler radar, and an inertial navigation system, in addition to its avionics and computerized systems. These systems allow the B-1B to navigate accurately and to perform precision bombing without assistance from the ground.

The B-1B can claim at least sixty-one world records. The aircraft has been celebrated for its large payload, distance, and speed. The B-1B has also participated in combat: in 1998 during Operation Desert Fox, in 1999 during Operation Allied Force in Kosovo, and in 2001 during Operation Enduring Freedom in Afghanistan.

In 2001 the air force began a plan to decommission B-1Bs to save money since each Lancer is expensive to maintain. Thirty-three B-1Bs were scheduled to be relocated to Air National Guard bases; however, the aircraft proved to be too valuable to the air force. As a result, retired B-1Bs are being upgraded and returned to active duty. The active B-1B fleet is located at Ellsworth Air Force Base in South Dakota, and Dyess Air Force Base in Texas. The National Museum of the United States Air Force has a B-1B on display. It originated from the 7th Bomb Wing at Dyess Air Force Base.

The Rockwell/Boeing B-1B Lancer has experienced the changing tides of military attitude firsthand. Disparaged during the Carter administration, revived by Ronald Reagan, it overcame criticism to become a versatile, multi-role/multi-mission bomber that continues to serve the U.S. Air Force.

Northrop Grumman B-2 Spirit

It is only fitting that the B-2 bomber's development was shrouded in secrecy. Like the stealthy nature that defines the B-2, the program credited with creating the wholly unconventional aircraft was a top secret undertaking; as such, all development was concealed from the public, press, and any military or manufacturing personnel who lacked the appropriate security clearance. The entire operation was as protected as the Manhattan Project; even outdoor prototype testing only occurred when United States intelligence could confirm Soviet satellites were out of view.

The idea of the B-2 stealth bomber arose from the desire for an aircraft that could fly into the heart of the Soviet Union without detection; so, like the stop-and-go B-1 program, the B-2 was a product of the Cold War. (Another aircraft that benefited from advancements in detection suppression was the Lockheed F-117 Nighthawk stealth fighter.)

Stealth technology entails designing an aircraft's structure in a manner that helps to reduce the appearance of its radar cross-section and heat signature, thus making it imperceptible to enemy radar and infrared detection devices.

Today, for an aircraft to be classified as stealth, it must have the following characteristics: Primarily, it needs to project that it is a smaller object than it really is; the heat it creates during flight must be unidentifiable; and it requires a trim physical profile. A stealth aircraft also cannot carry any external stores, and its engines must operate quietly, with nominal emissions and no identifiable exhaust smoke or contrail. A stealth aircraft is, for all intents and purposes, invisible. This anonymity allows a stealth aircraft to embark on a mission without giving the enemy the forewarning necessary to launch countermeasures. Stealth is especially effective for night missions.

The Advanced Technology Bomber program, as it was first known, was kicked off by Northrop in the 1970s. Northrop, later as the Northrop Grumman Corporation, spent nearly twenty years perfecting the world's first stealth bomber. It is one of the most technologically advanced aircraft ever produced for any nation's military, and it is also the world's most expensive. The U.S. Air Force originally intended to purchase 165 of the new bomber, but at over $1 billion dollars apiece, a significantly smaller number was procured. Today, the U.S. Air Force operates a fleet of only twenty-one of the elite stealth bombers, which are stationed at Whiteman Air Force Base in Missouri.

After years of speculation and wonder, the first flight of a B-2A occurred in July 1989. The aircraft is built on the premise of Jack Northup's iconic flying wing. The aircraft does not have a traditional cylindrical fuselage or tail structure;

RIGHT: A detailed look at the retractable nose gear of the B-2 Spirit of Louisiana, which arrived at Whiteman Air Force Base in 1997. All twenty-one Spirits are operated by the 509th Bomb Wing, Whiteman AFB, Missouri.

OPPOSITE: The B-2 Spirit is a multi-role, intercontinental, heavy bomber with a "low observable" stealth planform that can deliver both nuclear and a conventional bomb load. The high aerodynamic efficiency of its blended wing configuration has a direct line to the flying wing concept Jack Northrop used in his YB-49 jet bomber in the early 1950s. To note an historical irony, the wingspan on the B-2 is exactly the same as Northrop's flying wing bomber—172 feet.

rather the entire aircraft is one large, efficient lifting body with little drag. In addition, years of research went into the development of the lightweight but strong carbon fiber and radar absorbent material (RAM) that surround the aircraft, as well as into the plastic, paint, curved body panels, and "sawtooth" shape of control surfaces on the trailing-edge of the wing—all aspects of the design that contribute to the "low-observable" profile of the aircraft.

The B-2, as it is most commonly called, is powered by four General Electric F-118-GE-100 non-afterburning turbofan engines with 19,000 pounds of thrust that are situated within the wing. The engine intake and exhaust are covered by curved hoods that mask the engines' activity. To aid in the aircraft's stealth characteristics, the exhaust flow is cooled and controlled by a series of fans and chemical additives.

The B-2 can carry up to 40,000 pounds in its two internal bomb bays, which are located inside the center of the aircraft. Even the B-2's payload is advanced. Typically, the B-2 is armed with smart bombs or guided missiles, such as the joint direct attack munition (JDAM) or joint air-to-surface standoff missile (JASSM), that both use GPS to accurately locate a target.

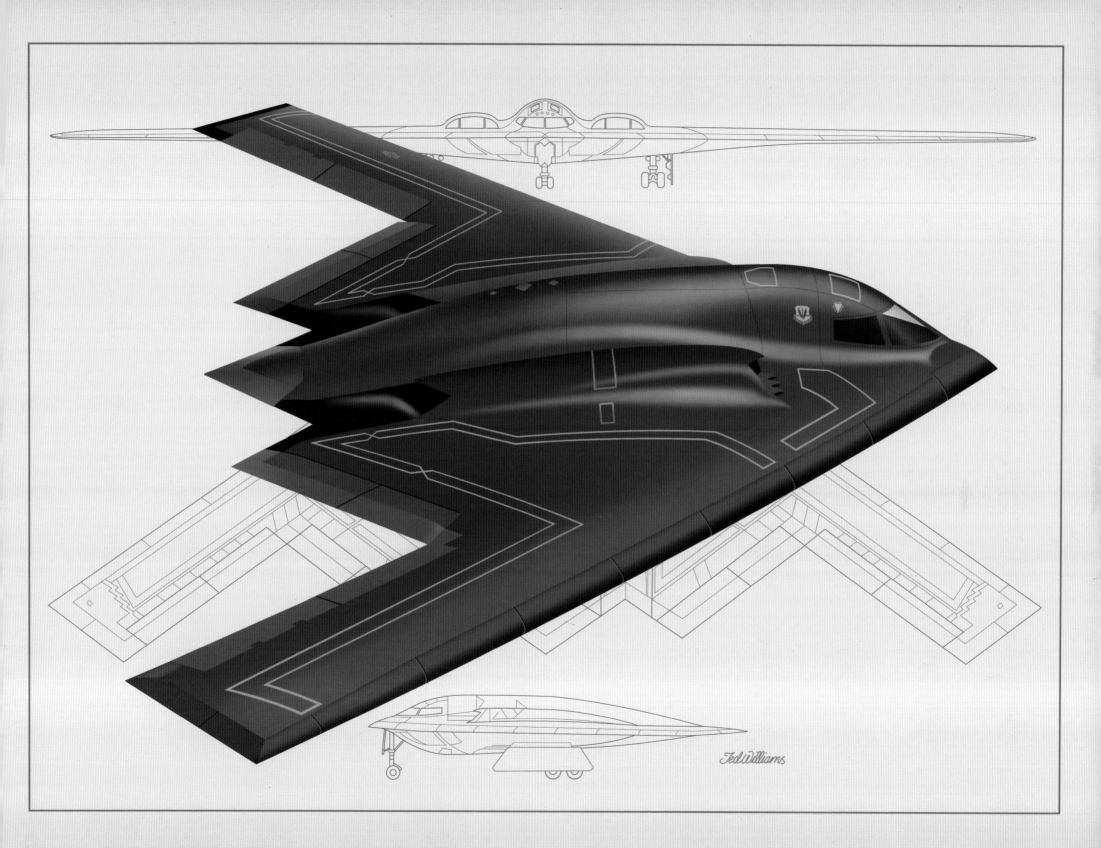

Ted Williams

The B-2 can carry either conventional or nuclear weapons. In 2007 the B-2 began a modification program to add massive ordnance penetrator (MOP), a new weapons technology from Boeing, to its capabilities. Other recent upgrades have included the inclusion of the generic weapons interface system (GWIS) that allows a B-2 to manage up to four different targets during one sortie.

A crew of two—a mission commander and pilot who are seated side-by-side on ejection seats—operate the aircraft using a series of sophisticated computer and video systems. Although the B-2's avionics suite is among the most advanced in the world, because it is a stealth bomber, the B-2 cannot communicate while in flight during a mission. Its transmissions must be undetectable, and all of its navigation and targeting must occur without any intervention from a ground source. Instead, the B-2 receives all information via GPS and military satellites. In 2007 testing began on a new radar antenna that can ignore commercial satellite activity.

The B-2 is a long-range bomber. It has an intercontinental range of at least 6,000 miles using onboard fuel stores. The B-2 can house 130,000 pounds of fuel within its wings. With in-flight refueling, a B-2 can remain in flight for nearly two consecutive days.

The U.S. Air Force began taking delivery of the B-2 in 1993. The first one was called the "Spirit of Missouri." Today the name "Spirit" applies to all B-2s. In 1999 the B-2 was called to duty over Serbia. It has also participated in Operation Enduring Freedom over Afghanistan in 2001 and in Operation Iraqi Freedom in 2003.

The air force does not plan to build any more new B-2s, but improvements to the fleet, including upgrades to the avionics suite and its radar systems, continue with the goal to keep the big bomber in service until 2020.

As political power centers shift and technology changes the way war is waged, the B-2 has been disparaged as a dinosaur from another era of military doctrine. If a missile can be launched hundreds of miles away from a target, why should the U.S. Air Force continue to maintain a fleet of expensive aircraft, such as the B-2, that requires crews to enter hostile territory? However, the B-2 remains the only heavy bomber that can fly without being seen—an invaluable asset that ensures mission success and the survivability of the crew. The air force asserts that the B-2 expense is justifiable; it claims two B-2s can do the work of seventy-five traditional bombers.

Come what may, the B-2 bomber continues to serve the U.S. Air Force. It is an engineering triumph and, for the present, the pinnacle of American bomber development.

Northrop B-2 Specifications

Type: Stealth strategic/multi-role bomber
Crew: Two
Power plant: Four General Electric F118-GE-100 engines with 19,000 pounds of thrust each
Performance: Maximum speeds, high subsonic; service ceiling, 50,000 feet; range, 6,900 miles
Weight: Empty, 153,700 pounds; maximum takeoff weight, 336,500 pounds
Dimensions: Span, 172 feet; length, 69 feet; height, 17 fee
Armament: More than 40,000 pounds of conventional and nuclear weapons

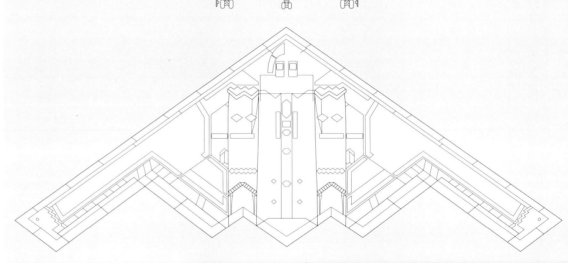

RIGHT: The B-2 Spirit of Oklahoma from Whiteman Air Force Base is participating in the Pacific U.S. Air Forces's joint and coalition exercises at Andersen Air Force Base in Guam. Weapons specialists are preparing to load a BDU-56 bomb.

ABOVE: Overhead view of the B-2 Spirit's cockpit. The aircraft's graceful appearance belies its aerodynamic instability. A Flight Control Computer with a quadruple redundant fly-by-wire system is needed to keep the B-2 in the air.

Bibliography

Books

Angelucci, Enzo. *Rand McNally Encyclopedia of Military Aircraft*. New York: Military Press, 1980.

Art, Robert J. *The TFX Decision; McNamara and the Military*. Boston, MA: Little, Brown, 1968.

Bauer, Eugene E. *Boeing in Peace and War*. Enumclaw, WA: TABA Publishing, 1990.

Bowers, Peter. *Curtiss Aircraft 1907–1947*. Annapolis, MD: Naval Institute Press, 1979.

Boyne, Walter J. *Beyond the Horizons: The Lockheed Story*. New York: St. Martin's Press, 1998.

Boyne, Walter J. *The Best of Wings*. Dulles, VA: Brassey's, Inc., 2001.

Boyne, Walter J. *The Influence of Air Power upon History*. Gretna, LA: Pelican Publishing, 2003.

Boyne, Walter J. *Weapons of Desert Storm*. Lincolnwood, IL: Publications International, 1991.

Breihan, John R., Stan Piet, and Roger S. Mason. *Martin Aircraft 1909–1960*. Santa Ana, CA: Jonathan Thompson/Publisher, 1995.

Doll, Thomas E. *SBC Helldiver in Action*. Carrollton, TX: Squadron/Signal Publications, 1995.

Douhet, Giulio, translated by Dino Ferrari. *The Command of the Air*. Washington, D.C.: Office of Air Force History, 1983.

Easterly, William M. *The Belgian Rattlesnake: The Lewis Automatic Machine Gun*. Cobourg, Ontario, Canada: Collector Grade Publications Incorporated, 1998.

Francillon, René J. *McDonnell Douglas Aircraft Since 1920: Volume I*. Annapolis, MD: Naval Institute Press, 1979.

Futrell, Robert Frank. *Ideas, Concepts, Doctrine: Basic Thinking in the United States Air Force*. Darby, PA: Diane Publishing Co., 1990.

Green, Michael. *Long Range Bombers: B-1B Lancer*. Mankato, MN: Capstone Press, 2008.

Hess, William N., Frederick A. Johnsen, and Chester Marshall. *Big Bombers of WWII*. Ann Arbor, MI: Lowe & B. Hould Publishers, 1998.

Jablonski, Edward. *Flying Fortress: The Illustrated Biography of the B-17 and the Men Who Flew Them*. New York: Doubleday & Company, Inc., 1965.

Jenkins, Dennis R. *Convair B-36 "Peacemaker"*. North Branch, MN: Specialty Press Publishers, 1999.

Johnsen, Frederick A. *Douglas A-26 Invader*. North Branch, MN: Specialty Press, 1999.

Kinzey, Bert. *SBD Dauntless: In Detail and Scale*. Waukesha, WI: Kalmbach Publishing, Co., 1995.

Knott, Richard C. *The American Flying Boat: An Illustrated History*. Annapolis, MD: Naval Institute Press, 1979.

Launius, Roger D, ed. *Innovation and the Development of Flight*. College Station, TX: Texas A&M University, 1999.

Maurer, Maurer. *Aviation in the U.S. Army, 1919-1939*. Washington, D.C.: Office of Air Force History, U.S. Air Force, 1987.

Polmar, Norman. *Historic Naval Aircraft: From the Pages of Naval History Magazine*. Dulles, VA: Brassey's, Inc., 2004.

Polmar, Norman, and Dana Bell. *One Hundred Years of World Military Aircraft*. Annapolis, MD: Naval Institute Press, 2004.

Polmar, Norman, and Timothy M. Laur, eds. *Strategic Air Command: People, Aircraft, and Missiles, 2nd ed.* Baltimore, MD: Nautical and Aviation Publishing Company of America, 1990.

Schatzberg, Eric. *Wings of Wood, Wings of Metal: Culture and Technical Choice in American Airplane Materials, 1914-1945*. Princeton, NJ: Princeton University Press, 1999.

Scott, Bill. *Inside the Stealth Bomber: The B-2 Story*. Blue Ridge Summit, PA: Aero, 1991.

Smallwood, William. *Warthog: Flying the A-10 in the Gulf War*. Dulles, VA: Brassey's, Inc., 1993.

Stoff, Joshua. *The Thunder Factory: An Illustrated History of the Republic Aviation Corporation*. Osceola, WI: Motorbooks International, 1990.

Sullivan, George. *Modern Bombers and Attack Planes*. New York: Facts On File, 1992.

Swanborough, Gordon, and Peter M. Bowers. *United States Military Aircraft Since 1908*. London: Putnam Aeronautical Books, 1971.

Swanborough, Gordon, and Peter M. Bowers. *United States Navy Aircraft Since 1911*. London: Putnam Aeronautical Books, 1990.

Sweetman, Bill. *Stealth Bomber: Invisible Warplane, Black Budget*. Osceola, WI: Motorbooks International, 1989.

Sweetman, Bill. *Inside the Stealth Bomber*. Osceola, WI: Motorbooks International, 1999.

Taylor, Michael J.H., and David Mondey. *Milestones of Flight*. London: Jane's Publishing Company, 1983.

Taylor, Michael J.H., ed. *Jane's Encyclopedia of Aviation*. New York: Portland House, 1989.

Williams, Amy E., illustrated by Ted Williams. *The American Fighter Plane*. New York: Metro Books, 2002

Articles

"A Pictorial History of USN Carriers and their Aircraft." *Air Classics Quarterly Review*. Vol. 2, no. 2 (Summer 1975).

Bodie, Warren M. "Breeching the Walls of Fortress Europe: The Taciturn "Tornado." World's First Operational Jet Bomber." *Airpower*. Vol. 3, no. 5 (September 1973): 36 – 55.

"Boeing B-28 Superfortress." *World War II*. Vol. 1, no. 7 (November 1971): 40 - 43.

"Bomber One." *Airpower*. Vol. 1, no. 1 (September 1971): 12 – 19, 58 – 61. [Portions of this article were excerpted from *U.S. Navy Dive and Torpedo Bombers*, Sentry Books.]

"Bomber B-25." *Air Classics*. Vol. 4, no. 4 (April 1968): 28 – 43.

Bowers, Peter M. "A Fortress is Forever." *Wings*. Vol. 7, no. 1 (February 1977): 24 – 51, 64.

Bowers, Peter M. "Keystone Bombers." *Aero Album*. (Summer 1972): 2 – 19.

Bowers, Peter M. "Martin's Mighty Mariner." *Wings*. Vol. 2, no. 6 (December 1972): 6 – 17.

Bowers, Peter M. "Sea Wings: The Classic Curtiss' Flying Boats." *Airpower*. Vol. 5, no. 5 (September 1975): 38 – 53.

Bowers, Peter M. "The Reluctant Dragon." *Airpower*. Vol. 10, no. 6 (November 1980): 28 – 41.

Bowers, Peter M. "Scout Bomber." *Wings*. Vol. 15, no. 2 (April 1985): 18 – 25, 55.

Bowers, Peter M. "The Forgotten Fortresses, Part II." *Airpower*. Vol. 4, no. 5 (September 1974): 8 – 31, 54 – 55.

Boyne, Walt. "B-10 Baltimore's Best." *Airpower*. Vol. 2, no. 3 (May 1972): 28 – 53, 66 - 67.

Boyne, Walt. "Cry Havoc: The Douglas A-20, Part I." *Wings*. Vol. 6, no. 3 (June 1976): 22 – 37, 52 – 54.

Boyne, Walt. "Cry Havoc: The Douglas A-20, Part II." *Airpower*. Vol. 6, no. 4 (July 1976): 50 – 66.

Boyne, Walt. "Death Angel: Boeing's Benign B-9." *Airpower*. Vol. 1, no. 2 (November 1971): 38 – 57.

Boyne, Walt. "Huff-Daland in 3D." *Wings*. Vol. 7, no. 6 (December 1977): 54 - 63.

Boyne, Walt. "Martin's Gallant Soldier the B-10." *Air Classics*. Vol. 3, no. 2 (1966 Annual): 28 – 31, 52 – 53.

Chester, Dave. "B-36 Restoration." *Air Classics*. Vol. 8, no. 5 (March 1972): 10 – 15, 65.

Cornelius, Art. "Skyraider." *Air Classics*. Vol. 6, no. 6 (August 1970): 32 – 41, 63 – 64.

Daniels, C. M. "The Twin Tailed Lockheeds." *Airpower*. Vol. 10, no. 6 (November 1980): 8 – 25, 41.

Dean, Jack. "Taming the Big Tailed Beast." *Wings*. Vol. 1, no. 1 (August 1971): 36 – 49, 62 – 63.

Doll, Thomas E. "The Devastator." *Air Classics*. Vol. 3, no. 2 (1966 Annual): 24 – 27, 50 – 51.

Freeman, Edgar. "Douglas A4 Skyhawk" *Air Classics*. Vol. 8, no. 6 (April 1972): 26 – 35.

Gault, Owen. "Taming the Beast—Curtis SB2C Helldiver." *Air Classics*. Vol. 8, no. 6 (April 1972): 10 – 15, 49 – 53.

Guyton, Boone T. "Vindicator." *Air Classics*. Vol. 10, no. 7 (July 1974): 14 – 31.

Hendrix, Lin. "Requiem for a Heavyweight." *Wings*. Vol. 8, no. 1 (February 1978): 20 – 36, 52 -53, 62.

Jacobsen, Meyers K. "Peacemaker." *Airpower*. Vol. 4, no. 6 (November 1974): 8 – 27, 50 – 55.

Janczarek, Ted. "North American's Classic Bomber." *Air Progress Pilot Reports*. (1979): 12 – 16.

Johnsen, Frederick A. "Agony Wagon." *Wings*. Vol. 2, no. 2 (April 1972): 8 – 19.

Johnsen, Frederick A. "Dominator." *Wings*. Vol. 4, no. 1 (February 1974): 8 – 17.

Johnson, E.R. "Paper Airplanes." *Aviation History* (May 2007): 50 – 57.

Marmo, Richard. "B-1: The Restoration of the Year." *Airpower*. Vol. 6, no. 6 (November 1976): 26 – 35.

McCullough, Anson. "Torpedo Bomber Devastator." *Air Classics*. Vol. 5, no. 1 (October 1968): 28 – 43, 73.

Miller, Jay. "History of the Hustler." *Airpower*. Vol. 6, no. 4 (July 1976): 18 – 39.

Miller, Jay. "F-111…Billion Dollar Blunder or Answer to the Loss of the B-1?" *Wings*. Vol. 9, no. 3 (June 1979): 22 – 30, 45.

Mizrahi, Joe. "Fortress in the Sky." *Wings*. Vol. 1, no. 1 (August 1971): 16 – 33.

Mizrahi, J. V. "Avenger." *Air Classics*. Vol. 5, no. 3 (February 1969): 38 – 52.

O'Leary, Michael. "The Reluctant Dragon." *Air Classics*. Vol. 10, no. 10 (October 1974): 30 – 37.

"PD-1/PM-1: Patrol Planes and Patrol Squadrons." *American Aviation Historical Society Journal*. Vol. 6, no. 3 (Fall 1961): 167 – 168, 216.

Phillips, Ward. "The Douglas TBD "Devastator"." *Fighting Wings of the Navy, Combat Illustrated*. No. 2. (Spring 1985): 14 – 21, 90 – 91.

Rawlings, Neal. "The Hudson Ventura Saga." *Air Classics*. Vol. 7, no. 6 (September 1971): 32 – 39.

Ryan, Frank. "B-26 Widow Maker." *Air Classics*. Vol. 3, no 2 (1966 Annual): 66 – 74.

Scarborough, William E. "P-Boat: The Consolidated PBY Catalina, Part I." *Wings*. Vol. 5, no. 2 (April 1975): 8 – 29, 52 – 55.

Scarborough, William E. "P-Boat: The Consolidated PBY Catalina, Part II." *Airpower*. Vol. 5, no. 3 (May 1975): 8 – 21, 54 – 55.

Seller, Donald J. "Trial By Fire." *Wings*. Vol. 9, no. 3 (June 1979): 10 – 21, 46 – 54.

Spenser, Jay P. "Flak Bait." *Airpower*. Vol. 8, no. 5 (September 1978): 36 – 57.

"The B-1 Bomber." *Air Classics*. Vol. 8, no. 11 (September 1972): 72 – 78.

"The B-25 Mitchell." *World War II*. Vol. 1, no. 7 (November 1971): 28 – 31.

Tillman, Barrett, "Intruder." *Wings*. Vol. 7, no. 1 (February 1977): 8 – 17, 65.

Tillman, Barrett. "Go in and Get a Hit: Flying the TBD Devastator and TBF Avenger." *Airpower*. Vol. 3, no. 4 (July 1973): 20 – 39, 65 – 66.

Tillman, Barrett. "Winged Excalibur: The Douglas SBD Dauntless." *Wings*. Vol. 7, no. 2 (April 1977): 20 – 41.

Trimble, Robert L. "Bolo: America's Forgotten Warrior." *Air Classics*. Vol. 16, no. 5 (May 1980): 22 – 33, 62 – 67.

Trimble, Robert L. "Dive Bomber: The Douglas SBD "Dauntless"." *Fighting Wings of the Navy, Combat Illustrated*. No. 2. (Spring 1985): 56 – 75.

Trimble, Robert L. "History of the Curtiss SB2C Helldiver, Part I." *Air Classics*. Vol. 17, no. 5 (May 1981): 12 – 23.

Trimble, Robert L. "Skyraider, Part I." *Air Classics*. Vol. 10, no. 12 (December 1974): 28 – 37, 56 – 61.

Trimble, Robert L. "Skyraider, Part II." *Air Classics*. Vol. 11, no. 1 (January 1975): 40 – 42, 48 – 53, 74 – 75.

Waag, Robert J. "Thunder From the Sky: The Story of North American's B-25 Mitchell." *Wings*. Vol. 2, no. 3 (June 1972): 36 – 59, 64, 66.

Westburg, Peter. "Curtiss A-8 Shrike." *Air Classics*. Vol. 11, no. 12 (December 1975): 14 – 25, 68 – 71.

Websites

http://www.afa.org
Air Force Magazine Online, Air Force Association

http://www.aero-web.org/
Aviation Enthusiast Corner, Specifications

http://www.blueangels.navy.mil
The Blue Angels, The U.S. Navy's Flight Demonstration Squadron

http://www.boeing.com/history/
Boeing, including history of McDonnell Douglas, North American Aviation

http://www.cradleofaviation.org/history/index.html
Cradle of Aviation Museum

http://www.geae.com/aboutgeae/history.html
GE Aircraft Engines

http://www.glennhcurtissmuseum.org/
Glenn H. Curtiss Museum

http://www.marylandaviationmuseum.org
The Glenn L. Martin Maryland Aviation Museum

http://movies.nytimes.com/movie/94717/Hell-Divers/overview
Hell Divers (1932)

http://www.historynet.com
HistoryNet

http://www.lockheedmartin.com/aboutus/history/index.html
Lockheed Martin Corporation

www.nationalaviation.org
National Aviation Hall of Fame (NAHF)

http://www.nationalmuseum.af.mil/
National Museum of the U.S. Air Force at Wright-Patterson Air Force Base, Dayton, OH

http://www.navalaviationmuseum.org
National Naval Aviation Museum, Naval Air Station Pensacola, Fl

http://www.history.navy.mil/
Naval Historical Center

http://www.northropgrumman.com/heritage/index.html
Northrop Grumman Corporation

http://www.nasa.gov/
The National Air and Space Administration

http://www.navy.mil
Official website of the United States Navy

http://www.pw.utc.com/
Pratt & Whitney, a United Technologies Company

http://www.nasm.si.edu/
Smithsonian National Air and Space Museum, Washington, D.C.

http://www.centennialofflight.gov
U.S. Centennial of Flight Commission

Photo Credits

All illustrations © Ted Williams

Associated Press: © Henri Huet: 147 top

© Boeing: 30 top inset, 31 top inset, 44, 47 left, 52, 55 top, 72, 74 right, 79, 82, 104, 126 right, 127, 128, 131, 140

Corbis: © Roger Ressmeyer: 11 top, 164; 46 bottom; © Museum of Flight: 70 bottom; © Bettmann: 123, 144; © George Hall: 132; © Philip Wallick: 167

Department of Defense: TSGT Michael J. Haggerty: 156; MSGT Patrick Nugent: 158-159; MSGT Val Gempis: 160

Getty Images: © Jack Delano/Library of Congress: 88; © Margaret Bourke-White/Time & Life Pictures: 114, 115 bottom right; © Joseph Scherschel/Time & Life Pictures: 115 top right

The Granger Collection, New York: 83

IPNstock: © Thomas Kraft/Transtock: 168

Library of Congress: © Howard R. Hollem: 51 top inset, 64; © Alfred T. Palmer: 60, 62 top left, 76; 130 inset

© Michael Marston ePixel Images: 159 top right

National Archives: 47 right, 50 top inset; © Charles Kerlee: 84; 147 bottom; LCpl G.A. Martines: 148

From AMERICA BY THE YARD: CIRKUT CAMERA by Robert B. MacKay. © 2006 by Robert B. MacKay. Used by permission of W. W. Norton & Company, Inc.: front and back endpapers

1000aircraftphotos.com: Capt. Robert E. Selff Memorial Collection/US Army Air Service photo: 18

Courtesy of Dave Ostrowski: 2-3, 7, 100, 14, 15, 16, 19, 20, 22, 23, 24, 27, 30-31 bottom, 35 background, 40, 42, 46 top, 50-51 bottom, 54, 55 bottom, 58, 59, 62 inset, 62-63, 66, 67, 70 top, 71, 78, 90, 91, 92, 94, 95, 98, 99, 102, 103 background, 106, 107, 110, 111 top, 115 left, 116, 118, 119, 126 left, 130 background, 134, 135, 136, 139, 150, 151 left, 159 bottom inset, 162 top, 163, 166

Photography Collection, Harry Ransom Humanities Research Center, The University of Texas at Austin/Photograph by E.O. Goldbeck: 4-5

© SuperStock: 1, 170-171 background

U.S. Air Force: Staff Sgt. Craig Seals: 8; 11 bottom, 32, 35 inset, 43, 142, 162 bottom; Master Sgt. Val Gempis: 170 inset

U.S. Naval Historical Center: Courtesy of Thomas E. Doll: 74 left; 75

US Naval Institute: 36, 38, 39, 48, 86, 87, 103 inset, 111 bottom, 120, 122, 143, 146

US Navy: MCSA Anthony R. Martinez: 151 right; PH3 Christopher Stephens: 154 inset; MC1 Alan Warner: 154 background; PHAN Ryan O'Connor: 155 top; PH3 (AW) Mark J. Rebilas: 155 bottom

Index